# Gradle Effective
# Implementation Guide

Empower yourself to automate your build

**Hubert Klein Ikkink**

BIRMINGHAM - MUMBAI

# Gradle Effective Implementation Guide

Copyright © 2012 Packt Publishing

First published: October 2012

Production Reference: 1181012

Published by Packt Publishing Ltd.
Livery Place
35 Livery Street
Birmingham B3 2PB, UK.

ISBN 978-1-84951-810-9

www.packtpub.com

Cover Image by Syarafuddin (syarafuddin@yahoo.com)

# Credits

**Author**
Hubert Klein Ikkink

**Reviewers**
René Gröschke

Rajmahendra Hegde

Michał Huniewicz

James L. Williams

**Acquisition Editor**
Martin Bell

**Lead Technical Editor**
Sweny M. Sukumaran

**Technical Editors**
Dipesh Panchal

Unnati Shah

Dominic Pereira

**Copy Editors**
Brandt D'Mello

Insiya Morbiwala

Aditya Nair

**Project Coordinator**
Sai Gamare

**Proofreader**
Maria Gould

Clyde Jenkins

Mario Cecere

**Indexer**
Rekha Nair

**Production Coordinator**
Nitesh Thakur

**Cover Work**
Nitesh Thakur

# About the Author

**Hubert Klein Ikkink** was born in 1973 and lives in Tilburg, the Netherlands, with his beautiful wife and gorgeous children. He is also known as mrhaki, which is simply the initials of his name prepended by mr. He studied Information Systems and Management at the Tilburg University. After finishing his studies he started to work at a company which specialized in knowledge-based software. There he started writing his first Java software (yes, an applet!) in 1996. Over the years his focus switched from applets, to servlets, to Java Enterprise Edition applications, to Spring-based software.

In 2008 he wanted to have fun again when writing software. The larger projects he was working on were more about writing configuration XML files, tuning performance and less about real development in his eyes. So he started to look around and noticed Groovy as a good language to learn about. He could still use existing Java code, libraries, and his Groovy classes in Java. The learning curve isn't steep and to support his learning phase he wrote down interesting Groovy facts in his blog with the title Groovy Goodness. He posts small articles with a lot of code samples to understand how to use Groovy. Since November 2011 he is also a DZone Most Valuable Blogger (MVB); DZone also posts his blog items on their site.

In 2010, 2011, and 2012 Hubert was invited to speak at Gr8Conf in Copenhagen, Denmark. This is a very good conference with all the project leaders of Groovy and Groovy-related projects. In November 2010 he presented a Gradle talk at the J-Fall conference of the Dutch Java User Group. In November 2011 he presented about the new features in Groovy 1.8 at the same conference. The conference is visited by 1000 Java developers and he got the chance to educate some of them about the greatness of Gradle and Groovy.

Hubert works for a company called JDriven in the Netherlands. JDriven focuses on technologies that simplify and improve development of enterprise applications. Employees of JDriven have years of experience with Java and related technologies and are all eager to learn about new technologies. Hubert works on projects using Grails and Java combined with Groovy and Gradle.

# Acknowledgement

It was a great honor to be asked by Packt Publishing to write this book. I knew beforehand it would be a lot of work and somehow needed to be combined with my daytime job. I couldn't have written the book without the help of a lot of people and I would like to thank them.

First of all I would like to thank my family for supporting me while writing this book. They gave me space and time to write the book. Thank you for your patience and a big kiss for Kim, Britt, and Liam; I love you. I also like to thank my colleagues at JDriven. They reviewed the pages I wrote and helped me by asking questions and showing interest in the progress of the book. Of course I like to thank all the people at Gradleware for making Gradle such a great build tool and René Gröschke for reviewing the chapters in the book.

Finally I'd like to thank the great staff at Packt Publishing. Sai Gamare kept me on schedule and made sure everything was submitted on time. I'd also like to thank all the editors for reviewing the book. They really helped me to keep focus and be concise with the text.

# About the Reviewers

**René Gröschke** has been working as a Software Engineer for more than eight years now. He has worked on several international projects and regularly shares his passion and experience of agile methodologies and software craftsmanship with other developers at different national and international conferences or with bachelor students of the Baden-Wuerttemberg Cooperative State University (DHBW) in Germany.

Supporting Gradle and the Gradle community by providing plugins, patches, screencasts, and talks since the early days, René has turned his hobby into his occupation and is now part of the core developer team of Gradle working for Gradleware. From time to time, he's contributing to other open source projects, such as Macports or Griffon.

**Rajmahendra Hegde** has been a Java Developer since 2000. He is currently working for Logica as Project Lead/Architect. He is a User Group lead for Java User Group – Chennai. He has contributed to JSRs and Scalaxia.com. He is the committer for Visage. His primary areas of interest are JEE, JavaFX, JVM Languages (Groovy, Scala, and Visage), NetBeans, and Gradle. You can follow him at `@rajonjava`.

**Michał Huniewicz** is a Software Developer, with several years of experience in the JVM technologies. He has been involved in projects for a variety of industries, including banking, press, finance, telecoms, and the government. He was also the head developer of an award-winning community portal. Apart from being an active blogger (http://blog.m1key.me/), he is a passionate photographer and traveller. He holds an M.Sc. degree in Computer Science from Adam Mickiewicz University. Currently, he lives in London.

I would like to thank my parents, Rita and Andrzej, for their continued support and for having faith in me.

**James L. Williams** is a developer based in Silicon Valley and a frequent international conference speaker. He is the author of the book *Learning HTML5 Game Programming* for *Addison-Wesley*. He blogs at http://jameswilliams.be/blog and tweets as @ecspike.

# www.PacktPub.com

## Support files, eBooks, discount offers and more

You might want to visit www.PacktPub.com for support files and downloads related to your book.

Did you know that Packt offers eBook versions of every book published, with PDF and ePub files available? You can upgrade to the eBook version at www.PacktPub.com and as a print book customer, you are entitled to a discount on the eBook copy. Get in touch with us at service@packtpub.com for more details.

At www.PacktPub.com, you can also read a collection of free technical articles, sign up for a range of free newsletters and receive exclusive discounts and offers on Packt books and eBooks.

http://PacktLib.PacktPub.com

Do you need instant solutions to your IT questions? PacktLib is Packt's online digital book library. Here, you can access, read and search across Packt's entire library of books.

## Why Subscribe?

- Fully searchable across every book published by Packt
- Copy and paste, print and bookmark content
- On demand and accessible via web browser

## Free Access for Packt account holders

If you have an account with Packt at www.PacktPub.com, you can use this to access PacktLib today and view nine entirely free books. Simply use your login credentials for immediate access.

# Table of Contents

# Preface

Gradle is the next-generation build automation. Not only does Gradle use convention over configuration to provide good defaults, it is also adaptable for use in every situation you encounter in daily development. Build logic is described with a powerful DSL and empowers developers to create reusable and maintainable build logic.

We will see more about Gradle in this book. We will learn about Gradle's features with code samples throughout the book. We will learn how to write tasks, work with files, and write build scripts using the Groovy DSL. Next, we will learn how to use Gradle in projects to compile, package, test, check code quality and deploy applications. And finally, we will see how to integrate Gradle with continuous integration servers and development environments (IDEs).

After reading this book, we will know how to use Gradle in our daily development. We can write tasks, apply plugins, and write build logic using the Gradle build language.

## What this book covers

*Chapter 1, Starting with Gradle,* introduces Gradle and explains how to install Gradle. We will write our first Gradle script and learn about the command-line and GUI features of Gradle.

*Chapter 2, Creating Gradle Build Scripts,* looks at tasks as part of the Gradle build scripts. We will see how we can define tasks and use task dependencies to describe build logic.

*Chapter 3, Working with Gradle Build Scripts,* covers more functionality that we can apply in Gradle scripts. We will learn how to work with files and directories, apply logging to our build scripts, and use properties to parameterize our build scripts.

*Chapter 4, Using Gradle for Java Projects,* is all about using the Java plugin for Gradle projects. Gradle offers several tasks and configuration conventions that make working with Java projects very easy. We will see how we can customize the configuration for projects that cannot follow the conventions.

*Chapter 5, Dependency Management,* covers the support for dependencies by Gradle. We will learn how to use configurations to organize dependencies. We will also see how we can use repositories with dependencies in our build scripts.

*Chapter 6, Testing, Building, and Publishing Artifacts,* is an introduction to Gradle support for running tests from the build script. We will learn how we can build several artifacts for a project and publish the artifacts to a repository so other developers can reuse our code.

*Chapter 7, Multi-project Builds,* covers Gradle's support for multi-project builds. With Gradle, we can easily configure multiple projects that are related to each other. We will also see how Gradle can automatically build related or dependent projects if necessary.

*Chapter 8, Mixed Languages,* is about the Scala and Groovy plugins that are included with Gradle, to work with projects that have Scala or Groovy code.

*Chapter 9, Maintaining Code Quality,* introduces Gradle's code quality plugins. We will see how we can use and configure the plugins to include code analysis in our build process.

*Chapter 10, Writing Custom Tasks and Plugins,* covers what we need to do to write our own custom tasks and plugins. We will see how we can decouple the definition and usage of a custom task and plugin into separate source files. We will also learn how we can reuse our custom tasks and plugins in other projects

*Chapter 11, Using Gradle with Continuous Integration,* is an introduction to the support of several continuous integration tools for Gradle. We will learn how we can configure a continuous integration server to automatically invoke our Gradle build scripts.

*Chapter 12, IDE Support,* looks at how Gradle can generate project files for Eclipse and IntelliJ IDEA. We will also see how the IDEs support Gradle from within the IDE to run (for example) tasks, and keep track of dependencies defined in Gradle scripts.

# What you need for this book

In order to work with Gradle and the code samples in the book, we need at least a Java Development Kit (JDK 1.5 or higher), Gradle, and a good text editor. In *Chapter 1, Starting with Gradle*, we will see how we can install Gradle on our computer.

# Who this book is for

This book is for you if you work on Java (Scala or Groovy) applications and want to use build automation to compile, package, and deploy your application automatically. You might have worked with other build automation tools such as Maven or ANT, but this is not necessary to understand the topics in this book.

# Conventions

In this book, you will find a number of styles of text that distinguish between different kinds of information. Here are some examples of these styles, and an explanation of their meaning.

Code words in text are shown as follows: "In our first build we only have one task, so the command `gradle h` should work just fine."

A block of code is set as follows:

```
task helloWorld << {
  println 'Hello world.'
}
```

When we wish to draw your attention to a particular part of a code block, the relevant lines or items are set in bold:

```
apply plugin: 'java'

archivesBaseName = 'gradle-sample'
version = '1.0'

sourceSets {
    api
}

task apiJar(type: Jar) {
    appendix = 'api'
    from sourceSets.api.output
}
```

Any command-line input or output is written as follows:

```
hello-world $ gradle helloWorld
:helloWorld
Hello world.

BUILD SUCCESSFUL

Total time: 2.047 secs
```

**New terms** and **important words** are shown in bold. Words that you see on the screen, in menus or dialog boxes for example, appear in the text like this: "We select the plugin and click on the button **Install without restart**".

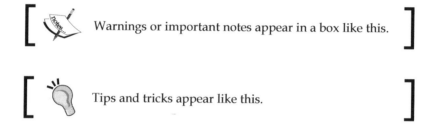

Warnings or important notes appear in a box like this.

Tips and tricks appear like this.

# Reader feedback

Feedback from our readers is always welcome. Let us know what you think about this book—what you liked or may have disliked. Reader feedback is important for us to develop titles that you really get the most out of.

To send us general feedback, simply send an e-mail to feedback@packtpub.com, and mention the book title via the subject of your message.

If there is a book that you need and would like to see us publish, please send us a note in the **SUGGEST A TITLE** form on www.packtpub.com or e-mail suggest@packtpub.com.

If there is a topic that you have expertise in and you are interested in either writing or contributing to a book, see our author guide on www.packtpub.com/authors.

# Customer support

Now that you are the proud owner of a Packt book, we have a number of things to help you to get the most from your purchase.

# Downloading the example code

You can download the example code files for all Packt books you have purchased from your account at `http://www.PacktPub.com`. If you purchased this book elsewhere, you can visit `http://www.PacktPub.com/support` and register to have the files e-mailed directly to you.

# Errata

Although we have taken every care to ensure the accuracy of our content, mistakes do happen. If you find a mistake in one of our books—maybe a mistake in the text or the code—we would be grateful if you would report this to us. By doing so, you can save other readers from frustration and help us improve subsequent versions of this book. If you find any errata, please report them by visiting `http://www.packtpub.com/support`, selecting your book, clicking on the **errata submission form** link, and entering the details of your errata. Once your errata are verified, your submission will be accepted and the errata will be uploaded on our website, or added to any list of existing errata, under the Errata section of that title. Any existing errata can be viewed by selecting your title from `http://www.packtpub.com/support`.

# Piracy

Piracy of copyright material on the Internet is an ongoing problem across all media. At Packt, we take the protection of our copyright and licenses very seriously. If you come across any illegal copies of our works, in any form, on the Internet, please provide us with the location address or website name immediately so that we can pursue a remedy.

Please contact us at `copyright@packtpub.com` with a link to the suspected pirated material.

We appreciate your help in protecting our authors, and our ability to bring you valuable content.

# Questions

You can contact us at `questions@packtpub.com` if you are having a problem with any aspect of the book, and we will do our best to address it.

# 1
# Starting with Gradle

When we develop software, we write code, compile code, test our code, package our code, and finally, distribute the code. We can automate these steps by using a build system. The big advantage is that we have a repeatable sequence of steps. Each time, the build system will follow the steps we have defined, so we can concentrate on writing the actual code and not worry about the other steps.

Gradle is such a build system. In this chapter, we will explain what Gradle is and how to use it in our development projects.

## Introducing Gradle

Gradle is a tool for build automation. With Gradle, we can automate the compiling, testing, packaging, and deployment of our software or other types of projects. Gradle is flexible but has sensible defaults for most projects. This means we can rely on the defaults, if we don't want something special, but can still use the flexibility to adapt a build to certain custom needs.

Gradle is already used by big open source projects, such as Spring, Hibernate, and Grails. Enterprise companies such as LinkedIn also use Gradle.

Let's take a look at some of Gradle's features.

# Declarative builds and convention over configuration

Gradle uses a **Domain Specific Language** (DSL) based on **Groovy** to declare builds. The DSL provides a flexible language that can be extended by us. Because the DSL is based on Groovy, we can write Groovy code to describe a build and use the power and expressiveness of the Groovy language. Groovy is a language for the **Java Virtual Machine (JVM)**, such as Java and Scala. Groovy makes it easy to work with collections, has closures, and has a lot of useful features. The syntax is closely related to the Java syntax. In fact, we could write a Groovy class file with Java syntax and it would compile. But, using the Groovy syntax makes it easier to express the code intent, and we need less boilerplate code than with Java. To get the most out of Gradle, it is best to learn the basics of the Groovy language, but it is not necessary to start writing Gradle scripts.

Gradle is designed to be a build language and not a rigid framework. The Gradle core itself is written in Java and Groovy. To extend Gradle we can use Java and Groovy to write our custom code. We can even write our custom code in Scala if we want to.

Gradle provides support for Java, Groovy, Scala, Web, and OSGi projects, out of the box. These projects have sensible convention over configuration settings that we probably already use ourselves. But we have the flexibility to change these configuration settings, if needed, in our projects.

# Support for Ant tasks and Maven repositories

Gradle supports Ant tasks and projects. We can import an Ant build and re-use all the tasks. But we can also write Gradle tasks dependent on Ant tasks. The integration also applies to properties, paths, and so on.

Maven and Ivy repositories are supported to publish or fetch dependencies. So, we can continue to use any repository infrastructure we already have.

# Incremental builds

With Gradle we have incremental builds. This means tasks in a build are only executed if necessary. For example, a task to compile source code will first check whether the sources since the last execution of the task have changed. If the sources have changed, the task is executed, but if the sources haven't changed, the execution of the task is skipped and the task is marked as being up to date.

Gradle supports this mechanism for a lot of the provided tasks. But we can also use this for tasks we write ourselves.

# Multi-project builds

Gradle has great support for multi-project builds. A project can simply be dependent on other projects or be a dependency for other projects. We can define a graph of dependencies between projects, and Gradle can resolve those dependencies for us. We have the flexibility to define our project layout as we want.

Gradle has support for partial builds. This means Gradle will figure out if a project that our project depends on needs to be rebuilt or not. And if the project needs rebuilding, Gradle will do this before building our own project.

# Gradle wrapper

The Gradle wrapper allows us to execute Gradle builds, even though Gradle is not installed on a computer. This is a great way to distribute source code and provide the build system with it, so that the source code can be built.

Also, in an enterprise environment, we can have a zero administration way for client computers to build the software. We can use the wrapper to enforce a certain Gradle version to be used, so the whole team is using the same version.

# Free and open source

Gradle is an open source project and it is licensed under the **Apache Software License (ASL)**.

# Getting started

In this section, we will download and install Gradle before writing our first Gradle build script.

Before we get and install Gradle, we must make sure we have a **Java Development Kit (JDK)** installed on our computer. Gradle requires JDK 5 or higher. Gradle will use the JDK found at the path set on our computer. We can check this by running the following command on the command line:

```
java -version
```

Although Gradle uses Groovy, we don't have to install Groovy ourselves. Gradle bundles the Groovy libraries with the distribution and will ignore a Groovy installation already available on our computer.

Gradle is available on the Gradle website, at http://www.gradle.org/downloads. From this page we can download the latest release of Gradle. Or, we can download a previous version if we want to. We can choose among three different distributions to download. We can download either the complete Gradle distribution, with binaries, sources, and documentation, or only the binaries, or only the sources.

To get started with Gradle, we download the standard distribution with the binaries, sources, and documentation. At the time of writing this book, the current release is 1.1. On computers with a Debian Linux operation sytem, we can install Gradle as a Debian package. On computers with Mac OS X, we can use MacPorts or Homebrow to install Gradle.

# Installing Gradle

Gradle is packaged as a **ZIP** file for one of the three distributions. So, when we have downloaded the Gradle full distribution ZIP file, we must unzip the file. After unpacking the ZIP file we have the following:

- Binaries in the bin directory
- Documentation with the user guide, Groovy DSL, and the API documentation in the docs directory
- A lot of samples in the samples directory
- Source code for Gradle in the src directory
- Supporting libraries for Gradle in the lib directory
- A directory named init.d where we can store Gradle scripts that need to be executed each time we run Gradle

Once we have unpacked the Gradle distribution to a directory, we can open a command prompt. We change the directory to bin, which we extracted from the ZIP file. To check our installation, we run gradle -v and we get output, listing the JDK used and the library versions of Gradle:

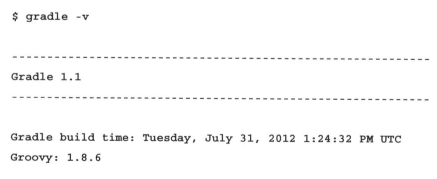

```
$ gradle -v


------------------------------------------------------------

Gradle 1.1

------------------------------------------------------------


Gradle build time: Tuesday, July 31, 2012 1:24:32 PM UTC
Groovy: 1.8.6
```

```
Ant: Apache Ant(TM) version 1.8.4 compiled on May 22 2012
Ivy: 2.2.0
JVM: 1.6.0_33 (Apple Inc. 20.8-b03-424)
OS: Mac OS X 10.7.4 x86_64
```

Here we can check whether the displayed version is the same as the distribution version we have downloaded from the Gradle website.

To run Gradle on our computer we only have to add `$GRADLE_HOME/bin` to our `PATH` environment variable. Once we have done that, we can run the `gradle` command from every directory on our computer.

If we want to add JVM options to Gradle, we can use the environment variables `JAVA_OPTS` and `GRADLE_OPTS`. The former is a commonly used environment variable name to pass extra parameters to a Java application. Similarly, Gradle uses the `GRADLE_OPTS` environment variable to pass extra arguments to Gradle. Both environment variables are used so we can set them both with different values. This is mostly used to set, for example, an HTTP proxy or extra memory options.

# Writing our first build script

We now have a running Gradle installation. It is time to create our first Gradle build script. Gradle uses the concept of projects to define a related set of tasks. A Gradle build can have one or more projects. A project is a very broad concept in Gradle, but it is mostly a set of components we want to build for our application.

A project has one or more tasks. Tasks are a unit of work that need to be executed by the build. Examples of tasks are compiling source code, packaging class files into a JAR file, running tests, or deploying the application.

We now know that a task is part of a project, so to create our first task we also create our first Gradle project. We use the `gradle` command to run a build. Gradle will look for a file named `build.gradle` in the current directory. This file is the build script for our project. We define those of our tasks that need to be executed in this build script file.

We create a new file, `build.gradle`, and open it in a text editor. We type the following code to define our first Gradle task:

```
task helloWorld << {
  println 'Hello world.'
}
```

With this code we define a `helloWorld` task. The task will print the words "Hello world." to the console. `println` is a Groovy method to print text to the console and is basically a shorthand version of the Java method `System.out.println`.

The code between the brackets is a closure. A closure is a code block that can be assigned to a variable or passed to a method. Java doesn't support closures, but Groovy does. And because Gradle uses Groovy to define the build scripts, we can use closures in our build scripts.

The `<<` syntax is, technically speaking, operator shorthand for the method `leftShift()`, which actually means "add to". So, we are defining here that we want to add the closure (with the statement `println 'Hello world.'`) to our task with the name `helloWorld`.

First we save `build.gradle`, and then with the command `gradle helloWorld`, we execute our build:

```
hello-world $ gradle helloWorld
:helloWorld
Hello world.


BUILD SUCCESSFUL


Total time: 2.047 secs
```

The first line of output shows our line **Hello world**. Gradle adds some more output, such as the fact that the build was successful and the total time of the build. Because Gradle runs in the JVM, it must be started each time we run a Gradle build.

We can run the same build again, but with only the output of our task, by using the Gradle command-line option `--quiet` (or `-q`). Gradle will suppress all messages except error messages. When we use `--quiet` (or `-q`), we get the following output:

```
hello-world $ gradle --quiet helloWorld
Hello world.
```

# Default Gradle tasks

We created our simple build script with one task. We can ask Gradle to show us the available tasks for our project. Gradle has several built-in tasks we can execute. We type `gradle -q tasks` to see the tasks for our project:

```
hello-world $gradle -q tasks


------------------------------------------------------

All tasks runnable from root project

------------------------------------------------------


Help tasks
----------

dependencies - Displays the dependencies of root project 'hello-world'.

help - Displays a help message

projects - Displays the sub-projects of root project 'hello-world'.

properties - Displays the properties of root project 'hello-world'.

tasks - Displays the tasks runnable from root project 'hello-world'
(some of the displayed tasks may belong to subprojects).


Other tasks
-----------

helloWorld


To see all tasks and more detail, run with --all.
```

Here, we see our task `helloWorld` in the **Other tasks** section. The Gradle built-in tasks are displayed in the **Help tasks** section. For example, to see some general help information, we execute the `help` task:

```
hello-world $ gradle -q help


Welcome to Gradle 1.1.


To run a build, run gradle <task> ...


To see a list of available tasks, run gradle tasks


To see a list of command-line options, run gradle --help
```

The `properties` task is very useful to see the properties available to our project. We haven't defined any property ourselves in the build script, but Gradle provides a lot of built-in properties. The following output shows some of the properties:

```
hello-world $ gradle -q properties


------------------------------------------------------

Root project

------------------------------------------------------


additionalProperties: {}

allprojects: [root project 'hello-world']

ant: org.gradle.api.internal.project.DefaultAntBuilder@6af37a62

antBuilderFactory: org.gradle.api.internal.project.DefaultAntBuilderFacto
ry@16e7eec9

artifacts: org.gradle.api.internal.artifacts.dsl.
DefaultArtifactHandler@54edd9de

asDynamicObject: org.gradle.api.internal.DynamicObjectHelper@4b7aa961

buildDir: /Users/mrhaki/Projects/gradle-book/samples/chapter1/hello-
world/build

buildDirName: build

buildFile: /Users/mrhaki/Projects/gradle-book/samples/chapter1/hello-
world/build.gradle

...
```

The `dependencies` task will show dependencies (if any) for our project. Our first project doesn't have any dependencies when we run the task, as the output shows:

```
hello-world $ gradle -q dependencies


------------------------------------------------------

Root project

------------------------------------------------------


No configurations
```

The `projects` task will display sub-projects (if any) for a root project. Our project doesn't have any sub-projects. So when we run the task `projects`, the output shows us that our project has no sub-projects.

```
hello-world $ gradle -q projects


------------------------------------------------------

Root project

------------------------------------------------------


Root project 'hello-world'
No sub-projects


To see a list of the tasks of a project, run gradle <project-path>:tasks
For example, try running gradle :tasks
```

# Task name abbreviation

Before we look at more Gradle command-line options, it is good to learn about a real timesaving feature of Gradle: task name abbreviation. With task name abbreviation, we don't have to type the complete task name on the command line. We only have to type enough of the name to make it unique within the build.

In our first build we only have one task, so the command `gradle h` should work just fine. But then, we didn't take into account the built-in task `help`. So, to uniquely identify our `helloWorld` task, we use the abbreviation `hello`:

```
hello-world $ gradle -q hello
Hello world.
```

We can also abbreviate each word in a camel case task name. For example, our task name `helloWorld` can be abbreviated to `hW`:

```
hello-world $gradle -q hW
HelloWorld
```

This feature saves us the time spent in typing the complete task name and can speed up the execution of our tasks.

# Executing multiple tasks

With just a simple build script, we already learned that we have a couple of default tasks besides our own task that we can execute. To execute multiple tasks we only have to add each task name to the command line. Let's execute our custom task `helloWorld` and the built-in task `tasks`, as follows:

```
hello-world $ gradle helloWorld tasks
:helloWorld
Hello world.
:tasks


------------------------------------------------------
All tasks runnable from root project
------------------------------------------------------


Help tasks
----------
dependencies - Displays the dependencies of root project 'hello-world'.
help - Displays a help message
projects - Displays the sub-projects of root project 'hello-world'.
properties - Displays the properties of root project 'hello-world'.
tasks - Displays the tasks runnable from root project 'hello-world'
(some of the displayed tasks may belong to subprojects).


Other tasks
-----------
helloWorld


To see all tasks and more detail, run with --all.


BUILD SUCCESSFUL

Total time: 1.718 secs
```

We see the output of both the tasks. First, `helloWorld` is executed, followed by `tasks`. When executed, we see the task names prepended with a colon (:) and the output on the following lines.

Gradle executes the tasks in the same order as they are defined on the command line. Gradle will execute a task only once during the build. So even if we define the same task multiple times, it will be executed only once. This rule also applies when tasks have dependencies on other tasks. Gradle will optimize the task execution for us, and we don't have to worry about that.

# Command-line options

The `gradle` command is used to execute a build. This command accepts several command-line options. We know the option `--quiet` (or `-q`) to reduce the output of a build. If we use the option `--help` (or `-h` or `-?`), we see the complete list of options:

```
hello-world $ gradle --help


USAGE: gradle [option...] [task...]


-?, -h, --help          Shows this help message.

-a, --no-rebuild        Do not rebuild project dependencies.

-b, --build-file        Specifies the build file.

-C, --cache             Specifies how compiled build scripts should be
cached. Possible values are: 'rebuild' and 'on'. Default value is 'on'
[deprecated - Use '--rerun-tasks' or '--recompile-scripts' instead]

-c, --settings-file     Specifies the settings file.

--continue              Continues task execution after a task failure.
[experimental]

-D, --system-prop       Set system property of the JVM (e.g.
-Dmyprop=myvalue).

-d, --debug             Log in debug mode (includes normal stacktrace).

--daemon                Uses the Gradle daemon to run the build. Starts
the daemon if not running.

--foreground            Starts the Gradle daemon in the foreground.
[experimental]

-g, --gradle-user-home  Specifies the gradle user home directory.

--gui                   Launches the Gradle GUI.

-I, --init-script       Specifies an initialization script.

-i, --info              Set log level to info.

-m, --dry-run           Runs the builds with all task actions disabled.

--no-color              Do not use color in the console output.

--no-daemon             Do not use the Gradle daemon to run the build.
```

```
--no-opt                 Ignore any task optimization. [deprecated - Use
'--rerun-tasks' instead]

--offline                The build should operate without accessing
network resources.

-P, --project-prop       Set project property for the build script (e.g.
-Pmyprop=myvalue).

-p, --project-dir        Specifies the start directory for Gradle.
Defaults to current directory.

--profile                Profiles build execution time and generates a
report in the <build_dir>/reports/profile directory.

--project-cache-dir      Specifies the project-specific cache directory.
Defaults to .gradle in the root project directory.

-q, --quiet              Log errors only.

--recompile-scripts      Force build script recompiling.

--refresh                Refresh the state of resources of the type(s)
specified. Currently only 'dependencies' is supported. [deprecated - Use
'--refresh-dependencies' instead.]

--refresh-dependencies   Refresh the state of dependencies.

--rerun-tasks            Ignore previously cached task results.

-S, --full-stacktrace    Print out the full (very verbose) stacktrace for
all exceptions.

-s, --stacktrace         Print out the stacktrace for all exceptions.

--stop                   Stops the Gradle daemon if it is running.

-u, --no-search-upward   Don't search in parent folders for a settings.
gradle file.

-v, --version            Print version info.

-x, --exclude-task       Specify a task to be excluded from execution.
```

# Logging options

Let's look at some of the options in more detail. The options `--quiet` (or `-q`), `--debug` (or `-d`), `--info` (or `-i`), `--stacktrace` (or `-s`), and `--full-stacktrace` (or `-S`) control the amount of output we see when we execute tasks. To get the most detailed output we use the option `--debug` (or `-d`). This option provides a lot of output with information about the steps and classes used to run the build. The output is very verbose, therefore we will not use it much.

To get a better insight into the steps that are executed for our task, we can use the `--info` (or `-i`) option. The output is not as verbose as with `--debug`, but it can give a better understanding of the build steps:

```
hello-world $ gradle --info helloWorld
Starting Build
Settings evaluated using empty settings file.
Projects loaded. Root project using build file '/Users/gradle/hello-
world/build.gradle'.
Included projects: [root project 'hello-world']
Evaluating root project 'hello-world' using build file '/Users/gradle/
hello-world/build.gradle'.
All projects evaluated.
Selected primary task 'helloWorld'
Tasks to be executed: [task ':helloWorld']
:helloWorld
Task ':helloWorld' has not declared any outputs, assuming that it is
out-of-date.
Hello world.


BUILD SUCCESSFUL


Total time: 1.535 secs
```

If our build throws exceptions, we can see the stack trace information with the options `--stacktrace` (or -s) and `--full-stacktrace` (or -S). The latter option will output the most information and is the most verbose. The options `--stacktrace` and `--full-stracktrace` can be combined with the other logging options.

# Changing the build file and directory

We created our build file with the name `build.gradle`. This is the default name for a build file. Gradle will look for a file with this name in the current directory, to execute the build. But we can change this with the command-line options `--build-file` (or -b) and `--project-dir` (or -p).

Let's run the Gradle command from the parent directory of our current directory:

```
hello-world $ cd ..
$ gradle --project-dir hello-world -q helloWorld
Hello world.
```

And we can also rename `build.gradle` to, for example, `hello.build` and still execute our build:

```
hello-world $ mv build.gradle hello.build
hello-world $ gradle --build-file -q helloWorld
Hello world.
```

# Running tasks without execution

With the option `--dry-run` (or `-m`), we can run all the tasks without really executing them. When we use the dry run option, we can see which tasks are executed, so we get an insight into which tasks are involved in a certain build scenario. And we don't have to worry if the tasks are actually executed. Gradle builds up a **Directed Acyclic Graph** (**DAG**) with all the tasks before any task is executed. The DAG is built so that tasks will be executed in order of dependencies and so that a task is executed only once.

```
hello-world $ gradle --dry-run helloWorld
:helloWorld SKIPPED


BUILD SUCCESSFUL


Total time: 1.437 secs
```

# Gradle daemon

We already learned that Gradle is executed in a Java Virtual Machine, and each time we invoke the `gradle` command, a new Java Virtual Machine is started, the Gradle classes and libraries are loaded, and the build is executed. We can reduce the build execution time if we don't have to load a JVM, Gradle classes, and libraries, each time we execute a build. The command-line option, `--daemon`, starts a new Java process that will have all Gradle classes and libraries already loaded, and then we execute the build. The next time when we run Gradle with the `--daemon` option, only the build is executed, because the JVM, with the required Gradle classes and libraries, is already running.

The first time we execute `gradle` with the `--daemon` option, the execution speed will not improve, because the Java background process has not started as yet. But the next time around, we will see a major improvement:

```
hello-world $ gradle --daemon helloWorld
:helloWorld
```

```
Hello world.

BUILD SUCCESSFUL

Total time: 0.59 secs
```

Even though the daemon process has started, we can still run Gradle tasks without using the daemon. We use the command-line option `--no-daemon` to run a Gradle build without utilizing the daemon:

```
hello-world $ gradle --no-daemon helloWorld
:helloWorld
Hello world.

BUILD SUCCESSFUL

Total time: 1.496 secs
```

To stop the daemon process, we use the command-line option `--stop`:

```
$ gradle --stop
Stopping daemon.
Gradle daemon stopped.
```

This will stop the Java background process completely.

To always use the `--daemon` command-line option, without typing it every time we run the `gradle` command, we can create an alias—if our operating system supports aliases. For example, on a Unix-based system we can create an alias and then use the alias to run the Gradle build:

```
hello-world $ alias gradled='gradle --daemon'
hello-world $ gradled helloWorld
:helloWorld
Hello world.

BUILD SUCCESSFUL

Total time: 0.59 secs Instead
```

Instead of using the `--daemon` command-line option, we can use the Java system property `org.gradle.daemon` to enable the daemon. We can add this property to environment variable `GRADLE_OPTS`, so that it is always used when we run a Gradle build.

```
hello-world $ export GRADLE_OPTS="-Dorg.gradle.daemon=true"
hello-world $ gradle helloWorld
:helloWorld
Hello world.

BUILD SUCCESSFUL

Total time: 0.707 secs
```

# Profiling

Gradle also provides the command-line option `--profile`. This option records the time that certain tasks take to complete. The data is saved in an HTML file in the directory `build/reports/profile`. We can open this file in a web browser and see the time taken for several phases in the build process. The following image shows the HTML contents of the profile report:

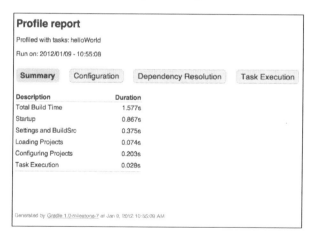

# Understanding the Gradle user interface

Finally, we take a look at the `--gui` command-line option. With this option, we start a graphical shell for our Gradle builds. Until now, we have used the command line to start a task. With the Gradle GUI, we have a graphical overview of the tasks in a project, and we can execute them by simply double-clicking on them.

To start the GUI, we invoke the following command:

```
hello-world $ gradle --gui
```

A window is opened with a graphical overview of our task tree. We have only one task, which is listed in the task tree, as shown in the following screenshot:

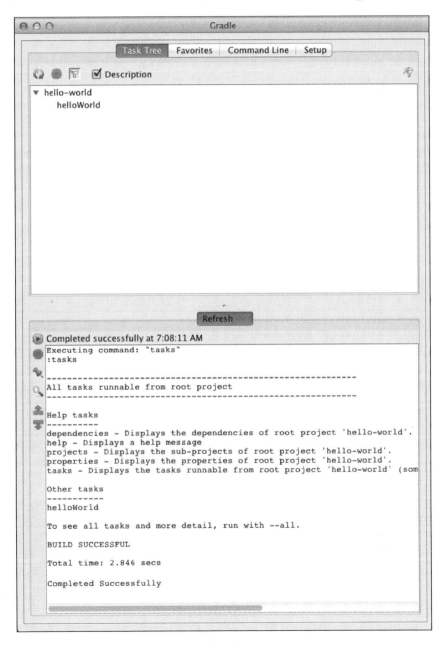

The output of a running task is shown in the bottom part of the window. When we start the GUI for the first time, the `tasks` task is executed and we see the output in the window.

# Task Tree

The **Task Tree** tab shows projects and tasks found in our build project. We can execute a task by double-clicking on the task name.

By default all tasks are shown, but we can apply a filter to show or hide certain projects and tasks. The **Filter** button opens a new dialog window where we can define which tasks and properties are part of the filter. The **Toggle filter** button makes the filter active or inactive.

We can also right-click on the project and task names. This opens a context menu where we can choose whether to execute the task, add it to the favorites, hide it (adds it to the filter), or edit the build file. If we click on **Edit File**, and if the `.gradle` extension is associated with a text editor in our operating system, the editor is opened with the content of the build script. These options can be seen in the following screenshot:

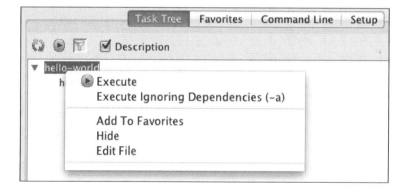

# Favorites

The **Favorites** tab stores tasks we want to execute regularly. We can add a task by right-clicking on the task in the **Task Tree** tab and selecting the **Add To Favorites** menu option. Alternatively, we can open the **Favorites** tab, click on the **Add** button and manually enter the project and task name we want to add to our favorites list. We can see the **Add Favorite** dialog window in the following screenshot:

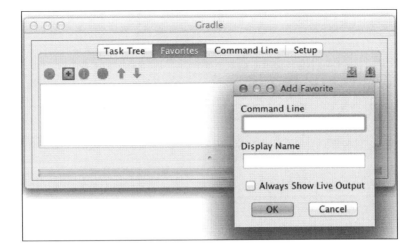

# Command Line

On the **Command Line** tab, we can enter any Gradle command we normally would enter on the command prompt. The command can be added to **Favorites** as well. We can see the **Command Line** tab contents in the following screenshot:

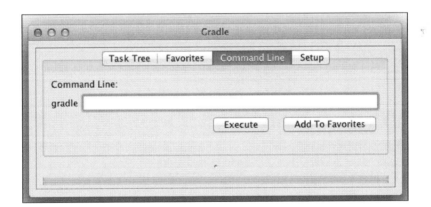

# Setup

The last tab is the **Setup** tab. Here, we can change the project directory, which is set by default to the current directory.

We learned about the different logging levels as command-line options previously in this chapter. In the GUI, we can select the logging level from the **Log Level** drop-down box with the different log levels. We can choose one of **Debug**, **Info**, **Lifecyle**, and **Error** as the log levels. The **Error** log level only shows errors and is the least verbose, while **Debug** is the most verbose log level. The **Lifecyle** log level is the default log level.

Here we can also set how detailed the exception stack trace information should be. In the section **Stack Trace Output** we can choose between the following three options:

- **Exceptions only:** For showing only exceptions when they occur; this is the default value
- **Standard Stack Trace:** For showing more stack trace information for the exceptions
- **Full Stack Trace:** For the most verbose stack trace information for exceptions

If we enable the option **Only Show Output When Errors Occur**, we get output from the build process only if the build fails; otherwise we don't get any output.

Finally, we can define a different way to start Gradle for the build, with the option **Use Custom Gradle Executor**. For example, we can define a different batch or script file with extra setup information to run the build process. The following screenshot shows the **Setup** tab page along with all the options we can set:

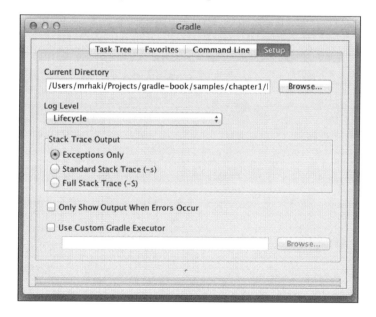

# Summary

So now, we have learned how to install Gradle on our computers. We have written our first Gradle build script with a simple task.

We have seen how to use the tasks built-in to Gradle to get more information about a project. We learned how to use the command-line options to help us run the build scripts. And, we have looked at the Gradle graphical user interface and how we can use it to run Gradle build scripts.

In the next chapter we will take a further look at tasks. We will learn how to add actions to a task. We will write more complex tasks where tasks will depend on other tasks. And we will learn how Gradle builds up a task graph internally and how we can use this in our projects.

# 2
# Creating Gradle Build Scripts

In Gradle, projects and tasks are two important concepts. A Gradle build always consists of one or more projects. A project defines some sort of component we want to build. There are no defining rules about what the component is. It can be a JAR file with utility classes to be used in other projects, or a web application to be deployed to the corporate intranet. A project doesn't have to be about building and packaging code; it can also be about doing things such as copying files to a remote server or deployment of applications to servers.

A project has one or more tasks. A task is a small piece of work that is executed when we run a build, for example, compiling source code, packaging code in an archive file, generating documentation, and so on.

In this chapter we will learn how to define a project with tasks and use it as a Gradle build.

## Writing a build script

In the first chapter we have already written our first build script. Let's create a similar build script with a simple task. Gradle will look for a file with the name `build.gradle`, in the current directory. The file `build.gradle` contains the tasks that make up our project. In this example, we define a simple task that prints out a simple message to the console:

```
project.description = 'Simple project'

task simple << {
    println 'Running simple task for project ' + project.description
}
```

If we run the build we see the following output in the console:

```
$ gradle simple
:simple
Running simple task for project Simple project

BUILD SUCCESSFUL

Total time: 2.08 secs
```

A couple of interesting things happen with this small build script. Gradle reads the script file and creates a `Project` object. The build script configures the `Project` object, and finally the set of tasks to be executed is determined and executed.

So, it is important to note that Gradle creates a `Project` object for us. The `Project` object has several properties and methods, and it is available in our build scripts. We can use the variable name `project` to reference the `Project` object, but we can also leave out this variable name to reference properties and methods of the `Project` object. Gradle will automatically try to map properties and methods in the build script to the `Project` object.

In our simple build script we assign the value `Simple project` to the project property `description`. We used the explicit project variable name and the Groovy property assignment syntax. The following build script uses a different syntax to get the same result:

```
setDescription("Simple project")

task simple << {
    println 'Running simple task for project ' + project.
getDescription()
}
```

Here, we use the Java syntax to set and get the value of the description property of the project object. We are very flexible in our syntax, but we will stick with the Groovy syntax for the rest of the book, because it results in more readable build scripts.

# Defining tasks

A project has one or more tasks to execute some actions, so a task is made up of actions. These actions are executed when the task is executed. Gradle supports several ways to add actions to our tasks.

We can use the `doFirst` and `doLast` methods to add actions to our task, and we can use the left shift operator (<<) as a synonym for the `doLast` method. With the `doLast` method or the left shift operator (<<) we add actions at the end of the list of actions for the task. With the `doFirst` method we can add actions to the beginning of the list of actions. The following script shows how we can use the several methods:

```
task first {
    doFirst {
        println 'Running first'
    }
}

task second {
    doLast { Task task ->
        println "Running ${task.name}"
    }
}

task third << { taskObject ->
    println 'Running ' + taskObject.name
}
```

When we run the script, we get the following output:

```
$ gradle first second third
:first
Running first
:second
Running second
:third
Running third


BUILD SUCCESSFUL


Total time: 2.13 secs
```

For the task `second`, we add the action to print out text with the `doLast` method. The method accepts a closure as an argument. The `task` object is passed to the closure as a parameter. This means we can use the `task` object in our actions. In the sample build file, we get the value for the name property of the task and print it to the console.

Maybe it is a good time to look more closely at closures, because they are an important part of Groovy and are used throughout Gradle build scripts. **Closures** are basically reusable pieces of code that can be assigned to a variable or passed to a method. A closure is defined by enclosing the piece of code between curly brackets ({ . . . }). We can pass one or more parameters to closures. If the closure has only one argument, an implicit parameter, it, can be used to reference the parameter value. We could have written the second task as follows, and the result would still be the same:

```
task second {
    doLast {
        // Using implicit 'it' closure parameter
        println "Running ${it.name}"
    }
}
```

We can also define a name for the parameter and use that name in the code. This is what we did for the tasks second and third, wherein we named the closure parameter task and taskObject respectively. The resulting code is more readable if we define the parameter name explicitly in our closure:

```
task second {
    doLast { Task task ->
        // Using explicit name 'task' as closure parameter
        println "Running ${task.name}"
    }
}
```

# Defining actions with the Action interface

Gradle often has more than one way of defining something, as we will see throughout the book. Besides using closures to add actions to a task, we can also use a more verbose way by passing an implementation class of the org. gradle.api.Action interface. The Action interface has one method: execute. This method is invoked when the task is executed. The following piece of code shows a reimplementation of the first task in our build script:

```
task first {
    doFirst(
        new Action() {
            void execute(task) {
                println "Running ${task.name}"
            }
        }
    )
}
```

It is good to know that we have choices when we define actions for a task, but the closure syntax is denser and more readable.

# Build scripts are Groovy code

We must keep in mind that Gradle scripts use Groovy. This means we can use all the Groovy's good stuff in our scripts. We already saw in our sample script the use of the so-called Groovy `GString`. The `GString` is defined as a `string` with double quotes and can contain references to variables defined in a `${...}` section. The variabled reference is resolved when we get the value of the `GString`.

But other great Groovy constructs can also be used in Gradle scripts. The following sample script shows some of these constructs:

```
task numbers << {
    (1..4).each { number ->
        def squared = number * number
        println "Square of ${number} = ${squared}"
    }
}

task list {
    doFirst {
        def list = ['Groovy', 'Gradle']
        println list.collect { it[0].toLowerCase() }.join('&')
    }
}
```

And when we run the script we get the following output:

```
$ gradle -q numbers list
:numbers
Square of 1 = 1
Square of 2 = 4
Square of 3 = 9
Square of 4 = 16
:list
g&g

BUILD SUCCESSFUL

Total time: 2.129 secs
```

# Defining dependencies between tasks

Until now, we have defined tasks independent of each other. But in our projects we need dependencies between tasks. For example, a task to package compiled class files is dependent on the task to compile the class files. The build system should then first run the compile task, and when the task is finished, the package task must be executed.

In Gradle, we can add task dependencies with the `dependsOn` method for a task. First, let's look at a simple task dependency:

```
task first << { task ->
    println "Run ${task.name}"
}

task second << { task ->
    println "Run ${task.name}"
}

// Define dependency of task second on task first
second.dependsOn 'first'
```

Note that we define the dependency of task `second` on task `first`, in the last line. When we run the script, we see that the `first` task is executed before the `second` task:

```
$ gradle second
:first
Run first
:second
Run second


BUILD SUCCESSFUL


Total time: 2.145 secs
```

Another way to define the dependency between tasks is to set the `dependsOn` property instead of using the `dependsOn` method. There is a subtle difference; Gradle just offers several ways to achieve the same result. In the following piece of code, we use the property to define the dependency of task `second`. And for task `third`, we immediately define the property when we define the task:

```
task first << { task ->
    println "Run ${task.name}"
}

task second << { task ->
    println "Run ${task.name}"
}

// Use property syntax to define dependency.
// dependsOn expects a collection object.
second.dependsOn = ['first']

// Define dependsOn when we create the task:
task third(dependsOn: 'second') << { task ->
    println "Run ${task.name}"
}
```

When we run task `third` on the command line, we see that all three tasks are executed:

```
$ gradle -q third
Run first
Run second
Run third
```

The dependency between tasks is "lazy". We can define a dependency on a task that is defined later in the build script. Gradle will set up all task dependencies during the configuration phase and not during the execution phase. The following script shows that the order of the tasks doesn't matter in the build script:

```
task third(dependsOn: 'second') << { task ->
    println "Run ${task.name}"
}

task second(dependsOn: 'first') << { task ->
    println "Run ${task.name}"
}

task first << { task ->
    println "Run ${task.name}"
}
```

We now have our build script with three tasks. But each task does the same thing—it prints out a string with the name of the task. It is good to keep in mind that our build script is just code, and code can be organized and refactored to create cleaner code. This applies to Gradle build scripts as well. It is important to take a good look at your build scripts and see if things can be organized better and if code can be reused instead of repeated. Even our simple build script can be rewritten like this:

```
def printTaskName = { task ->
    println "Run ${task.name}"
}


task third(dependsOn: 'second') << printTaskName


task second(dependsOn: 'first') << printTaskName


task first << printTaskName
```

This might seem trivial, but it is important to understand that we can apply the same coding techniques we use in our application code to our build code.

# Defining dependencies via tasks

In our build scripts, we defined the task dependencies using the task name. But, there are more ways in which to define a task dependency. We can use the `task` object instead of the task name to define a task dependency:

```
def printTaskName = { task ->
    println "Run ${task.name}"
}

task first << printTaskName

task second(dependsOn: first) << printTaskName
```

# Defining dependencies via closures

We can also use a closure to define the task dependencies. The closure must return a single task name or `task` object, or a collection of task names or `task` objects. Using this technique, we can really fine-tune the dependencies for our task. For example, in the following build script, we define a dependency for task `second` on all tasks in the project with task names that have the letter "f" in the task name:

```
def printTaskName = { task ->
    println "Run ${task.name}"
}

task second << printTaskName
second.dependsOn {
    project.tasks.findAll { task ->
        task.name.contains 'f'
    }
}

task first << printTaskName

task beforeSecond << printTaskName
```

When we run the build project we get the following output:

```
:beforeSecond
Run beforeSecond
:first
Run first
:second
Run second

BUILD SUCCESSFUL

Total time: 2.515 secs
```

# Setting default tasks

To execute a task we use the task name on the command line when we run Gradle. So, if our build script contains a task with the name `first`, we can run the task with the following command:

```
$ gradle first
```

But, we can also define a default task or multiple default tasks that need to be executed, even if we don't explicitly set the task name. So, if we run the `gradle` command without arguments, the default task of our build script will be executed.

To set the default task or tasks, we use the method `defaultTasks`. We pass the names of the tasks that need to be executed, to the method. In the following build script, we make the tasks `first` and `second` the default tasks:

```
defaultTasks 'first', 'second'

task first {
    doLast {
        println "I am first"
    }
}

task second {
    doFirst {
        println "I am second"
    }
}
```

We can run our build script and get the following output:

```
$ gradle
:first
I am first
:second
I am second

BUILD SUCCESSFUL

Total time: 2.097 secs
```

# Organizing tasks

In *Chapter 1, Starting with Gradle*, we already learned that we could use the `tasks` task of Gradle to see which tasks are available for a build. Let us suppose we have the following simple build script:

```
defaultTasks 'second'

task first << {
    println "I am first"
}

task second(dependsOn: first) << {
    println "I am second"
}
```

Nothing fancy here. Task `second` is the default task and depends on task `first`. When we run the `tasks` task on the command line, we get the following output:

```
$ gradle -q tasks


------------------------------------------------------------
All tasks runnable from root project
------------------------------------------------------------


Default tasks: second


Help tasks
----------
dependencies - Displays the dependencies of root project 'chapter2'.
help - Displays a help message
projects - Displays the sub-projects of root project 'chapter2'.
properties - Displays the properties of root project 'chapter2'.
tasks - Displays the tasks runnable from root project 'chapter2'
(some of the displayed tasks may belong to subprojects).


Other tasks
-----------
second


To see all tasks and more detail, run with --all.
```

We see our task with the name `second` in the section **Other tasks**, but not the task with the name `first`. To see all tasks, including the tasks other tasks depend on, we must add the option `--all` to the `tasks` command:

```
$ gradle tasks --all
...
Default tasks: second
...
Other tasks
-----------
second
    first
...
```

Now we see our task with the name `first`. Gradle even indents the dependent tasks so we can see that the task `second` depends on the task `first`.

At the beginning of the output, we see the line:

```
Default tasks: second
```

Gradle shows us which task is the default task in our build.

# Adding a description to tasks

To describe our task, we can set the `description` property of a task. The value of the `description` property is used by the `tasks` task of Gradle. Let's add a description to our two tasks:

```
defaultTasks 'second'

task first(description: 'Base task') << {
    println "I am first"
}

task second(dependsOn: first, description: 'Secondary task') << {
    println "I am second"
}
```

Now when we run the `tasks` task, we get a more descriptive output:

```
$ gradle tasks --all
...
Other tasks
-----------
second - Secondary task
    first - Base task
...
```

# Grouping tasks together

With Gradle, we can also group tasks together in so-called **task groups**. A task group is a set of tasks that belong together logically. The task group is used, for example, in the output of the `tasks` task we used earlier. Let's expand our sample build script by grouping the two tasks together in a sample task group. We must assign a value to the `group` property of a task:

```
defaultTasks 'second'
```

```
def taskGroup = 'base'
task first(description: 'Base task', group: taskGroup) << {
    println "I am first"
}

task second(dependsOn: first, description: 'Secondary task', group:
taskGroup) << {
    println "I am second"
}
```

Next time when we run the `tasks` task, we can see our tasks grouped together in a section **Base tasks**:

```
$ gradle tasks --all
...
Base tasks
----------
first - Base task
second - Secondary task [first]
...
```

Note that the task dependency is appended to the `description` property of task `second`.

# Adding tasks in other ways

Until now, we have added tasks to our build project using the `task` keyword followed by the name of the task. But there are more ways to add tasks to our project. We can use a `string` value with the task name to define a new task:

```
task 'simple' << { task ->
    println "Running ${task.name}"
}
```

We can also use variable expressions to define a new task. If doing so, we must use parentheses, because otherwise the expression cannot be resolved. The following sample script defines a variable `simpleTask` with the `string` value `simple`. This expresssion is used to define the task. The result is that our project now contains a task with the name `simple`:

```
def simpleTask = 'simple'

task(simpleTask) << { task ->
    println "Running ${task.name}"
}
```

We can run the `tasks` task to see our newly created task:

```
$ gradle -q tasks
...
Other tasks
-----------
simple
...
```

We can also use the power of Groovy to add new tasks. We can use Groovy's `GString` notation to dynamically create a task name. It is just like using expressions in the previous sample, but expressed in a Groovy `GString`:

```
def simpleTask = 'simple'

task "${simpleTask}" << { task ->
    println "Running ${task.name}"
}

// Or use loops to create multiple tasks
['Dev', 'Acc', 'Prod'].each { environment ->
    task "deployTo${environment}" << { task ->
        println "Deploying to ${environment}"
    }
}
```

If we run the `tasks` task, we can see we have four new tasks:

```
$ gradle -q tasks
...
Other tasks
-----------
deployToAcc
deployToDev
deployToProd
simple
...
```

Another way to add a new task is through the `tasks` property of a project. Remember that, in our build script, we have access to the `Project` object. Either we use the `project` variable explicitly, or we use methods and properties of the `Project` object implicitly, without using the `project` variable. The `tasks` property of a project is basically a container for all tasks in our project. In the following build script, we use the `add` method to add a new task:

```
def printTaskName = { task ->
    println "Running ${task.name}"
}

// Use project variable.
project.tasks.add(name: 'first') << printTaskName

// Let Gradle resolve tasks to project variable.
tasks.add(name: 'second', dependsOn: 'first') << printTaskName
```

# Using task rules

We have seen how we can add tasks dynamically to our build project. But we can also define so-called **task rules**. These rules are very flexible and allow us to add tasks to our project based on several parameters and project properties.

Suppose we want to add an extra task for every task in our project that shows the description of a task. If we have a task `first` in our project, we want to add a task `descFirst` to show the `description` property of the task `first`. With task rules, we define a pattern for new tasks. In our sample this is `desc<TaskName>`; it is the prefix `desc` followed by the name of the existing task. The following build script shows the implementation of the task rule:

```
task first(description: 'First task')

task second(description: 'Second task')

tasks.addRule("Pattern: desc<TaskName>: show description of a task.")
{ taskName ->
    if (taskName.startsWith('desc')) {
        def targetTaskName = taskName - 'desc'
        def targetTaskNameUncapitalize = targetTaskName[0].
toLowerCase() + targetTaskName[1..-1]
        def targetTask = project.tasks.findByName(targetTaskNameUncap
italize)
        if (targetTask) {
            task(taskName) << {
                println "Description of task ${targetTask.name} ->
${targetTask.description}"
            }
        }
    }
}
```

If we run the `tasks` task, we see an extra `Rules` section in the output:

```
$ gradle tasks
...
Rules
-----
Pattern: desc<TaskName>: show description of a task.
...
```

So, we know we can invoke `descFirst` and `descSecond` for our project. Note that those two extra tasks are not shown in the `Other tasks` section, but the `Rules` section shows the pattern we can use.

If we execute the `descFirst` and `descSecond` tasks, we get the following output:

```
$ gradle descFirst descSecond
:descFirst
Description of task first -> First task
:descSecond
Description of task second -> Second task

BUILD SUCCESSFUL

Total time: 2.223 secs
```

# Accessing tasks as project properties

Each task that we add is also available as a `Project` property, and we can reference this property like we can any other property in our build script. We can, for example, invoke methods or get and set property values of our task through the property reference. This means we are very flexible in how we create our tasks and add behaviour to the tasks. In the following script, we use the `Project` property reference to a task to change the `description` property:

```
task simple << { task ->
    println "Running ${task.name}"
}

// The simple task is available as project property.
simple.description = 'Print task name'
```

```
simple.doLast {
    println "Done"
}
project.simple.doFirst {
    println "Start"
}
```

When we run our task from the command line, we get the following output:

```
$ gradle -q simple
Start
Running simple
Done
```

# Adding additional properties to tasks

A `task` object already has several properties and methods. But we can add any arbitrary new property to a task and use it. In the following sample, we print the value of the task property message. The value of the property is assigned with the statement `simple.message = 'world'`:

```
task simple << {
    println "Hello ${message}"
}
simple.message = 'world'
```

When we run the task we get the following output:

```
$ gradle -q simple
Hello world
```

# Avoiding common pitfalls

A common mistake when creating a task and adding actions for that task is that we forget the left shift operator (<<). Then we are left with a valid syntax in our build script, so we don't get an error when we execute the task. But instead of adding actions, we have configured our task. The closure we use is then interpreted as a configuration closure. All methods and properties in the closure are applied to the task. We can add actions for our tasks in the configuration closure, but we must use the `doFirst` and `doLast` methods. We cannot use the left shift operator (<<).

The following tasks do the same thing, but note the small subtle differences when we define the tasks:

```
def printTaskName = { task ->
    println "Running ${task.name}"
}

task 'one' {
    // Invoke doFirst method to add action.
    doFirst printTaskName
}

// assign action through left-shift operator (<<)
task 'two' << printTaskName

task 'three' {
    // This line will be displayed during configuration
    // and not when we execute the task,
    // because we use the configuration closure
    // and forgot the << operator.
    println "Running three"
}

defaultTasks 'one', 'two'
```

# Skipping tasks

Sometimes, we want tasks to be excluded from a build. In certain circumstances, we just want to skip a task and continue executing other tasks. We can use several methods to skip tasks in Gradle.

# Using onlyIf predicates

Every task has a method `onlyIf` that accepts a closure as an argument. The result of the closure must be `true` or `false`. If the task must be skipped, the result of the closure must be `false`, otherwise the task is executed. The `task` object is passed as a parameter to the closure. Gradle evaluates the closure just before the task is executed.

The following build file will skip the task `longrunning`, if the file is executed during weekdays, but will execute it during the weekend:

```
import static java.util.Calendar.*

task longrunning {
    onlyIf { task ->
        def now = Calendar.instance
        def weekDay = now[DAY_OF_WEEK]
        def weekDayInWeekend = weekDay in [SATURDAY, SUNDAY]
        return weekDayInWeekend
    }
    doLast {
        println "Do long running stuff"
    }
}
```

If we run our build during weekdays, we get the following output:

```
$ gradle longrunning
:longrunning SKIPPED


BUILD SUCCESSFUL


Total time: 2.448 secs
```

And if we run the build during the weekend, we see that the task is executed:

```
$ gradle longrunning
:longrunning
Do long running stuff


BUILD SUCCESSFUL


Total time: 1.823 secs
```

We can invoke the `onlyIf` method multiple times for a task. If one of the predicates returns `false`, the task is skipped. Besides using a closure to define the condition that determines if the task needs to be executed or not, we can use an implementation of the `org.gradle.api.specs.Spec` interface. The `Spec` interface has one method: `isSatisfiedBy`. We must write an implementation and return `true` if the task must be executed or `false` if we want the task to be skipped. The current `task` object is passed as a parameter to the `isSatisfiedBy` method.

In the following sample we check if a file exists. And if the file exists we can execute the task, otherwise the task is skipped:

```
def file = new File('data.sample')

task 'handleFile' << {
    println "Work with file ${file.name}"
}

handleFile.onlyIf(new Spec() {
    boolean isSatisfiedBy(task) {
        file.exists()
    }
})
```

# Skipping tasks by throwing StopExecutionException

Another way to the skip execution of a task is to throw a StopExecutionException exception. If such an exception is thrown, the build will stop the current task and continue with the next task. We can use the doFirst method to add a precondition check for a task. In the closure, when we pass to the doFirst method, we can check for a condition and throw a StopExecutionException exception if necessary.

In the following build script, we check if the script is executed during working hours. If so, the exception is thrown and task first is skipped:

```
def printTaskName = { task ->
    println "Running ${task.name}"
}

task first << printTaskName

first.doFirst {
    def today = Calendar.instance
    def workingHours = today[Calendar.HOUR_OF_DAY] in 8..17

    if (workingHours) {
        throw new StopExecutionException()
    }
}

task second(dependsOn: 'first') << printTaskName
```

If we run our script during working hours and look at the output of our build script, we will notice that we cannot see the task has been skipped. If we use the `onlyIf` method, Gradle will add `SKIPPED` to a task that is not executed:

```
$ gradle second
:first
:second
Running second

BUILD SUCCESSFUL

Total time: 2.174 secs
```

# Enabling and disabling tasks

We have seen how we can skip tasks with the `onlyIf` method or by throwing `StopExecutionException`. But we can also use another method to skip a task. Every task has an `enabled` property. By default, the value of the property is `true`, which means the task is enabled and is executed. We can change the value and set it to `false` to disable the task and skip its execution.

In the following sample, we check for the existence of a directory, and if it exists, the `enabled` property is set to `true`, if not, it is set to `false`:

```
task 'listDirectory' {
    def dir = new File('assemble')
    enabled = dir.exists()
    doLast {
        println "List directory contents: ${dir.listFiles().
join(',')}"
    }
}
```

If we run the task and the directory doesn't exist, we get the following output:

```
$ gradle listDirectory
:listDirectory SKIPPED

BUILD SUCCESSFUL

Total time: 2.112 secs
```

If we run the task, and this time the directory exists, containing a single file with the name `sample`, we get the following output:

```
$ gradle lD
:listDirectory
List directory contents: assemble/sample


BUILD SUCCESSFUL


Total time: 2.118 secs
```

# Skipping from the command line

Until now, we have defined the rules to skip a task in the build file. But we can use the `--exclude-tasks` (`-x`) command-line option if we run the build. We must define, as an argument, which task we want to exclude from the tasks to be executed.

The following script has three tasks with some task dependencies:

```
def printTaskName = { task ->
    println "Run ${task.name}"
}

task first << printTaskName

task second(dependsOn: first) << printTaskName

task third(dependsOn: [second, first]) << printTaskName
```

If we run the `gradle` command and exclude task `second`, we get the following output:

```
$ gradle third -x second
:first
Run first
:third
Run third


BUILD SUCCESSFUL


Total time: 1.618 secs
```

If our task `third` didn't depend on task `first`, only task `third` would be executed.

# Skipping tasks that are up-to-date

Until now, we have defined conditions that are evaluated to determine whether a task needs to be skipped or not. But with Gradle, we can be even more flexible. Suppose we have a task that works on a file and generates some output based on the file. For example, a compile task fits this pattern. In the following sample build file, we have task convert that will take an XML file, parse the contents, and write data to a text file.

```
task(convert) {
    def source = new File('source.xml')
    def output = new File('output.txt')
    doLast {
        def xml = new XmlSlurper().parse(source)
        output.withPrintWriter { writer ->
            xml.person.each { person ->
                writer.println "${person.name},${person.email}"
            }
        }
        println "Converted ${source.name} to ${output.name}"
    }
}
```

We can run this task a couple of times. Each time, the data is read from the XML file and written to the text file:

```
$ gradle -q convert
Converted source.xml to output.txt
$ gradle -q convert
Converted source.xml to output.txt
```

But our input file hasn't changed between the task invocations, so the task doesn't have to be executed. We want the task to be executed only if the source file has changed or the output file is missing or has changed since the last run of the task.

Gradle supports this pattern; this support is known as **incremental build** support. A task only needs to be executed if necessary. This is a very powerful feature of Gradle. It will really speed up a build process, because only those tasks that need to be executed are executed.

We need to change the definition of our task, so that Gradle can determine whether the task needs to be executed based on changes in the input file or output file of the task. A task has the properties inputs and outputs that are used for this purpose. To define an input file, we invoke the file method of the inputs property with the value of our input file. We set the output file by invoking the file method of the outputs property.

Let's rewrite our task to make it support Gradle's incremental build feature:

```
task(convert) {
    def source = new File('source.xml')
    def output = new File('output.txt')

    // Define input file
    inputs.file source

    // Define output file
    outputs.file output

    doLast {
        def xml = new XmlSlurper().parse(source)
        output.withPrintWriter { writer ->
            xml.person.each { person ->
                writer.println "${person.name},${person.email}"
            }
        }
        println "Converted ${source.name} to ${output.name}"
    }
}
```

When we run the build file a couple of times, we see that our task is skipped the second time we run it, because the input and output file haven't changed:

```
$ gradle convert
: convert
Converted source.xml to output.txt

BUILD SUCCESSFUL

Total time: 2.623 secs
$ gradle convert
:convert UP-TO-DATE

BUILD SUCCESSFUL

Total time: 1.53 secs
```

We have defined a single file for the `inputs` and `outputs` properties. But Gradle supports more ways to define values for these properties. The `inputs` property has methods to add a directory, multiple files, or even properties to be watched for changes. The `outputs` property has methods to add a directory or multiple files to be monitored for changes. And if these methods are not appropriate for our build, we can even use the method `upToDateWhen` for the `outputs` property. We pass a closure or implementation of the `org.gradle.api.specs.Spec` interface to define a predicate that determines whether the output of the task is up-to-date.

The following build script uses some of these methods:

```
project.version = '1.0'

task createVersionDir {
    def outputDir = new File('output')

    // If project.version changes then the
    // task is no longer up-to-date
    inputs.property 'version', project.version

    outputs.dir outputDir

    doLast {
        println "Making directory ${outputDir.name}"
        mkdir outputDir
    }
}

task convertFiles {
    // Define multiple files to be checked as inputs.
    inputs.files 'input/input1.xml', 'input/input2.xml'
    // Or use inputs.dir 'input' to check a complete directory.

    // Use upToDateWhen method to define predicate.
    outputs.upToDateWhen {
        // If output directory contains any file which name
        // starts with output and has the txt extension,
        // then the task is up-to-date.
        new File('output').listFiles().any { it.name ==~ /output.*\.
txt$/ }
    }

    doLast {
        println "Running convertFiles"
    }
}
```

# Summary

In this chapter we learned how to create tasks in a build project. We created tasks with actions in several ways and learned how to configure tasks.

We skipped tasks by using predicates, throwing `StopExecutionException`, and enabling or disabling a task. And we even learned how to skip tasks from the command line.

A very powerful feature of Gradle is the incremental build support. If a task is up-to-date, it isn't executed. We can define the rules for determining the up-to-date state in the tasks definition.

In the next chapter, we will take a more in-depth look at the Gradle `Project` object.

# 3
# Working with Gradle Build Scripts

A Gradle script is a program. We use a Groovy DSL to express our build logic. Gradle has several useful built-in methods for handling files and directories, because we often deal with files and directories in our build logic.

In this chapter we will learn how we can use Gradle's features to work with files and directories. Also, we will take a look at how we can set properties in a Gradle build and use Gradle's logging framework. Finally, we see will how we can use the Gradle wrapper task to distribute a configurable Gradle with our build scripts.

## Working with files

It is very common in a build script that we have to work with files and directories. For example, when we need to copy a file from one directory to another, or when we first create a directory to store the output of a task or program.

## Locating files

To locate a file or directory relative to the current project, we can use the `file()` method. This method is actually a method of the `Project` object that is connected to our build script. In the previous chapter we learned how we could use an explicit reference to the `project` variable or simply invoke methods and properties of the `Project` object implicitly.

The `file()` method will resolve the location of a file or directory relative to the current project and not the current working directory. This is very useful because we can run a build script from a different directory than the location of the actual build script. File or directory references that are returned by the `file()` method are then resolved relative to the project directory.

We can pass any object as an argument to the `file()` method. Usually, we will pass a `String` or `java.io.File` object.

In the next example we will demonstrate how we can use the `file()` method to get a reference to a `File` object:

```
// Use String for file reference.
File wsdl = file('src/wsdl/sample.wsdl')

// Use File object for file reference.
File xmlFile = new File('xml/input/sample.xml')
def inputXml = project.file(xmlFile)
```

There are many more ways in which we can use the `file()` method. We can pass a URL or URI instance as an argument. Only `file:` URLs are now supported by Gradle. We can also use closure to define the file or directory. Finally, we could also pass an instance of the `java.util.concurrent.Callable` interface, where the return value of the `call()` method is a valid reference to a file or directory:

```
import java.util.concurrent.Callable

// Use URL instance to locate file.
URL url = new URL('file:/README')
File readme = file(url)

// Or a URI instance.
URI uri = new URI('file:/README')
def readmeFile = file(uri)

// Use a closure to determine the
// file or directory name.
def fileNames = ['src', 'web', 'config']
def configDir = file {
    fileNames.find { fileName ->
        fileName.startsWith('config')
    }
}

// Use Callable interface.
def source = file(new Callable<String>() {
    String call() {
        'src'
    }
})
```

With the `file()` method we create a new `File` object; this object can reference a file or a directory. We can use the `isFile()` or the `isDirectory()` method of the `File` object to see if we are dealing with a file or a directory. In case we want to check if the file or directory really exists, we use the `exists()` method. Because our Gradle build script is written in Groovy, we can also use the extra properties and methods added by Groovy to the `File` class. For example, we can use the `text` property to read the contents of a file. However, we can only test the `File` object after we have used the `file()` method to create it. What if we want to stop the build if a directory doesn't exist or if we are dealing with a file and we expected to be dealing with a directory? In Gradle we can pass an extra argument to the `file()` method, of type `org.gradle.api.PathValidation`. Gradle then validates if the created `File` object is valid for the `PathValidation` instance; if it isn't, the build is stopped and we get a nice error message telling us what went wrong.

Suppose we want to work with a directory named `config`, in our build script. The directory must be present, otherwise the build will stop:

```
def dir = project.file(new File('config'), PathValidation.DIRECTORY)
```

Now we can run the build and see from the output that the directory doesn't exist:

```
$ gradle -q build.gradle
...
* What went wrong:
A problem occurred evaluating root project 'chapter3'.
Cause: Directory '/samples/chapter3/config' does not exist.
...
```

We can also use the `PathValidation` argument to test if a `File` object is really a file and not a directory. Finally, we can check if the `File` object references an existing file or directory. If the file or directory doesn't exist, an exception is thrown and the build stops:

```
// Check file or directory exists.
def readme = project.file('README', PathValidation.EXISTS)

// Check File object is really a file.
def license = project.file('License.txt', PathValidation.FILE)
```

# Using file collections

We can also work with a set of files or directories instead of just a single file or directory. In Gradle, a set of files is represented by the `ConfigurableFileCollection` interface. The nice thing is that a lot of classes in the Gradle API implement this interface.

We can use the `files()` method to define a file collection in our build script. This method is defined in the `Project` object we can access in our build script. The `files()` method accepts many different types of arguments, which makes it very flexible to use. For example, we can use `String` and `File` objects to define a file collection.

As with the `file()` method, paths are resolved relative to the project directory:

```
// Use String instances.
ConfigurableFileCollection multiple = files('README', 'licence.txt')

// Use File objects.
ConfigurableFileCollection userFiles = files(new File('README'), new
File('INSTALL'))

// We can combine different argument types.
def combined = files('README', new File('INSTALL'))
```

But these are not the only arguments we can use. We can pass a URI or URL object, just as we could with the `file()` method:

```
def urlFiles = files(new URI('file:/README'), new URL('file:/
INSTALL'))
```

We can also use an array, `Collection`, or `Iterable` object with filenames or another `ConfigurableFileCollection` instance as an argument:

```
// Use a Collection with file or directory names.
def listOfFileNames = ['src', 'test']
def mainDirectories = files(listOfFileNames)

// Use an array.
mainDirectories = files(listOfFileNames as String[])

// Or an implementation of the Iterable interface.
mainDirectories = files(listOfFileNames as Iterable)
```

```
// Combine arguments and pass another file collection.
def allDirectories = files(['config'], mainDirectories)
```

We can also use a closure or an instance of the `Callable` interface to define a list of files:

```
import java.util.concurrent.Callable

def dirs = files {
    [new File('src'), file('README')].findAll { it.directory }
}

def rootFiles = files(new Callable<List<File>>() {
    List<File> call() {
        [new File('src'), file('README'), file('INSTALL')].findAll {
it.file }
    }
})
```

Finally, we can pass a `Task` object as an argument to the `files()` method. The output property of the task is used to determine the file collection. Let's look at the `convert` task we created in the previous chapter. This task has an `outputs` property with a single file, but this could also be multiple files or a directory. To get the file collection object in our build script, we simply pass the `Task` instance as an argument to the `files()` method:

```
task(convert) {
    def source = new File('source.xml')
    def output = new File('output.txt')

    // Define input file
    inputs.file source

    // Define output file
    outputs.file output

    doLast {
        def xml = new XmlSlurper().parse(source)
        output.withPrintWriter { writer ->
            xml.person.each { person ->
                writer.println "${person.name},${person.email}"
            }
        }
    }
```

```
        println "Converted ${source.name} to ${output.name}"
    }
}

// Get the file collection from
// the task outputs property.
def taskOutputFiles = files(convert)
```

It is also important to note that the file collection is lazy. This means the paths in the collection are not resolved when we define the collection. The paths in the collection are only resolved when the files are actually queried and used in the build script.

The `ConfigurableFileCollection` interface has useful methods to manipulate the collection, for example, we can use the + and - operators to add or remove elements from the collection, respectively:

```
// Define collection.
def fileCollection = files('README', 'INSTALL')

// Remove INSTALL file from collection.
def readme = fileCollection - files('INSTALL')

// Add new collection to existing collection.
def moreFiles = fileCollection + files(file('config', PathValidation.
DIRECTORY))
```

To get the absolute path names for the elements in `ConfigurableFileCollection`, we can use the `asPath` property. The path names are separated by the operating system's path separator. On a Microsoft Windows operating system, the semi-colon (`;`) is used as a path separator, and in Linux or Mac OS X operating systems, the colon (`:`) is used. This means we can simply use the `asPath` property on any operating system and Gradle will automatically use the correct path separator:

```
task 'collectionPath' << {
    def fileCollection = files('README', 'INSTALL')
    println fileCollection.asPath
}
```

When we run the build script on Mac OS X, we get the following output:

```
$ gradle -q collectionPath
/samples/chapter3/README:/samples/chapter3/INSTALL
```

To get the `File` objects that make up the file collection, we can use the `files` property. We can also cast the collection to a list of `File` objects using the `as` keyword; if we know our collection is made up of just a single file or directory, then we can use the `singleFile` property to get the `File` object:

```
def fileCollection = files('README', [new File('INSTALL')])

// Get all elements as File objects.
def allFiles = fileCollection.files

// Or use casting with as keyword.
def fileObjects = fileCollection as File[]

def singleFileCollection = files('INSTALL')

// Get single file as File object.
def installFile = singleFileCollection.singleFile
```

Finally, we can apply a filter to our file collection with the `filter()` method. We pass a closure that defines which elements are to be in the filtered collection. The filtered collection is a live collection. This means that if we add new elements to the original collection, the filter closure is applied again for our filtered collection. In the following example we have the `filterFiles` task, where we define a file collection of two files with the names INSTALL.txt and README. Next, we define a new file collection with a filter that contains all files that have the filename extension .txt. This collection is a live, filtered collection because when we add a new file to the original collection, the filtered collection is also updated:

```
task 'filterFiles' << {
    def rootFiles = files('INSTALL', 'README')

    // Filter for files smaller than 5KB
    def smallFiles = rootFiles.filter {
        it.name.endsWith 'txt'
    }

    rootFiles = rootFiles + files('LICENSE.txt')

    // smallFiles now contains 2 files:
    // INSTALL and LICENSE
}
```

# Working with file trees

In Gradle we can also work with file collections organized as a tree, for example, a directory tree on a disk or hierarchical content in a ZIP file. A hierarchical file collection is represented by a `ConfigurableFileTree` interface. This interface extends the `ConfigurableFileCollection` interface that we saw earlier.

To create a new file tree, we use the `fileTree()` method in our project. We can use several ways to define the file tree.

 If we don't provide a base directory, the current project directory is used as the base directory of the file tree.

We can use the `include` and `includes` properties and methods to define a matching pattern to include a file (or files) in the file tree. With the `exclude` and `excludes` properties and methods, we can use the same syntax to exclude a file or multiple files from the file tree. The matching pattern style is described as an ANT-style matching pattern because the ANT build tool uses this style to define a syntax for matching filenames in file trees. The following patterns can be used:

- `*` to match any number of characters
- `?` to match any single character
- `**` to match any number of directories or files

The following example demonstrates how we can create a file tree:

```
// Create file tree with base directory 'src/main'
// and only include files with extension .java
def srcDir = fileTree('src/main').include('**/*.java')

// Use map with arguments to create a file tree.
def resources = fileTree(dir: 'src/main', excludes: ['**/*.java,
'**/*.groovy'])

// Create file tree with project directory as base
// directory and use method includes() on tree
// object to include 2 files.
FileTree base = fileTree()
base.includes ['README', 'INSTALL']

// Use closure to create file tree.
def javaFiles = fileTree {
    from 'src/main/java'
    exclude '*.properties'
}
```

To filter a file tree, we can use the `filter()` method like we do with file collections, but we can also use the `matching()` method. We pass a closure to the `matching()` method or an instance of the `org.gradle.api.tasks.util.PatternFilterable` interface. We can use the `include`, `includes`, `exclude`, and `excludes` methods to either include or exclude files from the file tree:

```
def sources = fileTree {
    from 'src'
}

def javaFiles = sources.matching {
    include '**/*.java'
}

def nonJavaFiles = sources.matching {
    exclude '**/*.java'
}

def nonLanguageFiles = sources.matching {
    exclude '**/*.scala', '**/*.groovy', '**/*.java'
}

def modifiedLastWeek = sources.matching {
    lastWeek = new Date() - 7
    include { FileTreeElement file ->
        file.lastModified > lastWeek.time
    }
}
```

We can use the `visit()` method to visit each tree node. We can check if the node is a directory or a file. The tree is then visited in breadth-wise order:

```
FileTree testFiles = fileTree(dir: 'src/test')

testFiles.visit { FileVisitDetails fileDetails ->
    if (fileDetails.directory) {
        println "Entering directory ${fileDetails.relativePath"
    } else {
        println "File name: ${fileDetails.name}"
    }
}

def projectFiles = fileTree()
```

```
projectFiles.visit(new FileVisitor() {
    void visitDir(FileVisitDetails details) {
        println "Directory: ${details.path}"
    }

    void visitFile(FileVisitDetails details) {
        println "File: ${details.path}, size: ${details.size}"
    }
})
```

# Copying files

To copy files in Gradle, we can use the `Copy` task. We must assign a set of source files to be copied and the destination of those files. This is defined with a **copy spec**. A copy spec is defined by the `org.gradle.api.file.CopySpec` interface. The interface has a `from()` method we can use to set the files or directories we want to copy. With the `into()` method we specify the destination directory or file.

The following example shows a simple `Copy` task called `simpleCopy` with a single source directory `src/xml` and a destination directory `definitions`:

```
task simpleCopy(type: Copy) {
    from 'src/xml'
    into 'definitions'
}
```

The `from()` method accepts the same arguments as the `files()` method. When the argument is a directory, all files in that directory—but not the directory itself—are copied to the destination directory. If the argument is a file, then only that file is copied.

The `into()` method accepts the same arguments as the `file()` method. To include or exclude files, we use the `include()` and `exclude()` methods of the `CopySpec` interface. We can apply the ANT-style matching patterns just like we do with the `fileTree()` method.

The following example defines a task with the name `copyTask` and uses the `include()` and `exclude()` methods to select the set of files to be copied:

```
def getTextFiles = {
    '**/*.txt'
}

def getDestinationDir = {
    file('dist')
```

```
    }

    task copyTask(type: Copy) {
        // Copy from directory
        from 'src/webapp'

        // Copy single file
        from 'README.txt'

        // Include files with html extension.
        include '**/*.html', '**/*.htm'

        // Use closure to resolve files.
        include getTextFiles

        exclude 'INSTALL.txt'

        // Copy into directory dist
        // resolved via closure.
        into getDestinationDir
    }
```

Another way to copy files is with the `Project.copy()` method. The `copy()` method accepts a `CopySpec` interface implementation, just like the `Copy` task. Our `simpleCopy` task could also have been written like this:

```
    task simpleCopy << {
        copy {
            from 'src/xml'
            into 'definitions'
        }
    }
```

# Renaming files

With the `rename()` method of the `CopySpec` interface, we can rename files as they are copied. The method accepts a closure argument, with the closure argument being the name of the file. We can return a new filename to change the filename or return a null value to keep the original filename:

```
    task copyAndRename(type: Copy) {
        from 'src'
```

```
        rename { String fileName ->
            if (fileName.endsWith('txt')) {
                String original = fileName
                String originalWithoutExtension = original - '.txt'
                originalWithoutExtension + '.text'
            }
        }

        into 'dist'
    }
```

Besides using a closure to rename files during the copy action, we can use a `String` value as a regular expression or a `java.util.regexp.Pattern` object as a regular expression. We also provide the replacement `String` value when a filename matches the pattern. If the regular expression captures groups, we must use the `$1` syntax to reference a group. If a file doesn't match the regular expression, the original filename is used:

```
task copyAndRenameRegEx(type: Copy)

copyAndRenameRegEx {
    from 'src'

    // Change extension .txt to .text.
    rename '(.*).txt', '$1.text'

    // Rename files that start with sample-
    // and remove the sample- part.
    rename ~/^sample-(.*)/, '$1'

    into 'dist'
}
```

# Filtering files

To filter files we must use the `filter()` method of the `CopySpec` interface. We can pass a closure to the `filter()` method. Each line of the file is passed to the closure, and we must return a new `String` value to replace that line. Besides a closure, we can pass an implementation of the `java.io.FilterReader` interface. The ANT build tool already has several filter implementations that we can use in a Gradle build. We must import the `org.apache.tools.ant.filters.*` package to access the ANT filters. We can pass along the properties for a filter with this method invocation:

```
import org.apache.tools.ant.filters.*

task filterFiles(type: Copy) {
    from 'src/filter.txt'
    into 'dist'

    // Closure to replace each line.
    filter { line ->
        "I say: $line"
    }

    // Use ANT filter ReplaceTokens.
    filter(ReplaceTokens, tokens: [message: 'Hello'])
}
```

We set the following contents for src/filter.txt:

```
@message@ everyone
```

If we execute the filterFiles task, we get the resulting filter.txt file in the dist directory:

```
I say: Hello everyone
```

We can use the expand() method to expand property references in a file. The file is transformed with a groovy.text.SimpleTemplateEngine object, which is part of Groovy. Properties are defined as $property or ${property} and we can even include code such as ${new Date()} or ${value ? value : 'default'}.

In the following example we use the expand() method to replace the property languages in the file src/expand.txt:

```
task expandFiles(type: Copy) {
    from 'src/expand.txt'
    into 'dist'

    // Set property languages
    expand languages: ['Java', 'Groovy', 'Scala']

    rename 'expand.txt', 'expanded.txt'
}
```

We execute the `expandFiles` task with the following contents for `src/expand.txt`:

```
A list of programming languages: ${languages.join(', ')}
```

Then, we get the following new contents in the file `dist/expanded.txt`:

```
A list of programming languages: Java, Groovy, Scala.
```

# Archiving files

To create an archive file, we can use the `Zip`, `Tar`, `Jar`, `War`, and `Ear` tasks. To define the source files for the archive and the destination inside the archive files, we use a `CopySpec` interface, just like with copying files. We can use the `rename()`, `filter()`, `expand()`, `include()`, and `exclude()` methods in the same way. So, we don't have to learn anything new; we can use what we have already learned.

To set the filename of the archive, we use any of these properties: `baseName`, `appendix`, `version`, `classifier`, and `extension`. Gradle will use the following pattern to create a filename: `[baseName]-[appendix]-[version]-[classifier].[extension]`. If a property is not set, then it is not included in the resulting filename. To override the default filename pattern, we can set the `archiveName` property and assign our own complete filename, which is used for the resulting archive file.

In the following example, we create a ZIP archive with the `archiveZip` task. We include all the files from the `dist` directory and put them in the root of the archive. The name of the file is set by the individual properties that follow Gradle's pattern:

```
task archiveDist(type: Zip) {
    from 'dist'

    // Create output filename.
    baseName = 'dist-files'
    appendix = 'archive'
    extension = 'zip'
    version = '1.0'
    classifier = 'sample'
}
```

When we run the `archiveDist` task, a new file called `dist-files-archive-1.0-sample.zip` is created in the root of our project. To change the destination directory of the archive file, we must set the `destinationDir` property. In the following example, we set the destination directory to `build/zips`. We also put the files in a `files` directory inside the archive file with the `into()` method. The name of the file is now set by the `archiveName` property:

```
task archiveFiles(type: Zip) {
    from 'dist'

    // Copy files to a directory inside the archive.
    into 'files'

    // Set destination directory.
    destinationDir = file("$buildDir/zips")

    // Set complete filename.
    archiveName = 'dist-files.zip'
}
```

To create a TAR archive with the optional gzip or bzip2 compression, we must use the `tarFiles` task. The syntax is the same as the task for type `Zip`, but we have an extra property `compression` that we can use to set the type of compression (gzip, bzip2) we want to use. If we don't specify the `compression` property, no compression is used to create the archive file.

In the following example, we create a `tarFiles` task of type `Tar`. We set the compression property to `gzip`. After running this task, we get a new file called `dist/tarballs/dist-files.tar.gz`:

```
task tarFiles(type: Tar) {
    from 'dist'

    // Set destination directory.
    destinationDir = file("$buildDir/tarballs")

    // Set filename properties.
    baseName = 'dist-files'
    extension = 'tar.gz'

    compression = Compression.GZIP // or Compression.BZIP2
}
```

The `Jar`, `War`, and `Ear` task types follow the same pattern as the `Zip` and `Tar` task types. Each type has some extra properties and methods to include files specific for that type of archive. We will see examples of these tasks when we look at how we can use Gradle in Java projects.

# Project properties

In a Gradle build file we can access several properties that are defined by Gradle, but we can also create our own properties. We can set the value of our custom properties directly in the build script and also by passing values via the command line.

The default properties we can access in a Gradle build are displayed in the following table:

| Name | Type | Default value |
| --- | --- | --- |
| project | Project | The project instance. |
| name | String | The name of the project directory. The name is read-only. |
| path | String | The absolute path of the project. |
| description | String | Description of the project. |
| projectDir | File | The directory containing the build script. The value is read-only. |
| buildDir | File | Directory with the name build in the directory containing the build script. |
| group | Object | Not specified. |
| version | Object | Not specified. |
| ant | AntBuilder | An AntBuilder instance. |

The following build file has a task to show the value of the properties:

```
version = '1.0'
group = 'Sample'
description = 'Sample build file to show project properties'

task defaultProperties << {
    println "Project: $project"
    println "Name: $name"
    println "Path: $path"
    println "Project directory: $projectDir"
    println "Build directory: $buildDir"
    println "Version: $version"
    println "Group: $project.group"
    println "Description: $project.description"
    println "AntBuilder: $ant"
}
```

When we run the build, we get the following output:

```
$ gradle defaultProperties
:defaultProperties
Project: root project 'chapter3'
Name: defaultProperties
Path: :defaultProperties
Project directory: /Users/mrhaki/Projects/gradle-book/samples/chapter3
Build directory: /Users/mrhaki/Projects/gradle-book/samples/chapter3/
build
Version: 1.0
Group: Sample
Description: Sample build file to show project properties
AntBuilder: org.gradle.api.internal.project.DefaultAntBuilder@1ebafda6

BUILD SUCCESSFUL

Total time: 2.328 secs
```

# Defining custom properties in script

To add our own properties, we have to define them in an ext{} script block in a
build file. Prefixing the property name with ext. is another way to set the value.
To read the value of the property, we don't have to use the ext. prefix; we can
simply refer to the name of the property. The property is automatically added
to the internal project property as well.

In the following script, we add a property customProperty with a String value
custom. In the showProperties task, we show the value of the property:

```
ext.customProperty = 'custom'

// Or we can use ext{} script block.
ext {
    anotherCustomProperty = 'custom'
}

task showProperties {
    doLast {
```

```
        println customProperty
        println ext.customProperty
        println project.customProperty
    }
}
```

After running the script, we get the following output:

```
$ gradle sP
:showProperties
custom
custom


BUILD SUCCESSFUL


Total time: 2.419 secs
```

# Passing properties via the command line

Instead of defining the property directly in the build script, we can use the -P command-line option to add an extra property to a build. We can also use the -P command-line option to set a value for an existing property.

The following build script has a showProperties task that shows the value of an existing property and a new property:

```
task showProperties {
    doLast {
        println "Version: $version"
        println "Custom property: $customProperty"
    }
}
```

Let's run our script and pass the values for the existing version property and the non-existent customProperty:

```
$ gradle -Pversion=1.1 -PcustomProperty=custom showProperties
showProperties
Version: 1.1
Custom property: custom


BUILD SUCCESSFUL


Total time: 2.266 secs
```

# Defining properties via system properties

We can also use Java system properties to define properties for our Gradle build. We use the -D command-line option just like in a normal Java application. The name of the system property must start with org.gradle.project, then the name of the property we want to set, followed by the value.

We can use the same build script we created before:

```
task showProperties {
    doLast {
        println "Version: $version"
        println "Custom property: $customProperty"
    }
}
```

But this time we use different command-line options to get a result:

```
$ gradle -Dorg.gradle.project.version=2.0 -Dorg.gradle.project.
customProperty=custom showProperties
:showProperties
Version: 2.0
Custom property: custom

BUILD SUCCESSFUL

Total time: 1.656 secs
```

# Adding properties via environment variables

Using the command-line options provides much flexibility; however, sometimes we cannot use the command-line options because of environment restrictions or because we don't want to retype the complete command-line options each time we invoke the Gradle build. Gradle can also use environment variables set in the operating system to pass properties to a Gradle build.

The environment variable name starts with ORG_GRADLE_PROJECT_ and is followed by the property name. We use our build file to show the properties:

```
task showProperties {
    doLast {
        println "Version: $version"
        println "Custom property: $customProperty"
    }
}
```

Firstly, we set the ORG_GRADLE_PROJECT_version and ORG_GRADLE_PROJECT_
customProperty environment variables, then we run our showProperties task:

```
$ export ORG_GRADLE_PROJECT_version=3.1
$ export ORG_GRADLE_PROJECT_customProperty="Set by environment variable"
$ gradle showProp
:showProperties
Version: 3.0
Custom property: Set by environment variable

BUILD SUCCESSFUL

Total time: 1.668 secs
```

# Defining properties using an external file

Finally, we can also set the properties for our project in an external file. The file
needs to be named gradle.properties and it should be a plain text file with the
name of the property and its value on separate lines. We can place the file in the
project directory or in the Gradle user home directory. The default Gradle user
home directory is $USER_HOME/.gradle. A property defined in the properties
file in the Gradle user home directory overrides the property values defined
in a properties file in the project directory.

We will now create a gradle.properties file in our project directory, with the
following contents:

```
version = 4.0
customProperty = Property value from gradle.properties
```

We use our build file to show the property values:

```
task showProperties {
    doLast {
        println "Version: $version"
        println "Custom property: $customProperty"
    }
}
```

If we run the build file, we don't have to pass any command-line options;
Gradle will use gradle.properties to get values of the properties:

```
$ gradle showProperties
:showProperties
Version: 4.0
Custom property: Property value from gradle.properties

BUILD SUCCESSFUL

Total time: 1.623 secs
```

# Using logging

In *Chapter 1, Starting with Gradle,* we learned about several command-line options we can use to show either more or fewer log messages when we run a Gradle build. These messages were from the Gradle internal tasks and classes. We used a `println` method in our Gradle build scripts to see some output, but we can also use Gradle's logging mechanisms to have a more customizable way to define logging messages.

Gradle supports several logging levels that we can use for our own messages. The level of our messages is important because we can use the command-line options to filter the messages for log levels.

The following table shows the log levels that are supported by Gradle:

| Level | Used for |
|-----------|------------------------------|
| DEBUG | Debug messages |
| INFO | Information messages |
| LIFECYCLE | Progress information messages |
| WARNING | Warning messages |
| QUIET | Import information messages |
| ERROR | Error messages |

Every Gradle build file and task has a `logger` object. The `logger` object is an instance of a Gradle-specific extension of the **SLF4J** Logger interface. SLF4J is a Java logging library and stands for **Simple Logging Facade for Java**. This library provides a logging API that is independent of the underlying logging framework. A specific logging framework can be used at deploy time or runtime to output the actual log message.

To use the `logger` object in our Gradle build files, we only have to reference `logger` and invoke the method for the logging level we want to use, or we can use the common method `log()` and pass the log level as a parameter to this method.

Let's create a simple task and use the different log levels:

```
task logLevels << {
    // Simple logging sample.
    logger.debug 'debug: Most verbose logging level.'
    logger.log LogLevel.DEBUG, 'debug: Most verbose logging level.'

    logger.info 'info: Use for information messages.'
    logger.log LogLevel.INFO, 'info: Most verbose logging level.'

    logger.lifecycle 'lifecycle: Progress information messages'
    logger.log LogLevel.LIFECYCLE, 'lifecycle: Most verbose logging
level.'

    logger.warn 'warn: Warning messages like invalid configuration'
    logger.log LogLevel.WARN, 'warn: Most verbose logging level.'

    logger.quiet 'quiet: This is important but not an error'
    logger.log LogLevel.QUIET, 'quiet: Most verbose logging level.'

    logger.error 'error: Use for errors'
    logger.log LogLevel.ERROR, 'error: Most verbose logging level.'
}
```

When we run this task from the command line, we get the following output:

```
$ gradle logLevels
:logLevels
lifecycle: Progress information messages
lifecycle: Most verbose logging level.
warn: Warning messages like invalid configuration
warn: Most verbose logging level.
quiet: This is important but not an error
quiet: Most verbose logging level.
error: Use for errors
error: Most verbose logging level.

BUILD SUCCESSFUL

Total time: 2.356 secs
```

We notice that only the LIFECYCLE, WARN, QUIET, and ERROR log levels are shown if we don't add any extra command-line options. To see the INFO messages, we must use the --info command-line option. Then we get the following output:

```
$ gradle --info logLevels
Starting Build
Settings evaluated using empty settings file.
Projects loaded. Root project using build file '/chapter3/logging.
gradle'.
Included projects: [root project 'chapter3']
Evaluating root project 'chapter3' using build file '/chapter3/logging.
gradle'.
All projects evaluated.
Selected primary task 'logLevels'
Tasks to be executed: [task ':logLevels']
:logLevels
Task ':logLevels' has not declared any outputs, assuming that it is
out-of-date.
info: Use for information messages.
info: Most verbose logging level.
lifecycle: Progress information messages
lifecycle: Most verbose logging level.
warn: Warning messages like invalid configuration
warn: Most verbose logging level.
quiet: This is important but not an error
quiet: Most verbose logging level.
error: Use for errors
error: Most verbose logging level.


BUILD SUCCESSFUL


Total time: 1.879 secs
```

Notice that we also get more messages from Gradle itself. Earlier, we only saw the log messages from our script, but this time a lot of extra logging is shown about the build process itself.

To get even more output and our DEBUG level logging messages, we must use the `--debug` command-line option to invoke the `logLevels` task:

```
$ gradle --debug logLevels

...

06:23:16.578 [DEBUG] [org.gradle.api.internal.tasks.execution.
ExecuteActionsTaskExecuter] Executing actions for task ':logLevels'.

06:23:16.585 [DEBUG] [org.gradle.api.Task] debug: Most verbose logging
level.

06:23:16.590 [DEBUG] [org.gradle.api.Task] debug: Most verbose logging
level.

06:23:16.592 [INFO] [org.gradle.api.Task] info: Use for information
messages.

06:23:16.593 [INFO] [org.gradle.api.Task] info: Most verbose logging
level.

06:23:16.595 [LIFECYCLE] [org.gradle.api.Task] lifecycle: Progress
information messages

06:23:16.596 [LIFECYCLE] [org.gradle.api.Task] lifecycle: Most verbose
logging level.

06:23:16.598 [WARN] [org.gradle.api.Task] warn: Warning messages like
invalid configuration

06:23:16.599 [WARN] [org.gradle.api.Task] warn: Most verbose logging
level.

06:23:16.601 [QUIET] [org.gradle.api.Task] quiet: This is important but
not an error

06:23:16.602 [QUIET] [org.gradle.api.Task] quiet: Most verbose logging
level.

06:23:16.604 [ERROR] [org.gradle.api.Task] error: Use for errors

06:23:16.606 [ERROR] [org.gradle.api.Task] error: Most verbose logging
level.

06:23:16.607 [DEBUG] [org.gradle.api.internal.tasks.execution.
ExecuteAtMostOnceTaskExecuter] Finished executing task ':logLevels'

06:23:16.608 [DEBUG] [org.gradle.execution.DefaultTaskGraphExecuter]
Timing: Executing the DAG took 0.045 secs

06:23:16.611 [LIFECYCLE] [org.gradle.BuildResultLogger]

06:23:16.612 [LIFECYCLE] [org.gradle.BuildResultLogger] BUILD SUCCESSFUL

...
```

This time, we get a lot of messages and we really have to look closely for our own. The output format of the logging has also changed; notice that while only the log message was shown before, now the time, log level, and originating class for the log message are also displayed.

So, we know every Gradle project and task has a logger we can use. But we can also explicitly create a logger instance with the Logging class. If, for example, we define our own class and want to use it in a Gradle build, we can use the getLogger() method of the Logging class to get a Gradle logger object. We can use the extra lifecycle() and quiet() methods on this logger instance, just like in projects and tasks.

We will now add a class definition in our build file and use an instance of this class to see the output:

```
class Simple {
    private static final Logger logger = Logging.getLogger('Simple')

    int square(int value) {
        int square = value * value
        logger.lifecycle "Calculate square for ${value} = ${square}"
        return square
    }
}

logger.lifecycle 'Running sample Gradle build.'

task useSimple {
    doFirst {
        logger.lifecycle 'Running useSimple'
    }
    doLast {
        new Simple().square(3)
    }
}
```

We have used the logger of the project and task; in the class Simple, we use Logging.getLogger() to create a Gradle logger instance. When we run our script, we get the following output:

```
$ gradle useSimple
:useSimple
Running useSimple
Calculate square for 3 = 9

BUILD SUCCESSFUL

Total time: 1.605 secs
```

To see the originating class of the logger, we can use the `--debug` (or `-d`) command-line option. Then we will see not only the time the message was logged, but also the name of the logger:

```
$ gradle useSimple -d
...
06:48:58.130 [LIFECYCLE] [org.gradle.api.Project] Running sample Gradle
build.
...
06:49:45.395 [LIFECYCLE] [org.gradle.api.Task] Running useSimple
06:49:45.416 [LIFECYCLE] [Simple] Calculate square for 3 = 9
...
```

Notice that our project logger is named `org.gradle.api.Project`, the task logger is named `org.gradle.api.Task`, and our logger in the `Simple` class is named `Simple`.

# Controlling output

Before we used the `logger` instance for logging messages, we used the `println()` method. Gradle redirects the output sent to `System.out` — which is what we do when we use `println()` — to the logger with the log level `quiet`. That is why we get to see the `println()` output when we run a Gradle build. Gradle intercepts the output and uses its logging support.

When we run the following very simple Gradle build with the `--debug` option, we can see that Gradle has redirected the output to the QUIET log level:

```
println 'Simple logging message'
```

Let's see the output if we run the build:

```
$ gradle --debug
...
06:54:54.442 [QUIET] [system.out] Simple logging message
...
```

Gradle redirects standard error to log messages, with log level ERROR. This also applies to classes we use from external libraries in our Gradle build. If the code in those libraries uses standard output and error, Gradle will capture the output and error messages and redirect them to the `logger` instance.

We can configure this ourselves if we want to change which log level is used for the redirected output and error messages. Every project and task has an instance of the org.gradle.api.logging.LoggingManager class with the name logging. LoggingManager has the captureStandardOutput() and captureStandardError() methods that we can use to set the log level for output and error messages. Remember that Gradle will, by default, use the QUIET log level for output messages and the ERROR log level for error messages. In the following script, we change the log level for output messages to INFO:

```
logging.captureStandardOutput LogLevel.INFO
println 'This message is now logged with log level info instead of
quiet'

task redirectLogging {
    doFirst {
        // Use default redirect log level quiet.
        println 'Start task redirectLogging'
    }
    doLast {
        logging.captureStandardOutput LogLevel.INFO
        println 'Finished task redirectLogging'
    }
}
```

First we run the build without any extra command-line options:

```
$ gradle redirectLogging
:redirectLogging
Start task redirectLogging

BUILD SUCCESSFUL

Total time: 2.291 secs
```

Notice that the println statement we have defined in the doFirst method of our task is shown, but the output of the other println statements is not shown. We redirected the output of those println statements to Gradle's logging with log level INFO. The INFO log level is now shown by default.

Let's run the script again, but now we add the `--info` command-line option so we can see all the output of our `println` statements:

```
$ gradle redirectLogging --info
Starting Build
Settings evaluated using empty settings file.
Projects loaded. Root project using build file '/chapter3/
loggingredirect.gradle'.
Included projects: [root project 'chapter3']
Evaluating root project 'chapter3' using build file '/chapter3/
loggingredirect.gradle'.
This message is now logged with log level info instead of quiet
All projects evaluated.
Selected primary task 'redirectLogging'
Tasks to be executed: [task ':redirectLogging']
:redirectLogging
Task ':redirectLogging' has not declared any outputs, assuming that it is
out-of-date.
Start task redirectLogging
Finished task redirectLogging

BUILD SUCCESSFUL

Total time: 1.646 secs
```

# Using the Gradle wrapper

Normally, if we want to run a Gradle build, we must have Gradle installed on our computer. Also, if we distribute our project to others and they want to build the project, they must have Gradle installed on their computers. The Gradle wrapper can be used to allow others to build our project even if they don't have Gradle installed on their computers.

The wrapper is a batch script on the Microsoft Windows operating systems or shell script on other operating systems that will download Gradle and run the build using the downloaded Gradle.

By using the wrapper, we can make sure the correct Gradle version for the project is used. We can define the Gradle version, and if we run the build via the wrapper script file, the version of Gradle that we defined is used.

# Creating wrapper scripts

To create the Gradle wrapper batch and shell script, we must add a task to our build. The type of task is `org.gradle.api.tasks.wrapper.Wrapper`. We set the `gradleVersion` property to the Gradle version we want to use.

The following sample build file shows how we configure a `Wrapper` task:

```
task createGradleWrapper(type: Wrapper) {
    gradleVersion = '1.1'
}
```

Next, we can execute the `createGradleWrapper` task to generate the files from the command line:

```
$ gradle createGradleWrapper
:createGradleWrapper


BUILD SUCCESSFUL


Total time: 5.938 secs
```

After the execution of the task, we have two script files: `gradlew.bat` and `gradlew` in the root of our project directory. These scripts contain all the logic needed to run Gradle. If Gradle is not downloaded yet, the Gradle distribution will be downloaded and installed locally.

In the directory `gradle/wrapper` relative to our project directory we find the files `gradle-wrapper.jar` and `gradle-wrapper.properties`. The `gradle-wrapper.jar` file contains a couple of class files necessary to download and invoke Gradle. The `gradle-wrapper.properties` file contains settings, such as specifying the URL to download Gradle. The `gradle-wrapper.properties` file also contains the Gradle version number. If a new Gradle version is released, we only have to change the version in the `gradle-wrapper.properties` file and the Gradle wrapper will download the new version, so we can use it to build our project.

All the generated files are now part of our project. If we use a version control system, then we must add these files to the version control. Other people that check out our project can use the `gradlew` scripts to execute tasks from the project. The specified Gradle version is downloaded and used to run the build file.

We can even delete the `createGradleWrapper` task from our build file. If we want to use another Gradle version, we can set the `gradleVersion` property in the `gradle/wrapper/gradle-wrapper.properties` file.

# Customizing the Gradle wrapper

We can change the names of the script files that are generated with the `scriptFile` property of the `Wrapper` task. To change the name of the generated JAR and properties files, we can change the `jarFile` property:

```
task createGradleWrapper(type: Wrapper) {
    gradleVersion = '1.1'
    scriptFile = 'startGradle'
    jarFile = 'gradle-bin'
}
```

To change the URL from which the Gradle version must be downloaded, we can alter the `distributionUrl` property. For example, we could publish a fixed Gradle version on our company intranet and use the `distributionUrl` property to reference a download URL on our intranet. This way we can make sure all developers in the company use the same Gradle version:

```
task createGradleWrapper(type: Wrapper) {
    gradleVersion = '1.1 '
    distributionUrl = 'http://intranet/downloads/gradle-custom-bin.
zip'
}
```

# Summary

In this chapter we learned about the support that Gradle gives when working with files. We saw how to create a file or directory and a collection of files and directories. A file tree represents a hierarchical set of files.

We can add logging messages to our project and tasks and see the output when we run a Gradle build. We learned how to use different log levels to influence how much information is shown in the output. We also used `LoggingManager` to capture standard output and error messages and redirect them to custom log levels.

We learned how we can use the Gradle wrapper to allow users to build our projects even if they don't have Gradle installed. We learned how we can customize the wrapper to download a specific version of Gradle and use it to run our build.

In the next chapter, we will create a Java project and use the Java plugin to add a set of default tasks we can use to compile, test, and package our Java code.

# 4
# Using Gradle for Java Projects

We have seen how we can write tasks in a Gradle build and how we can execute them, but we haven't seen how we can do real-life tasks such as compiling source code or testing with Gradle.

In this chapter, we will learn how we can use the Gradle Java plugin to get tasks for compiling and packaging a Java project. We will also see how Gradle's build-by-convention features make it very easy to start and work with source code.

## Using plugins

In Gradle, we can apply plugins to our project. A plugin basically adds extra functionalities such as tasks and properties to our project. By using a plugin, functionality is decoupled from the core Gradle build logic. We can write our own plugins, but Gradle also ships with plugins that are ready out of the box. For example, Gradle has a Java plugin. This plugin adds tasks for compiling, testing, and packaging Java source code to our project.

The plugins that are packaged with a Gradle version are never updated or changed for that version, so if new functionality is added to a plugin, a whole new Gradle version will be released. In future versions of Gradle, this will change. This doesn't apply for the plugins we write ourselves. We can release new versions of our own plugins, independent of the Gradle version.

# Getting started

The Java plugin provides a lot of useful tasks and properties we can use for building a Java application or library. If we follow the convention-over-configuration support of the plugin, we don't have to write a lot of code in our Gradle build file to use it. If we want to, we can still add extra configuration options to override the default conventions defined by the plugin.

Let's start with a new build file and use the Java plugin. We only have to apply the plugin for our build:

```
apply plugin: 'java'
```

And that's it! By just adding this simple line, we now have a lot of tasks we can use to work with in our Java project. To see which tasks have been added by the plugin, we run the `tasks` command on the command line and look at the output:

```
$ gradle tasks
:tasks


------------------------------------------------------------
All tasks runnable from root project
------------------------------------------------------------


Build tasks
-----------
assemble - Assembles all Jar, War, Zip, and Tar archives.

build - Assembles and tests this project.

buildDependents - Assembles and tests this project and all projects that
depend on it.

buildNeeded - Assembles and tests this project and all projects it
depends on.

classes - Assembles the main classes.

clean - Deletes the build directory.

jar - Assembles a jar archive containing the main classes.

testClasses - Assembles the test classes.


Documentation tasks
--------------------
javadoc - Generates Javadoc API documentation for the main source code.
```

```
Help tasks
----------

dependencies - Displays the dependencies of root project 'sample'.

help - Displays a help message

projects - Displays the sub-projects of root project 'sample'.

properties - Displays the properties of root project 'sample'.

tasks - Displays the tasks runnable from root project 'sample'
(some of the displayed tasks may belong to subprojects).


Verification tasks
------------------

check - Runs all checks.

test - Runs the unit tests.


Rules
-----

Pattern: build<ConfigurationName>: Assembles the artifacts of a
configuration.

Pattern: upload<ConfigurationName>: Assembles and uploads the artifacts
belonging to a configuration.

Pattern: clean<TaskName>: Cleans the output files of a task.


To see all tasks and more detail, run with --all.


BUILD SUCCESSFUL


Total time: 0.911 secs
```

If we look at the list of tasks, we can see how many tasks are now available to us that we didn't have before; all this just by adding a simple line to our build file.

We have several task groups with their own individual tasks that can be used. We have tasks related to building source code and packaging in the **Build tasks** section. The task `javadoc` is used to generate Javadoc documentation, and is in the **Documentation tasks** section. The tasks for running tests and checking code quality are in the **Verification tasks** section. Finally, we have several rule-based tasks to build, upload, and clean artifacts or tasks in our Java project.

The tasks added by the Java plugin are the visible part of the newly added functionality to our project. But the plugin also adds a so-called `convention` object to our project.

A `convention` object has several properties and methods, which are used by the tasks of the plugin. These properties and methods are added to our project, and can be accessed like normal project properties and methods. So with the `convention` object, we can not only look at the properties used by the tasks in the plugin, but we can also change the value of the properties to reconfigure certain tasks.

# Using the Java plugin

To work with the Java plugin, we are first going to create a very simple Java source file. We can then use the plugin's tasks to build the source file. You can make this application as complex as you wish, but in order to stay on topic, we will make this as simple as possible.

By applying the Java plugin, we must now follow some conventions for our project directory structure. To build the source code, our Java source files must be in the `src/main/java` directory, relative to the project directory. If we have non-Java source files that need to be included in the JAR file, we must place them in the directory `src/main/resources`. Our test source files need to be in the `src/test/java` directory, and any non-Java source files needed for testing can be placed in `src/test/resources`. These conventions can be changed if we want or need it, but it is a good idea to stick to them so we don't have to write any extra code in our build file, which could cause errors.

Our sample Java project we will write is a Java class that uses an external property file to get a welcome message. The source file with the name `Sample.java` is located in the `src/main/java` directory:

```
// File: src/main/java/gradle/sample/Sample.java
package gradle.sample;

import java.util.ResourceBundle;

/**
 * Read welcome message from external properties file
 * <code>messages.properties</code>.
 */
public class Sample {

    public Sample() {
    }
```

```
    /**
     * Get <code>messages.properties</code> file
     * and read the value for <em>welcome</em> key.
     *
     * @return Value for <em>welcome</em> key
     *           from <code>messages.properties</code>
     */
    public String getWelcomeMessage() {
        final ResourceBundle resourceBundle = ResourceBundle.
getBundle("messages");
        final String message = resourceBundle.getString("welcome");
        return message;
    }
}
```

In the code, we use `ResourceBundle.getBundle()` to read our welcome message. The welcome message itself is defined in a properties file with the name `messages.properties`, which will go in the `src/main/resources` directory:

```
# File: src/main/resources/gradle/sample/messages.properties
welcome = Welcome to Gradle!
```

To compile the Java source file and process the properties file, we run the `classes` task. Note that the `classes` task has been added by the Java plugin. This is a so-called lifecycle task in Gradle. The `classes` task is actually dependent on two other tasks—`compileJava` and `processResources`. We can see this task dependency when we run the `tasks` command with the command-line option `--all`:

```
$ gradle tasks --all
...
classes - Assembles the main classes.
    compileJava - Compiles the main Java source.
    processResources - Processes the main resources.
...
```

Let's run the `classes` task from the command line:

```
$ gradle classes
:compileJava
:processResources
:classes

BUILD SUCCESSFUL

Total time: 3.301 secs
```

Here we can see that the tasks `compileJava` and `processResources` are executed, because the `classes` task depends on these tasks. The compiled class file and properties file are now in the directories `build/classes/main` and `build/resources/main`. The build directory is the default directory that Gradle uses to build output files.

If we execute the `classes` task again, we notice that the tasks support the incremental build feature of Gradle. As we haven't changed the Java source file or the properties file, and the output is still present, all the tasks can be skipped because they are up-to-date:

```
$ gradle classes
:compileJava UP-TO-DATE
:processResources UP-TO-DATE
:classes UP-TO-DATE


BUILD SUCCESSFUL


Total time: 2.212 secs
```

To package our class file and properties file, we invoke the `jar` task. This task is also added by the Java plugin and depends on the `classes` task. This means that if we run the `jar` task, the `classes` task is also executed. Let's try and run the `jar` task:

```
$ gradle jar
:compileJava UP-TO-DATE
:processResources UP-TO-DATE
:classes UP-TO-DATE
:jar


BUILD SUCCESSFUL


Total time: 2.401 secs
```

The default name of the resulting JAR file is the name of our project. So if our project is called `sample`, then the JAR file is called `sample.jar`. We can find the file in the `build/libs` directory. If we look at the contents of the JAR file, we see our compiled class file and the `messages.properties` file. Also, a manifest file is added automatically by the `jar` task:

```
$ jar tvf build/libs/sample.jar
     0 Tue Mar 13 09:08:32 CET 2012 META-INF/
    25 Tue Mar 13 09:08:32 CET 2012 META-INF/MANIFEST.MF
     0 Tue Mar 13 09:06:50 CET 2012 gradle/
     0 Tue Mar 13 09:06:50 CET 2012 gradle/sample/
   685 Tue Mar 13 09:06:50 CET 2012 gradle/sample/Sample.class
    89 Tue Mar 13 07:07:12 CET 2012 gradle/sample/messages.properties
```

We can also execute the `assemble` task to create the JAR file. The `assemble` task, another lifecycle task, is dependent on the `jar` task and can be extended by other plugins. We could also add dependencies on other tasks that create packages for a project other than just the JAR file, such as a WAR file or ZIP archive file:

```
$ gradle assemble
:compileJava UP-TO-DATE
:processResources UP-TO-DATE
:classes UP-TO-DATE
:jar UP-TO-DATE
:assemble UP-TO-DATE

BUILD SUCCESSFUL

Total time: 2.321 secs
```

To start fresh and clean all the generated output from the previous tasks, we can use the `clean` task. This task deletes the project build directory and all the generated files in that directory. So if we execute the `clean` task from the command line, Gradle will delete the build directory:

```
$ gradle clean
:clean

BUILD SUCCESSFUL

Total time: 2.059 secs
```

Note that the Java plugin also added some rule-based tasks. One of them was `clean<TaskName>`. We can use this task to remove the output files of a specific task. The `clean` task deletes the complete build directory, but with `clean<TaskName>`, we delete only the files and directories created by the named task. For example, to clean the generated Java class files of the `compileJava` task, we execute the `cleanCompileJava` task. Because this is a rule-based task, Gradle will determine that everything after `clean` must be a valid task in our project. The files and directories created by that task are then determined by Gradle and deleted:

```
$ gradle cleanCompileJava
:cleanCompileJava


BUILD SUCCESSFUL


Total time: 2.133 secs
```

# Working with source sets

The Java plugin also adds a new concept to our project—**source sets**. A source set is a collection of source files that are compiled and executed together. The files can be Java source files or resource files. Source sets can be used to group together files with a certain meaning in our project, without having to create a separate project. For example, we can separate the location of source files that describe the API of our Java project in a source set, and run tasks that only apply to the files in this source set.

Without any configuration, we already have the `main` and `test` source sets, which are added by the Java plugin. For each source set, the plugin also adds these three tasks: `compile<SourceSet>Java`, `process<SourceSet>Resources`, and `<SourceSet>Classes`. When the source set is named `main`, we don't have to provide the source set name when we execute a task. For example, `compileJava` applies to the `main` source test, but `compileTestJava` applies to the `test` source set.

Each source set also has some properties to access the directories and files that make up the source set. The following table shows the properties we can access in a source set:

| Source set property | Type | Description |
| --- | --- | --- |
| `java` | `org.gradle.api.file.SourceDirectorySet` | The Java source files for this project. Only files with the extension `.java` are in this collection. |
| `allJava` | `SourceDirectorySet` | By default, it is the same as the `java` property, so it contains all the Java source files. Other plugins can add extra source files to this collection. |
| `resources` | `SourceDirectorySet` | All the resource files for this source set. This contains all the files in the resources source directory, excluding any files with the extension `.java`. |
| `allSource` | `SourceDirectorySet` | By default, this is the combination of the resources and Java properties. It includes all the source files of this source set, both resource and Java source files. |
| `output` | `SourceDirectorySet` | The output files for the source files in the source set. It contains the compiled classes and processed resources. |
| `java.srcDirs` | `Set<File>` | Directories with Java source files. |
| `resources.srcDirs` | `Set<File>` | Directories with the resource files for this source set. |
| `output.classesDir` | `File` | The output directory with the compiled class files for the Java source files in this source set. |
| `output.resourcesDir` | `File` | The output directory with the processed resource files from the resources in this source set. |
| `name` | `String` | Read-only value with the name of the source set. |

We can access these properties via the `sourceSets` property of our project. In the following example, we will create a new task to display values for several properties:

```
apply plugin: 'java'

task sourceSetJavaProperties << {
    sourceSets {
        main {
            println "java.srcDirs = ${java.srcDirs}"
            println "resources.srcDirs = ${resources.srcDirs}"
            println "java.files = ${java.files.name}"
            println "allJava.files = ${allJava.files.name}"
            println "resources.files = ${resources.files.name}"
            println "allSource.files = ${allSource.files.name}"
            println "output.classesDir = ${output.classesDir}"
            println "output.resourcesDir = ${output.resourcesDir}"
            println "output.files = ${output.files}"
        }
    }
}
```

When we run the task `sourceSetJavaProperties`, we get the following output:

```
$ gradle sourceSetJavaProperties
:sourceSetJavaProperties
java.srcDirs = [/chapter4/sample/src/main/java]
resources.srcDirs = [/chapter4/sample/src/main/resources]
java.files = [Sample.java, SampleApp.java]
allJava.files = [Sample.java, SampleApp.java]
resources.files = [messages.properties]
allSource.files = [messages.properties, Sample.java, SampleApp.java]
output.classesDir = /chapter4/sample/build/classes/main
output.resourcesDir = /chapter4/sample/build/resources/main
output.files = [/chapter4/sample/build/classes/main, /chapter4/sample/
build/resources/main]


BUILD SUCCESSFUL


Total time: 2.82 secs
```

# Creating a new source set

We can create our own source set in a project. A source set contains all the source files that are related to each other. In our example, we will add a new source set to include a Java interface. Our `Sample` class will then implement the interface, but because we use a separate source set, we can later use this to create a separate JAR file with only the compiled interface class. We will name the source set `api`, because the interface is actually the API of our example project that we can share with other projects.

To define this source set, we only have to put the name in the `sourceSets` property of the project:

```
apply plugin: 'java'

sourceSets {
    api
}
```

Gradle will create three new tasks based on this source set—`apiClasses`, `compileApiJava`, and `processApiResources`. We can see these tasks after we execute the `tasks` command:

```
$ gradle tasks --all
...
apiClasses - Assembles the api classes.
    compileApiJava - Compiles the api Java source.
    processApiResources - Processes the api resources.
...
```

We have created our Java interface in the directory `src/api/java`, which is the source directory for the Java source files for the `api` source set. The following code allows us to see the Java interface:

```java
// File: src/api/java/gradle/sample/ReadWelcomeMessage.java
package gradle.sample;

/**
 * Read welcome message from source and return value.
 */
public interface ReadWelcomeMessage {

    /**
     * @return Welcome message
     */
    String getWelcomeMessage();
}
```

To compile the source file, we can execute the task `compileApiJava` or `apiClasses`:

```
$ gradle apiClasses
:compileApiJava
:processApiResources UP-TO-DATE
:apiClasses

BUILD SUCCESSFUL

Total time: 3.507 secs
```

The source file is compiled into the `build/classes/api` directory.

We will now change the source code of our `Sample` class and implement the `ReadWelcomeMessage` interface:

```java
// File: src/main/java/gradle/sample/Sample.java
package gradle.sample;

import java.util.ResourceBundle;

/**
 * Read welcome message from external properties file
 * <code>messages.properties</code>.
 */
public class Sample implements ReadWelcomeMessage {

    public Sample() {
    }

    /**
     * Get <code>messages.properties</code> file and read
     * value for <em>welcome</em> key.
     *
     * @return Value for <em>welcome</em> key from <code>messages.
properties</code>
     */
    public String getWelcomeMessage() {
        final ResourceBundle resourceBundle = ResourceBundle.
getBundle("messages");
        final String message = resourceBundle.getString("welcome");
        return message;
    }
}
```

Next, we run the `classes` task to recompile our changed Java source file:

```
$ gradle classes
:compileJava
/chapter4/sample/src/main/java/gradle/sample/Sample.java:10: cannot find
symbol
symbol: class ReadWelcomeMessage
public class Sample implements ReadWelcomeMessage {
                               ^

1 error


FAILURE: Build failed with an exception.


* What went wrong:
Execution failed for task ':compileJava'.
> Compile failed; see the compiler error output for details.


* Try:
Run with --stacktrace option to get the stack trace. Run with --info or
--debug option to get more log output.


BUILD FAILED


Total time: 3.325 secs
```

We get a compilation error! The Java compiler cannot find the `ReadWelcomeMessage` interface. But we just ran the `apiClasses` task and compiled the interface without errors. To fix this, we must define a **dependency** between the `classes` and `apiClasses` tasks. The `classes` task is dependent on the `apiClasses` tasks. First, the interface must be compiled, and then the class that implements the interface.

Next, we must add the output directory with the compiled interface class file, to the `compileClasspath` property of the main source set. Once we have done that, we know for sure that the Java compiler for compiling the `Sample` class picks up the compiled class file.

To do this, we will change the build file and add the task dependency between the two tasks and the main source set configuration:

```
apply plugin: 'java'

sourceSets {
    api
    main {
        compileClasspath = compileClasspath + files(api.output.
classesDir)
    }
}

classes.dependsOn apiClasses
```

Now we can run the `classes` task again, without errors:

```
$ gradle classes
:compileApiJava
:processApiResources UP-TO-DATE
:apiClasses
:compileJava
:processResources
:classes

BUILD SUCCESSFUL

Total time: 3.703 secs
```

# Custom configuration

If we use Gradle for an existing project, we might have a different directory structure than the default structure defined by Gradle, or it may be that we want to have a different structure for another reason. We can account for this by configuring the source sets and using different values for the source directories.

Suppose that we have a project with the following source directory structure:

```
+ resources
|   |
|   + java
|   |
|   + test
```

```
|
+ src
|  |
|  + java
|
+ test
   |
   + unit
   |  |
   |  + java
   |
   + integration
      |
      + java
```

We will need to reconfigure the main and test source sets, but we must also add a new integration-test source set. The following code reflects the directory structure for the source sets:

```
apply plugin: 'java'

sourceSets {
    main {
        java {
            srcDir 'src/java'
        }
        resources {
            srcDir 'resources/java'
        }
    }
    test {
        java {
            srcDir 'test/unit/java'
        }
        resources {
            srcDir 'resources/test'
        }
    }
    'integration-test' {
        java {
            srcDir 'test/integration/java'
        }
        resources {
            srcDir 'resources/test'
        }
    }
}
```

Notice how we must put the name of the `integration-test` source set in quotes; this is because we use a hyphen in the name. Gradle then converts the name of the source set into `integrationTest` (without the hyphen and with a capital T). To compile, for example, the source files of the integration `test` source set, we use the `compileIntegrationTestJava` task.

# Working with properties

We have now already learned that the Java plugin adds tasks and source sets to our Gradle project; however, we also get a lot of new properties that we can use. Custom properties of a plugin are set in a `Convention` object of type `org.gradle.api.plugins.Convention`. A `Convention` object is used by a plugin to expose properties and methods that we can use in our project. The `Convention` object of the plugin is added to the `convention` property of a project. The `convention` property of a Gradle project is a container for all the `Convention` objects from the plugins.

We can access the properties from the plugin's `Convention` object directly as project properties, or we can specify a complete path to the `Convention` object of the plugin, to get to a property or invoke a method.

For example, the `sourceSets` property is a property of the `Convention` object of the Java plugin. With the following task, `showConvention`, we see the different ways we have to access that property:

```
task showConvention << {
    println sourceSets.main.name
    println project.sourceSets.main.name
    println project.convention.plugins.java.sourceSets.main.name
}
```

To see all the properties available for us, we must invoke the `properties` task from the command line. The following output shows part of the output from the `properties` task:

```
$ gradle properties
...
targetCompatibility: 1.5
test: task ':test'
testClasses: task ':testClasses'
testReportDir: /chapter4/sample/build/reports/tests
```

```
testReportDirName: tests
testResultsDir: /chapter4/sample/build/test-results
testResultsDirName: test-results
version: unspecified
...
```

If we look through the list, we see a lot of properties that we can use to redefine the directories where output files of the `compile` or `test` tasks are stored. The following table shows the directory properties:

| Property name | Default value | Description |
| --- | --- | --- |
| distDirName | distributions | The directory name relative to the build directory, to store distribution files. |
| libsDirName | libs | The directory name to store generated JAR files, relative to the build directory. |
| dependencyCacheDirName | dependency-cache | Name of directory for storing cached information about dependencies, relative to the build directory. |
| docsDirName | docs | Name of the directory for storing generated documentation, relative to the build directory. |
| testReportDirName | tests | The directory name relative to the build directory, to store test reports. |
| testResultsDirName | test-results | Store test result XML files, relative to the build directory. |

The Java plugin also adds other properties to our project. These properties can be used to set the source and target compatibility of the Java version for compiling the Java source files, or to set the base filename for the generated JAR files.

The following table shows the convention properties of the Java plugin:

| Property name | Type | Default value | Description |
| --- | --- | --- | --- |
| archives BaseName | String | Name of the project | The base file name to use for archives created by archive tasks such as `jar`. |
| source Compatibility | String, Number, JavaVersion, Object | Java version of JDK used to run Gradle | The Java version compatibility to use when compiling Java source files with the `compile` task. |
| target Compatibility | String, Number, JavaVersion, Object | Value of source Compatibility | The version of Java to generate class files for. |
| sourceSets | SourceSet Container | - | Source sets for the project. |
| manifest | Manifest | Empty manifest | Manifest to include in all JAR files. |
| metaInf | List | Empty list | The list of files to include in the `META-INF` directory of all the JAR files created in the project. |

In our example project, we already saw that the generated JAR file was named after the project name, but with the `archivesBaseName` property, we can change that. We can also change the source compatibility to Java 6 for our project. Finally, we can also change the manifest that is used for the generated JAR file. The following build file reflects all the changes:

```
apply plugin: 'java'

archivesBaseName = 'gradle-sample'
version = '1.0'

sourceCompatibility = JavaVersion.VERSION_1_6   // Or '1.6' or 6
```

```
manifest = manifest {
    attributes(
        'Implementation-Version' : version,
        'Implementation-Title' : 'Gradle Sample'
    )
}

// Need to explicitly set manifest on jar task,
// but should be automatic.
jar.manifest.from manifest
...
```

If we now invoke the `assemble` task to create our JAR file and look into the `build/` `libs` directory, we can see that the JAR file is now named `gradle-sample-1.0.jar`:

```
$ gradle assemble
:compileApiJava
:processApiResources
:apiClasses
:compileJava
:processResources
:classes
:jar
:assemble

BUILD SUCCESSFUL

Total time: 4.022 secs
$ ls build/libs
gradle-sample-1.0.jar
```

If we run the same task with the command-line option `--info` to set the info log level, we see in the output that the Java 6 compiler is used:

```
$ gradle --info cleanCompileJava assemble
...
Compiling with JDK 6 Java compiler API.
...
```

To see the contents of the generated manifest file, we first extract the file from the JAR file and then look at the contents:

```
$ jar xvf build/libs/gradle-sample-1.0.jar
  inflated: META-INF/MANIFEST.MF
$ cat META-INF/MANIFEST.MF
Manifest-Version: 1.0
Implementation-Version: 1.0
Implementation-Title: Gradle Sample
```

# Creating documentation

To generate Javadoc documentation, we must use the `javadoc` task that is of type `org.gradle.api.tasks.javadoc.Javadoc`. The task generates documentation for the Java source files in the `main` source set. If we want to generate documentation for the source sets in our project, we must configure the `javadoc` task or add an extra `javadoc` task to our project.

Note that, in our project, we have an `api` and `main` source set with the Java source files. If we want to generate documentation for both the source sets, we have to configure the `javadoc` task in our project. The `source` property of the `javadoc` task is, by default, set to `sourceSets.main.allJava`. If we add `sourceSets.api.allJava` to the `source` property, our interface file is also processed by the `javadoc` task:

```
apply plugin: 'java'
...
javadoc {
    source sourceSets.api.allJava
}
...
```

Next, we can run the `javadoc` task, and the documentation is generated and put into the `build/docs/javadoc` directory:

```
$ gradle javadoc
:compileApiJava UP-TO-DATE
:processApiResources UP-TO-DATE
:apiClasses UP-TO-DATE
:compileJava UP-TO-DATE
:processResources UP-TO-DATE
:classes UP-TO-DATE
:javadoc
```

```
BUILD SUCCESSFUL
```

```
Total time: 3.425 secs
```

We can set more properties on the `javadoc` task. For example, we can set a title for the generated documentation with the `title` property. The default value is the name of the project followed by the project version number, if available.

To change the destination directory, we can set the `destinationDir` property of the `javadoc` task to the directory we want.

We can also use the `options` property to define a lot of properties we know from the Java SDK `javadoc` tool. The following example shows how we can set some of the options for the `javadoc` task in our project:

```
apply plugin: 'java'
...
javadoc {
    source sourceSets.api.allJava
    title = 'Gradle Sample Project'
    options.links = ['http://docs.oracle.com/javase/6/docs/api/']
    options.footer = "Generated on ${new Date().format('dd MMM
yyyy')}"
    options.header = "Documention for version ${project.version}"
}
...
```

# Assembling archives

If we want to package the output of the new `api` source set in our JAR file, we must define a new task ourselves. Gradle doesn't provide some magic to do this for us automatically; luckily, the task itself is very simple:

```
apply plugin: 'java'

archivesBaseName = 'gradle-sample'
version = '1.0'

sourceSets {
    api
}

task apiJar(type: Jar) {
    appendix = 'api'
    from sourceSets.api.output
}
...
```

The task `apiJar` is a `Jar` task. We define the `appendix` property that is used to generate the final filename of the JAR file. We use the `from()` method to point to the output directory of our `api` source set, so all generated output is included in the JAR file. When we run the task `apiJar`, a new JAR file `gradle-sample-api-1.0.jar` is generated in the `build/libs` directory:

```
$ gradle apiJar
:compileApiJava UP-TO-DATE
:processApiResources UP-TO-DATE
:apiClasses UP-TO-DATE
:apiJar


BUILD SUCCESSFUL


Total time: 2.998 secs
```

The base name of the JAR file is the project name, which is similar to one for the `jar` task. If we look at the contents, we see our compiled `ReadWelcomeMessage` class file:

```
$ jar tvf build/libs/sample-api.jar
     0 Tue Mar 13 11:27:10 CET 2012 META-INF/
    25 Tue Mar 13 11:27:10 CET 2012 META-INF/MANIFEST.MF
     0 Tue Mar 13 11:17:50 CET 2012 gradle/
     0 Tue Mar 13 11:17:50 CET 2012 gradle/sample/
   182 Tue Mar 13 11:17:50 CET 2012 gradle/sample/ReadWelcomeMessage.
class
```

Note also that we didn't define a task dependency between the tasks `apiJar` and `apiClasses`, but when we ran the `apiJar` task, Gradle automatically ran the `apiClasses` task. This happened because we used the `sourceSets.api.output` property to define which files needed to be included in the JAR file; Gradle noticed this and determined which task is responsible for creating the content in the `sourceSets.api.output` directory. The `apiClasses` task is the task that compiles the Java source files, and processes the resources into the build directory, so Gradle will first invoke the `apiClasses` task before the `apiJar` task.

# Summary

In this chapter, we have learned about the support for a Java project in Gradle. With just a simple line needed to apply the Java plugin, we get masses of functionality, which we can use for our Java code. We can compile our source files, package the compiled code into a JAR file, and generate documentation.

In the next chapter, we will see how we can add dependencies to external libraries. We will learn how to configure repositories, and how we can organize our dependencies with configurations.

# 5
# Dependency Management

When we develop our code, we usually use third-party or open source libraries. These libraries need to be available in the classpath of the compiler, otherwise we will get errors and our build will fail. Gradle provides support for dependency management, so we can define our dependencies in our build file. Gradle will then take care of the necessary configuration for our various tasks.

In this chapter, we will learn how we can use dependency management in our builds. We will see how to organize dependencies with configurations. We will also learn about repositories that host dependency artifacts, their dependencies, and how we can handle different repository layouts.

Then we will define dependencies using Gradle syntax, for modules with version information.

## Dependency configuration

Java has no real support for working with versioned libraries as dependencies. We cannot express in Java whether our class depends on `lib-1.0.jar` or `lib-2.0.jar`, for example. There are some open source solutions that deal with dependencies and allow us to express whether our Java code depends on `lib-1.0.jar` or `lib-2.0.jar`. The most popular are Maven and Apache Ivy. Maven is a complete build tool and has a mechanism for dependency management. Ivy is only about dependency management.

Both tools support repositories where versioned libraries are stored, together with metadata about those libraries. A library can have dependencies on other libraries and is described in the metadata of the library. The metadata is described in descriptor XML files. Ivy fully supports Maven descriptor files and repositories; it also adds some extra functionality. So with Ivy, you get what you would with Maven, and then some more. That is why Gradle uses the Ivy API under the hood to do dependency management. Gradle also adds some extra sugar on top of Ivy, so we can define and use dependencies in a very flexible way.

In a Gradle build file, we group dependencies together in a configuration. A configuration has a name, and configurations can extend each other. With a configuration, we can make logical groups of dependencies. For example, we can create a `javaCompile` configuration to include dependencies needed to compile the Java code. We can add as many configurations to our build as we want to. We don't define our dependencies directly in the configuration. A configuration, as with a label, can be used when we define a dependency.

Every Gradle build has a `ConfigurationContainer` object. This object is accessible via the `Project` property containers. We can use a closure to configure the container with `Configuration` objects. Each `Configuration` object has at least a name, but we can change more properties. We can set a resolution strategy, if a configuration has version conflicts with dependencies, or we can change the visibility of a configuration so that it will not be visible outside of our project.

In the following example, we create a new configuration with the name `commonsLib` to hold our dependencies and a configuration `mainLib` that extends `commonsLib`. The extended configuration `mainLib` gets all settings and dependencies from `commonsLib`, and we can assign extra dependencies as well:

```
configurations {
    commonsLib {
        description = 'Common libraries'
    }
    mainLib {
        description = 'Main libraries'
        extendsFrom commonsLib
    }
}

println configurations['mainLib'].name
println configurations.commonsLib.name
```

The output of the build shows the names of the configurations:

```
$ gradle -q
commonsLib
mainLib
```

Many plugins add new configurations to `ConfigurationContainer`. We used the Java plugin in the previous chapter, which added four configurations to our project. With the built-in task dependencies, we can get an overview of defined dependencies and configurations for a project.

The following build script uses the Java plugin:

```
apply plugin: 'java'
```

We get the following output if we execute the `dependencies` task:

```
$ gradle -q dependencies


------------------------------------------------------------
Root project
------------------------------------------------------------


archives - Configuration for archive artifacts.
No dependencies


compile - Classpath for compiling the main sources.
No dependencies


default - Configuration for default artifacts.
No dependencies


runtime - Classpath for running the compiled main classes.
No dependencies


testCompile - Classpath for compiling the test sources.
No dependencies


testRuntime - Classpath for running the compiled test classes.
No dependencies
```

Notice how we already have six configurations in our project. The following table shows the configuration and which tasks use the configuration:

| Configuration | Extends | Used by task | Description |
|---|---|---|---|
| compile | - | compileJava | Dependencies needed at compile time to compile the source files. |
| runtime | compile | - | Dependencies for runtime of the application, but not needed for compilation. |
| testCompile | compile | compileTestJava | Dependencies to compile test source files. |
| testRuntime | testCompile | test | All dependencies needed to run the tests. |
| archives | - | uploadArchives | Contains artifacts, such as JAR files created by the project. |
| default | runtime | - | Default configuration contains all runtime dependencies. |

If our code has a dependency on a library, we can set the dependency with the compile configuration. The dependency is then automatically available in the runtime, testCompile, testRuntime, and default configurations.

# Repositories

Dependencies are usually stored in some kind of repository. A repository has a layout that defines a pattern for the path of a versioned library module. Gradle knows, for example, the layout of a Maven repository. Ivy repositories can have customized layouts, and with Gradle, we can configure a customized layout. The repository can be accessible via the file system, HTTP, SSH, or other protocols.

We can declare several repository types in the Gradle build file. Gradle provides some preconfigured repositories, but it is also very easy to use a custom Maven or Ivy repository. We can also declare a simple file system repository to be used for resolving and finding dependencies. The following table shows the preconfigured and custom repositories we can use:

| Repository type | Description |
|---|---|
| Maven repository | Maven layout repository on a remote computer or file system. |
| Maven central repository | Preconfigured Maven layout repository to search for dependencies in the Maven central repository. |
| Maven local repository | Preconfigured Maven repository that finds dependencies in the local Maven repository. |
| Ivy repository | Ivy repository that can be located on a local or remote computer. |
| Flat directory repository | Simple repository on the local file system of the computer or a network share. |

We define a repository with the `repositories()` method. This method accepts a closure that is used to configure an `org.gradle.api.artifacts.dsl.RepositoryHandler` object.

# Adding Maven repositories

A lot of Java projects use Maven as a build tool and for Maven's dependency management features. A Maven repository stores libraries with version information and metadata described in a descriptor XML file. The layout of a Maven repository is fixed and follows the pattern `someroot/[organization]/[module]/[revision]/[module]-[revision].[ext]`. The organization section is split into subfolders based on the dots used in the organization name. For example, if the organization name is `org.gradle`, an `org` folder with the subfolder `gradle` needs to be in the Maven repository. A JAR library with the organization name `org.gradle`, module name `gradle-api`, and revision `1.0` is resolved via the path `someroot/org/gradle/gradle-api/1.0/gradle-api-1.0.jar`.

The Maven central repository is located at `http://repo1.maven.org/maven2` and contains a lot of libraries. Many open source projects deploy their artifacts to Maven's central repository. We can use the `mavenCentral()` method in the configuration closure for the `repositories()` method. The following example is a build file where we have defined the Maven central repository:

```
repositories {
    mavenCentral()
}
```

If we have used Maven before on our computer, there is a good chance we have a local Maven repository. Maven will use a hidden folder in our home directory to store downloaded dependency libraries. We can add this local Maven repository, with the method `mavenLocal()`, to the list of repositories. We can add the Maven local repository to our build file, as follows:

```
repositories {
    mavenLocal()
    mavenCentral()
}
```

Both the central and local Maven repositories are preconfigured Maven repositories. We can also add a custom repository that follows the Maven layout. For example, our company can have a Maven repository available via the intranet. We define the URL of the Maven repository with the `maven()` or `mavenRepo()` methods.

The example build file uses both methods to add two new Maven repositories available through our intranet:

```
repositories {
    maven {
        // Name is optional. If not set url property is used
        name = 'Main Maven repository'
        url = 'http://intranet/repo'
    }

    mavenRepo(name: 'Snapshot repository', url: 'http://intranet/
snapshots')
}
```

Both methods configure a repository via a combination of a closure and method arguments. Sometimes we must access a Maven repository that stores the metadata in descriptor XML files, but the actual JAR files are in a different location. To support this scenario, we must set the property `artifactUrls` and assign the addresses of the servers that store the JAR files:

```
repositories {
    maven {
        url: 'http://intranet/mvn'
        artifactUrls 'http://intranet/jars'
        artifactUrls 'http://intranet/snapshot-jars'
    }
}
```

To access a Maven repository with basic authentication, we can set the credentials when we define the repository:

```
repositories {
    maven(name: 'Secured repository') {
        credentials {
            username = 'username'
            password = 'password'
        }
        url = 'http://intranet/repo'
    }
}
```

It is not a good idea to store the username and password as plain text in the build file; this is because anyone can read our password, if stored in plain text. It is better if we define the properties in a file `gradle.properties`, in the Gradle user home directory, apply the correct security constraints on the property file, and use those properties in our build file:

```
repositories {
    maven(name: 'Secured repository') {
        credentials {
            // Define properties usernameSecuredRepo
            // and passwordSecuredRepo in
            // $USER_HOME/.gradle/gradle.properties
            username = usernameSecuredRepo
            password = passwordSecuredRepo
        }
        url = 'http://intranet/repo'
    }
}
```

# Adding Ivy repositories

An Ivy repository has a customizable layout; this means that there is no single predefined layout as with a Maven repository. The default layout for an Ivy repository has the pattern `someroot/[organization]/[module]/[revision]/[type]s/[artifact].[ext]`. The name of the organization is not split into subfolders, as with the Maven layout. So, our module `gradle` with the organization name `org.gradle` and artifact `gradle-api` with revision `1.0` is resolved via the path `someroot/org.gradle/gradle/1.0/jars/gradle-api.jar`.

We use the same `resources()` method to configure an Ivy repository. We use the method `ivy()` to configure the settings for an Ivy repository. We define the URL of the repository and optionally, a name:

```
repositories {
    ivy(url: 'http://intranet/ivy-repo', name: 'Our repository')

    ivy {
        url = 'http://intranet/ivy-snapshots'
    }
}
```

If our Ivy repository has a Maven layout, we can set the `layout` property to `maven`. We can use the same property to define a custom layout for a repository. We define the patterns that are used to resolve the descriptor XML files and the actual library files.

The following table shows the different layout names we can use and the default patterns for the preconfigured layouts:

| Layout name | Pattern Ivy descriptors | Pattern artifacts |
|---|---|---|
| gradle | someroot/[organization]/ [module]/[revision]/ivy-[revision].xml | someroot/[organization]/ [module]/[revision]/ [artifact]-[revision] (-[classifier])(.[ext]) |
| maven | someroot/[organization]/ [module]/[revision]/ivy-[revision].xml | someroot/[organization]/ [module]/[revision]/ [artifact]-[revision] (-[classifier])(.[ext]) |
| pattern | Custom | Custom |

The example build file uses the preconfigured layout names `gradle` and `maven` and also a custom pattern:

```
repositories {
    ivy {
        url = 'http://intranet/ivy-snapshots'
        layout = 'maven'
    }

    ivy {
        url = 'http://intranet/repository'
        layout = 'gradle'
    }
```

```
ivy {
    url = 'http://intranet/custom'
    layout('pattern') {
        // Pattern to resolve Ivy descriptor files.
        ivy '[module]/[revision]/ivy.xml'

        // Pattern to resolve files.
        artifact '[module]/[revision]/[artifact](.[ext])'
    }
}
}
```

Instead of using the `layout()` method to define a custom pattern, we can use the methods `ivyPattern()` and `artifactPattern()` to define the patterns for the Ivy repository:

```
repositories {
    ivy {
        url = 'http://intranet/custom'
        ivyPatterns '[module]/[revision]/ivy.xml'
        artifactPatterns '[module]/[revision]/[artifact](.[ext])'
    }
}
```

To access an Ivy repository that is secured with basic authentication, we must pass our credentials. Just like with the secured Maven repository, it is best to store the username and password as properties in the file $USER_HOME/.gradle/gradle.properties:

```
repositories {
    ivy {
        credentials {
            username = usernameFromGradleProperties
            password = passwordFromGradleProperties
        }
        url = 'http://intranet/custom'
        ivyPatterns '[module]/[revision]/ivy.xml'
        artifactPatterns '[module]/[revision]/[artifact](.[ext])'
        artifactPatterns '[module]/[revision]/[artifact](.[ext])'
    }
}
```

# Adding a local directory repository

To use a simple repository on the local file system or a network share mapped as local storage, we must use the flatDir() method. The flatDir() methods accepts arguments or a closure to configure the correct directory. We can assign a single directory or multiple directories.

Gradle will resolve files in the configured directory using the first match it finds with the following patterns:

- [artifact]-[version].[ext]
- [artifact]-[version]-[classifier].[ext]
- [artifact].[ext]
- [artifact]-[classifier].[ext]

The following example build file defines a flat directory repository:

```
repositories {
    flatDir(dir: '../lib', name: 'libs directory')

    flatDir {
        dirs '../project-files', '/volumes/shared-libs'
        name = 'All dependency directories'
    }
}
```

# Defining dependencies

We learned how to use dependency configurations to group together dependencies; we saw how we must define repositories so dependencies can be resolved, but we haven't yet learned how to define the actual dependencies. We define dependencies in our build project with the dependencies{} script block. We define a closure to pass to the dependencies{} script block, with the configuration of the dependency.

We can define different types of dependencies. The following table shows the types we can use:

| Dependency type | Method | Description |
| --- | --- | --- |
| External module dependency | - | A dependency on an external module or library in a repository. |
| Project dependency | project() | Dependency on another Gradle project. |

| Dependency type | Method | Description |
| --- | --- | --- |
| File dependency | `files()`, `fileTree()` | Dependency on a collection of files on the local computer. |
| Client module dependency | `module()` | A dependency on an external module where the artifacts are stored in a repository but the meta information about the module is in the build file. We can override meta information using this type of dependency. |
| Gradle API dependency | `gradleApi()` | Dependency on the Gradle API of the current Gradle version. We use this dependency when we develop Gradle plugins and tasks. |
| Local Groovy dependency | `localGroovy()` | Dependency on the Groovy libraries used by the current Gradle version. We use this dependency when we develop Gradle plugins and tasks. |

# Using external module dependencies

The most used dependency is the external module dependency. We can define a module dependency in different ways. For example, we can use arguments to set a group name, module name, and revision of the dependency. Or, we can use the `String` notation to set the group name, module name, and revision in a single string. We always assign a dependency to a specific dependency configuration. The dependency configuration must be defined by ourselves or by a plugin we have applied to our project.

In the following example build file, we will use the Java plugin, so we get a `compile` and `runtime` dependency configuration. We will also assign several external module dependencies to each configuration using the different syntax rules:

```
apply plugin: 'java'

repositories {
    mavenCentral()
}

dependencies {
```

```
        compile group: 'org.springframework', name: 'spring-core',
    version: '3.1.1.RELEASE'

        runtime 'org.springframework:spring-aop:3.1.1.RELEASE'
}
```

Remember that a Gradle build file is a Groovy script file, so we can define variables to set values and use them in the `dependencies{}` script block configuration closure. If we rewrite the previous build file, we get:

```
apply plugin: 'java'

repositories {
    mavenCentral()
}

ext {
    springVersion = '3.1.1.RELEASE'
    springGroup = 'org.springframework'
}

dependencies {
    compile group: springGroup, name: 'spring-core', version:
springVersion

    runtime "$springGroup:spring-aop:$springVersion"
}
```

Gradle will look for the descriptor file in the Maven central repository. If the file is found, the artifact of the module and the dependencies of the module are downloaded and made available to the dependency configuration.

To see the dependencies and the transitive dependencies, we invoke the built-in task `dependencies`. We get the following output:

```
$ gradle -q dependencies
...
compile - Classpath for compiling the main sources.
\--- org.springframework:spring-core:3.1.1.RELEASE [default]
     +--- org.springframework:spring-asm:3.1.1.RELEASE
[compile,master,runtime]
     \--- commons-logging:commons-logging:1.1.1 [compile,master,runtime]
...
runtime - Classpath for running the compiled main classes.
+--- org.springframework:spring-core:3.1.1.RELEASE [default]
```

```
|    +--- org.springframework:spring-asm:3.1.1.RELEASE
[compile,master,runtime]
|    \--- commons-logging:commons-logging:1.1.1 [compile,master,runtime]
\--- org.springframework:spring-aop:3.1.1.RELEASE [default]
     +--- org.springframework:spring-core:3.1.1.RELEASE
[compile,runtime,master] (*)
     +--- org.springframework:spring-asm:3.1.1.RELEASE
[compile,master,runtime] (*)
     +--- aopalliance:aopalliance:1.0 [compile,master,runtime]
     \--- org.springframework:spring-beans:3.1.1.RELEASE
[compile,master,runtime]
          \--- org.springframework:spring-core:3.1.1.RELEASE
[compile,master,runtime] (*)
...

(*) - dependencies omitted (listed previously)
```

To only download the artifact of an external dependency and not the transitive dependencies, we can set the property `transitive` to `false`, for the dependency. We can set the property with a closure or as an extra property in the argument list:

```
apply plugin: 'java'

repositories {
    mavenCentral()
}

dependencies {
    // Configure transitive property with closure.
    compile('org.slf4j:slf4j-simple:1.6.4') {
        transitive = false
    }

    // Or we can use the transitive property
    // as method argument.
    compile group: 'org.slf4j', name: 'slf4j-simple', version:
    '1.6.4', transitive: false
}
```

We can also exclude some transitive dependencies, with the `exclude()` method. Gradle will look at the descriptor file of the module and exclude any dependencies that we have added with the `exclude()` method.

For example, in the following build file we exclude the transitive dependency `org.slf4j:sl4j-api`:

```
apply plugin: 'java'

repositories {
    mavenCentral()
}

dependencies {
    // Configure transitive property with closure.
    compile('org.slf4j:slf4j-simple:1.6.4') {
        exclude 'org.slf4j:slf4j-api'
    }
}
```

To only get an artifact of an external module dependency we can use the "artifact-only" notation. We must also use this notation when a repository doesn't have a module descriptor file and we want to get the artifact. We must add an @ symbol before the extension of the artifact. Gradle will not look at the module descriptor file, if available, when we use this notation:

```
apply plugin: 'java'

repositories {
    mavenCentral()
}

dependencies {
    // Use artifact-only notation with @ symbol.
    runtime('org.slf4j:slf4j-simple:1.6.4@jar')

    // Or we can use the ext property
    // as method argument.
    runtime group: 'org.slf4j', name: 'slf4j-simple', version:
'1.6.4', ext: 'jar'
}
```

We can even set the transitive behavior on a complete configuration. Each configuration has a property `transitive`. We can set the value to `true` or `false` to change the transitive behavior for each dependency we define in the configuration. In the following sample build file, we set the `transitive` property on the runtime configuration:

```
apply plugin: 'java'

repositories {
    mavenCentral()
}

dependencies {
  compile('org.slf4j:slf4j-simple:1.6.4')
}


configurations.compile.transitive = false
```

In a Maven repository, we can use classifiers for a dependency. For example, the module descriptor file defines the classifiers jdk16 and jdk15 for different JDK versions of the library. We can use the classifier in a Gradle dependency definition to select the dependency with the given classifier:

```
apply plugin: 'java'

repositories {
    mavenCentral()
}

dependencies {
    // Use artifact-only notation with @ symbol
    // together with classifier jdk16.
    compile('sample:simple:1.0:jdk16@jar')

    // Or we can use the classifier property
    // as method argument.
    compile group: 'sample', name: 'simple', version: '1.0',
classifier: 'jdk16'
}
```

The module descriptor of a module in a Maven repository can only have one artifact, but in an Ivy repository, we can define multiple artifacts for a single module. Each set of artifacts is grouped together in a configuration. The default configuration contains all artifacts belonging to the module. If we don't specify the configuration property when we define the dependency for an Ivy module, the default configuration is used. We must specify the configuration property if we want to use artifacts belonging to that specific configuration:

```
apply plugin: 'java'

repositories {
```

```
    ivy {
        url = 'http://intranet/custom'
        ivyPatterns '[module]/[revision]/ivy.xml'
        artifactPatterns '[module]/[revision]/[artifact](.[ext])'
    }
}

dependencies {
    // Use configuration property in method arguments.
    testCompile group: 'sample', name: 'logging', version: '1.0',
configuration: 'test'

    // Or we use a closure to set the property.
    testCompile('sample:logging:1.0') {
        configuration = 'test
    }
}
```

# Using project dependencies

Gradle projects can be dependent on each other. To define such a dependency we use
the `project()` method and use the name of the other project as an argument. Gradle
will look for a default dependency configuration in that project and use that as a
dependency. We can use the `configuration` property to use different dependency
configurations as a dependency for each project:

```
apply plugin: 'java'

dependencies {
    compile project(':projectA')

    compile project(':projectB') {
        configuration = 'compile'
    }
}
```

# Using file dependencies

We can add dependencies using `FileCollection`. We can use the methods `file()`,
`files()`, and `fileTree()` to add dependencies to a configuration. The dependency
must be resolved to an actual artifact.

The following example uses file dependencies for the compile configuration:

```
apply plugin: 'java'

dependencies {
    compile files('spring-core.jar', 'spring-aap.jar')
    compile fileTree(dir: 'deps', include: '*.jar')
}
```

# Using client module dependencies

Normally, Gradle will use a descriptor XML file for dependencies found in the repository to see which artifacts and optional transitive dependencies need to be downloaded. But those descriptor files can be misconfigured, and so we may want to override the descriptors ourselves to ensure the dependencies are correct. To do this we must use the `module()` method to define the transitive dependencies of a dependency. Gradle will then use our own configuration and not the one provided by the module in a repository:

```
apply plugin: 'java'

ext {
    springGroup = 'org.springframework'
    springRelease = '3.1.1.RELEASE'
}
dependencies {
    compile module("$springGroup:spring-context:$springRelease") {
        dependency("$springGroup:spring-aop:$springRelease") {
            transitive = false
        }
    }
}
```

# Using Gradle and Groovy dependencies

When we develop Grails plugins and tasks, we can define a dependency on the Gradle API and the Groovy libraries used by the current Gradle version. We can use the methods `gradleApi()` and `localGroovy()` to do this.

The following example defines the dependencies in the compile dependency configuration of a project:

```
apply plugin: 'groovy'

// Dependency configuration for developing
```

```
// Gradle plugins and tasks with Groovy.
dependencies {
    // Gradle API available for compile task.
    compile gradleApi()

    // Groovy libraries used by Gradle version.
    groovy localGroovy()
}
```

# Accessing configuration dependencies

We can access the dependencies for a dependency configuration in a build file or task through the `configurations` property of the `Project` object. We can use the `dependencies()` and `allDependencies()` methods to get a reference to the dependencies:

```
apply plugin: 'java'

repositories {
    mavenCentral()
}

dependencies {
    runtime "org.springframework:spring-aop:3.1.1.RELEASE"
}

task 'dependencyInfo' << {
    println "-- Runtime dependencies --"
    configurations.runtime.dependencies.each {
        println "${it.group}:${it.name}:${it.version}"
    }

    println "-- Runtime allDependencies --"
    configurations.runtime.allDependencies.each {
        println "${it.group}:${it.name}:${it.version}"
    }
}
```

# Setting dynamic versions

Until now, we have set a version for a dependency explicitly with a complete version number. To set a minimum version number, we can use a special dynamic version syntax. For example, to set the dependency version to a minimum of 2.1 for a dependency, we use a version value `2.1.+`. Gradle will resolve the dependency to the latest version after version 2.1, or to version 2.1 itself. In the following example, we will define a dependency on a `spring-core` version of at least 3.1:

```
apply plugin: 'java'

repositories {
    mavenCentral()
}

dependencies {
    compile group: 'org.springframework', name: 'spring-core',
version: '3.1.+'
}
```

We can also reference the latest released version of a module with `latest.integration`. We can also set a version range with a minimum and maximum version number. The following table shows the ranges we can use:

| Range | Description |
| --- | --- |
| [1.0, 2.0] | All versions greater than or equal to 1.0 and lower than or equal to 2.0 |
| [1.0, 2.0[ | All versions greater than or equal to 1.0 and lower than 2.0 |
| ]1.0, 2.0] | All versions greater than 1.0 and lower than or equal to 2.0 |
| ]1.0, 2.0[ | All versions greater than 1.0 and lower than 2.0 |
| [1.0, ) | All versions greater than or equal to 1.0 |
| ]1.0, ) | All versions greater than 1.0 |
| (, 2.0] | All versions lower than or equal to 2.0 |
| (, 2.0[ | All versions lower than 2.0 |

The following example build file will use version 3.0.7.RELEASE as the latest release, which is greater than 3.0 and less than 3.1:

```
apply plugin: 'java'

repositories {
    mavenCentral()
}

dependencies {
    compile group: 'org.springframework', name: 'spring-core',
version: '[3.0, 3.1['
}
```

# Resolving version conflicts

If we have a project with a lot of dependencies and those dependencies have transitive dependencies, version conflicts can easily arise. If one module has a dependency on `sample:logging:1.0` and another on `sample:logging:2.0`, Gradle will, by default, use the newest version number.

To change the default behavior, we set the `resolutionStrategy` property of a dependency configuration. We can instruct Gradle to fail the build if a conflict arises. This is very useful for debugging version conflicts.

In the following example build file, we instruct Gradle to fail the build if a version conflicts arises for all configurations:

```
apply plugin: 'java'

configurations.all {
    resolutionStrategy {
        failOnVersionConflict()
    }
}
```

To force a certain version number to be used for all dependencies (even transitive dependencies), we can use the `force()` method of `resolutionStrategy`. With this method we can make sure that, for a given module, the preferred version is always used:

```
apply plugin: 'java'

configurations.compile {
```

```
    resolutionStrategy {
        force 'org.springframework:spring-core:3.1.0.RELEASE'
    }
}
```

# Adding optional ANT tasks

We can re-use existing **ANT (Another Neat Tool)** tasks in Gradle build files.
Gradle uses Groovy's AntBuilder for ANT integration. But, if we want to use an
optional ANT task we must do something extra, because the optional tasks and their
dependencies are not in the Gradle classpath. Luckily, we only have to define our
dependencies for the optional task in the `build.gradle` file, and we can then define
and use the optional ANT task.

In the following sample, we are using the `scp` ANT optional task. We define a
new configuration with the name `sshAntTask` and assign the dependencies to
this configuration. Then, we can define the task and set the `classpath` property
to the classpath of the configuration. We use the `asPath` property to convert the
configuration classpath for the ANT task. In the sample, we also see how we can
ask for user input when the script is run. The passphrase for the ssh keyfile is a
secret and we don't want to keep it in a file somewhere, so we ask the user for it.
The Java method `System.console()` returns a reference to the console, and with
the `readPassword()` method, we can get the value for the passphrase:

```
// We define a new configuration with the name 'sshAntTask'.
// This configuration is used to define our dependencies.
configurations {
    sshAntTask
}

repositories.mavenCentral()

// Assign dependencies to the sshAntTask configuration.
dependencies {
    sshAntTask 'org.apache.ant:ant-jsch:1.7.1', 'jsch:jsch:0.1.29'
}

// Sample task which uses the scp ANT optional task.
task update {
    description = 'Update files on remote server.'

    // Get passphrase from user input.
    def console = System.console()
```

```
        def passphrase = console.readPassword('%s: ', 'Please enter the
    passphrase for the keyfile')

        // Redefine scp ANT task, with the classpath property set to our
    newly defined
        // sshAntTask configuration classpath.
        ant.taskdef(name: 'scp', classname: 'org.apache.tools.ant.
    taskdefs.optional.ssh.Scp',
                classpath: configurations.sshAntTask.asPath)

        // Invoke the scp ANT task. (Use gradle -i update to see the
    output of the ANT task.)
        ant.scp(todir: 'mrhaki@servername:/home/mrhaki',
                keyfile: '${user.home}/.ssh/id_rsa',
                passphrase: passphrase as String, // Use phassphrase
    entered by the user.
                verbose: 'true') {
            fileset(dir: 'work') {
                include(name: '**/**')
            }
        }
    }
}
```

# Using dependency configurations as files

Each dependency configuration implements the `FileCollection` interface of Gradle. This means we can use a configuration reference if we need a list of files somewhere. The files that make up the resolved dependency configuration are then used.

Let's create a new build file and use a dependency configuration as the value for the `from()` method. We create a new task of type `Copy` and copy all dependencies of a new configuration, `springLibs`, to a directory:

```
repositories.mavenCentral()

configurations {
    springLibs
}

dependencies {
    springLibs 'org.springframework:spring-web:3.1.1.RELEASE'
}

task copyCompileDeps(type: Copy) {
    from configurations.springLibs
    into "$buildDir/compileLibs"
}
```

# Summary

In this chapter we have learned about dependency management support in Gradle. We have seen how to create a dependency configuration or use dependency configurations provided by a plugin.

To get the real dependency artifacts and their transitive dependencies, we must define repositories that store those files. Gradle allows very flexible repository configurations to be used.

Finally, we saw how to define the actual dependencies for a dependency configuration. We learned how to resolve version conflicts between dependencies and how to use those dependencies in a Gradle build.

In the next chapter, we will look at how we can run tests for our code and how we can execute Java applications from our build. We will also learn how we can publish our own project to a repository.

# 6

# Testing, Building, and Publishing Artifacts

An important part of developing software is writing tests for our code. In this chapter, we will learn how we can run our test code as part of the build process. Gradle supports both JUnit and TestNG testing frameworks. We can even run tests in parallel to shorten the time of the build, resulting in quick builds.

We will also learn how to run a Java application as part of a Gradle build. We can use the application plugin to automatically execute a Java application as part of the build.

After we have written and tested our code, it is time to publish the code so others can use it. We will build a package and deploy our code to a company repository or any other repository.

## Testing

Gradle has built-in support for running tests for our Java projects. When we add the Java plugin to our project, we get new tasks to compile and run tests. We also get the dependency configurations `testCompile` and `testRuntime`. We use these dependencies to set the classpath for running the tests in our code base.

Let's write a simple JUnit test for a sample Java class. The implementation of `gradle.sample.Sample` has the method `getWelcomeMessage()`, where we read a text from a property file and then return the value. The following example contains the code for the `Sample` class:

```
// File: src/main/java/gradle/sample/Sample.java
package gradle.sample;

import java.util.ResourceBundle;

/**
 * Read welcome message from external properties file
 * <code>messages.properties</code>.
 */
public class Sample {

    public Sample() {
    }

    /**
     * Get <code>messages.properties</code> file and read
     * value for <em>welcome</em> key.
     *
     * @return Value for <em>welcome</em> key from <code>messages.
properties</code>
     */
    public String getWelcomeMessage() {
        final ResourceBundle resourceBundle = ResourceBundle.
getBundle("gradle.sample.messages");
        final String message = resourceBundle.getString("welcome");
        return message;
    }
}
```

Next, we must add the resource property file that is used by the `Sample` class. We create the file `messages.properties` in the `src/main/resources/gradle/sample` directory, with the following contents:

```
# File: src/main/resources/gradle/sample/messages.properties
welcome = Welcome to Gradle!
```

Our test is very simple. We create a `Sample` object and invoke the `getWelcomeMessage()` method. We compare the returned value with a value we expect to be returned. The following sample contains the test to check the value of the `getWelcomeMessage()` method with the expected `String` value `Welcome to Gradle`. We need to create the file `SampleTest.java` in the directory `src/test/java/gradle/sample`:

```java
// File: src/test/java/gradle/sample/
package gradle.sample;

import org.junit.Assert;
import org.junit.Test;

public class SampleTest {

    @Test
    public void readWelcomeMessage() {
        final Sample sample = new Sample();
        final String realMessage = sample.getWelcomeMessage();

        final String expectedMessage = "Welcome to Gradle.";

        Assert.assertEquals("Get text from properties file",
expectedMessage, realMessage);
    }
}
```

The Gradle build script for these files is very simple. We first apply the Java plugin, and because we are keeping to Gradle's configuration conventions, we don't have to configure or define much else. Our test is written as a JUnit test. JUnit is one of the most used test frameworks for Java projects. To make sure the required JUnit classes are available to compile and run the test class, we must add JUnit as a dependency to our project. The Java plugin adds testCompile and testRuntime configurations we can use. We add the JUnit dependency to the testCompile configuration. All JUnit classes are now available to compile the test classes.

The following sample build file contains all the necessary code to execute the test:

```
apply plugin: 'java'

repositories {
    mavenCentral()
}

dependencies {
    // Add at least version 4.8 of JUnit as dependency.
    testCompile 'junit:junit:[4.8,)'
}
```

To run our test, we only have to invoke the `test` task that is added by the Java plugin, from the command line:

```
$ gradle test
:compileJava
:processResources
:classes
:compileTestJava
:processTestResources UP-TO-DATE
:testClasses
:test

gradle.sample.SampleTest > readWelcomeMessage FAILED
    org.junit.ComparisonFailure at SampleTest.java:15

1 test completed, 1 failed

FAILURE: Build failed with an exception.

* What went wrong:
Execution failed for task ':test'.
> There were failing tests. See the report at file:///Users/mrhaki/
Projects/gradle-book/samples/chapter6/sample/build/reports/tests.

* Try:
Run with --stacktrace option to get the stack trace. Run with --info or
--debug option to get more log output.

BUILD FAILED

Total time: 1.629 secs
```

If we look at the output, we see that the test has failed, but we don't see why. One way to find out is to re-run the `test` task with extra logging. We can enable the `info` logging level with `--info` (or `-i`) arguments, as shown in the following command:

```
$ gradle test --info
...
Gradle Worker 1 executing tests.
```

```
Test readWelcomeMessage(gradle.sample.SampleTest) FAILED: org.junit.
ComparisonFailure: Get text from properties file expected:<Welcome to
Gradle[.]> but was:<Welcome to Gradle[!]>
Test gradle.sample.SampleTest FAILED
Gradle Worker 1 finished executing tests.
1 test completed, 1 failure
...
```

Now we can see why our test failed. In our test, we expected a dot (.) at the end of the `String` instead of the exclamation mark (!) we got from the property file. To fix our test, we must change the contents of the property file and replace the exclamation mark with a dot. Before we do that, we will use a different way to see the test results. Until now, we looked at the output on the command line after running the `test` task. In the directory `build/reports/test`, there is an HTML file report available with the results of our test run.

If we open the file `build/reports/test/index.html` in a web browser, we get a clear overview of the tests that have run and failed:

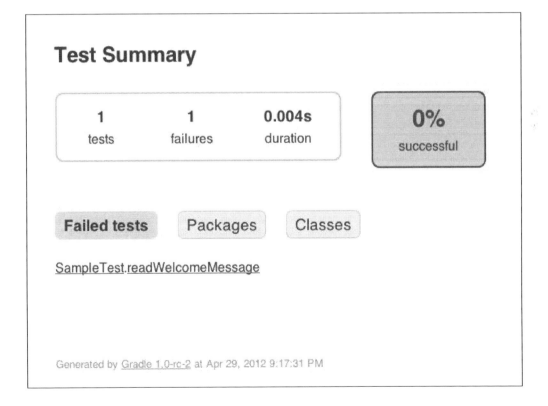

We can click on the method name of a failed test to see the details. Here we see again the message stating that the expected `String` value had a dot instead of an exclamation mark at the end of the line:

Let's change the contents of the `messages.properties` file and use a dot instead of an exclamation mark at the end of the line:

```
# File: src/main/resources/gradle/sample/messages.properties
welcome = Welcome to Gradle.
```

Now we run the `test` task again, from the command line:

```
$ gradle test
:compileJava UP-TO-DATE
:processResources
:classes
:compileTestJava
:processTestResources UP-TO-DATE
:testClasses
:test

BUILD SUCCESSFUL

Total time: 1.714 secs
```

The Gradle build did not fail this time and is successful. Our test has run, and we get the expected result from the `getWelcomeMessage()` method.

The following screenshot shows that the tests are 100 percent successful and are also documented in the generated test HTML reports:

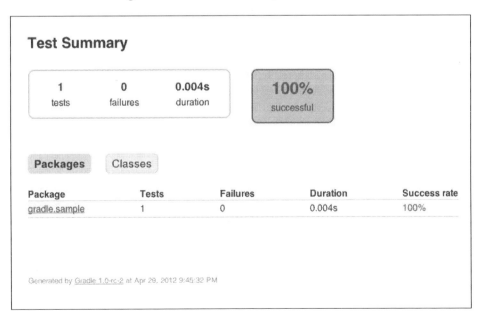

# Using TestNG for testing

We have written a test with the JUnit test framework. Gradle also supports tests that are written with the TestNG test framework. Gradle scans the test classpath for all class files and checks if they have specific JUnit or TestNG annotations. If a test class or super class extends `TestCase` or `GroovyTestCase` or is annotated with the `@RunWith` annotation, the test class is also determined to be a JUnit test.

For Gradle to use either JUnit or TestNG tests when we run the `test` task, we invoke the `useJUnit()` or `useTestNG()` methods, respectively, to force Gradle to use the correct testing framework. Gradle uses JUnit as testing framework by default, so we don't have to use the `useJUnit()` method when we use JUnit or JUnit-compatible test frameworks to test our code.

Let's write a new test, but this time we will use TestNG annotations and classes. The following sample class is the same test as we saw before, but written with the TestNG framework:

```java
// File: src/test/java/gradle/sample/SampleTestNG.java
package gradle.sample;

import org.testng.annotations.Test;
import org.testng.AssertJUnit;

public class SampleTestNG {

    @Test
    public void readWelcomeMessage() {
        final Sample sample = new Sample();
        final String realMessage = sample.getWelcomeMessage();

        final String expectedMessage = "Welcome to Gradle.";

        AssertJUnit.assertEquals("Get text from properties file",
expectedMessage, realMessage);
    }

}
```

We need to add the TestNG dependency to the `testCompile` dependency configuration. Furthermore, we invoke the `useTestNG()` method on our `test` task, so Gradle will pick up our new test. We create a new build file and add the following:

```
apply plugin: 'java'

repositories {
    mavenCentral()
}

dependencies {
    testCompile 'junit:junit:[4.8,)'
    testCompile 'org.testng:testng:6.5.1'
}

test.useTestNG()
```

Now we can run the `test` task again, but this time Gradle will use our TestNG test:

```
$ gradle test
:compileJava UP-TO-DATE
:processResources UP-TO-DATE
:classes UP-TO-DATE
:compileTestJava UP-TO-DATE
:processTestResources UP-TO-DATE
:testClasses
:test

BUILD SUCCESSFUL

Total time: 0.988 secs
```

The generated HTML test report is in the directory `build/reports/tests`. We can open the file `index.html` in our web browser and see the output that is generated by the TestNG framework. The following screenshot shows an example of the output that we can view:

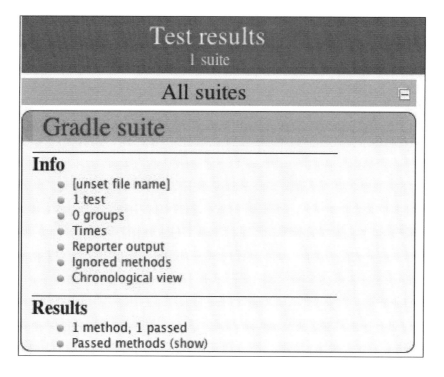

Gradle cannot use the `test` task to run both the JUnit and TestNG tests at the same time. If we have both types of tests in our project and we want to run them, we must add a new task of type `Test`. This new task can run the specific tests for one of the frameworks.

We add a new task of type `Test` to run the TestNG tests in our build file:

```
apply plugin: 'java'

repositories {
    mavenCentral()
}

dependencies {
    testCompile 'junit:junit:[4.8,)', 'org.testng:testng:6.5.1'
}
```

```
task testNG(type: Test) {
    useTestNG()
}

test.dependsOn testNG
```

To add configuration options for TestNG, we can pass a closure to the `useTestNG()` method. The closure has an argument of type `org.gradle.api.tasks.testing.testng.TestNGOptions`. The following table shows the options we can set:

| Option name | Type | Description |
| --- | --- | --- |
| excludeGroups | Set | Set of groups to exclude. |
| includeGroups | Set | Set of groups to include. |
| javadocAnnotations | boolean | When `true`, Javadoc annotations are used for these tests. |
| listeners | Set | Set of qualified classes that are TestNG listeners. |
| parallel | String | The parallel mode to use for running tests. `method` or `tests` are valid options. |
| suiteName | String | Sets the default name of the test suite, if one is not specified in a `suite.xml` file or in the source code. |
| suiteXmlBuilder | MarkupBuilder | `MarkupBuilder` to create a suite XML. |
| suiteXmlWriter | StringWriter | `StringWriter` to write out XML. |
| testName | String | Sets the default name of the test, if one is not specified in a `suite.xml` file or in the source code. |
| testResources | List | List of all directories containing test sources. |
| threadCount | int | The number of threads to use for this run. |
| useDefaultListeners | boolean | Whether the default listeners and reporters should be used. |

The following sample build file uses some of these options to configure TestNG:

```
apply plugin: 'java'

repositories {
    mavenCentral()
}

dependencies {
    testCompile 'org.testng:testng:6.5.1'
}

test {
    useTestNG { options ->
        options.excludeGroups = ['functional'] as Set
        options.parallel = 'method'
        options.threadCount = 4
    }
}
```

# Configuring the test process

The tests that are executed by the test task run in a separate, isolated JVM process. We can use several properties to control this process. We can set system properties and JVM arguments, and we can configure the Java class that needs to be executed to run the tests.

To debug the tests, we can set the debug property of the test task. Gradle will start the test process in debug mode and will listen on port 5005 for a debug process to attach to. This way, we can run our tests and use an IDE debugger to step through the code.

By default, Gradle will fail the build if any test fails. If we want to change this setting, we must set the ignoreFailures property to true. Our build will then not fail, even if we have errors in our tests. The generated test reports will still have the errors. It is bad practice to ignore failures, but it is good to know the option is there if we need it.

The following build file configures the test task with the properties just discussed:

```
apply plugin: 'java'

repositories {
    mavenCentral()
}
```

```
dependencies {
    testCompile 'junit:junit:[4.8,)'
}

test {
    // Add System property to running tests.
    systemProperty 'sysProp', 'value'

    // Use the following JVM arguments for each test process.
    jvmArgs '-Xms256m', '-Xmx512m'

    // Enable debugging mode.
    debug = true

    // Ignore any test failues and don't fail the build.
    ignoreFailures = true

    // Enable assertions for test with the assert keyword.
    enableAssertions = true
}
```

Gradle can execute tests in parallel. This means Gradle will start multiple test processes concurrently. A test process only executes a single test at a time. By enabling parallel test execution, the total execution time of the test task can drastically decrease, if we have a lot of tests. We must use the maxParallelForks property to set how many test processes we want to run in parallel. The default value is 1, which means that the tests don't run in parallel.

Each test process sets a system property of the name org.gradle.test.worker with a unique value. We could use this value to generate unique files for a test process.

If we have a lot of tests that are executed by a single test process, we might get heap size or PermGen problems. With the property forkEvery, we can set how many tests need to run in a single test process, before a new test process is started to execute more tests. So, if Gradle sees that the number of tests exceeds the given number assigned to the forkEvery property, the test process is restarted and the following set of tests is executed.

Let's create a new build file and configure it such that we can run four test processes in parallel and relaunch the test process after 10 tests:

```
apply plugin: 'java'

repositories {
    mavenCentral()
```

```
}

dependencies {
    testCompile 'junit:junit:[4.8,)'
}

test {
    forkEvery = 10
    maxParallelForks = 4
}
```

# Determining tests

To determine which files are tests, Gradle will inspect the compiled class files. If a class or its methods have the @Test annotation, Gradle will treat it as a JUnit or TestNG test. If the class extends TestCase or GroovyTestCase or is annotated with @RunWith, Gradle will handle it as a JUnit test. Abstract classes are not inspected.

We can disable this automatic inspection with the scanForTestClasses property of the test task. If we set the property to false, Gradle will use the implicit include rules **/*Tests.class and **/*Test.class and the exclude rule **/Abstract*.class.

We can also set our own include and exclude rules to find tests. We use the include() method of the test task to define our own rule for test classes. If we want to exclude certain class files, we can use the exclude() method to define the exclude rules.

In the following build file, we disable the automatic class inspection for test classes and set the include and exclude rules for test classes, explicitly:

```
apply plugin: 'java'

repositories {
    mavenCentral()
}

dependencies {
    testCompile 'junit:junit:[4.8,)'
}

test {
    // Disable automatic inspections.
```

```
    scanForTestClasses = false

    // Include test classes.
    include '**/*Test.class', '**/*Spec.class'

    // Exclude test classes.
    exclude '**/Abstract*.class', '**/Run*.class'
}
```

# Logging test output

We already noticed that the output that is shown on the command line isn't much if we simply run the test task. We must set the logging level to info or debug, to get more information about the output that is generated by the tests. We can configure the test task to show more output with the testLogging property. This property is of type org.gradle.api.tasks.testing.logging.TestLoggingContainer. We can set different options for each log level. If we don't specify a log level, the lifecyle log level is implied. The property is marked as experimental, which means the features can change in future versions of Gradle.

TestLoggingContainer has the option showStandardStreams, which we can set to true or false. If we set the value of the property to true, we get the output from System.out and System.err when we run the test tasks.

We can also use the events() method to set which events are logged on the command-line output. For example, we can configure that we also want to see the passed tests with the String value passed as an argument. We can use the arguments standardOut and standardError to get the same effect as with the showStandardStreams property. Other valid arguments are failed, started, and skipped.

If a test fails, we only see the line number of the test that failed. To get more output for a failed test, we can set the option exceptionFormat to full. Then, we get the exception message with, say, the assertion failed message. The default value is short, which only shows the line number. With the property stackTraceFilters, we can determine how much of the stack trace is logged.

We can also set the maximum and minimum granularity of the log messages with the minGranularity and maxGranularity properties. We use the value 0 for the Gradle-generated test suite, 1 for the generated test suite per test JVM, 2 for a test class, and 3 for a test method.

The following sample build file sets some of the options that are available:

```
apply plugin: 'java'

repositories {
    mavenCentral()
}

dependencies {
    testCompile 'junit:junit:[4.8,)'
}

test {
    // Set exception format to full
    // instead of default value 'short'.
    testLogging.exceptionFormat 'full'

    // We can also a script block to configure
    // the testLogging property.
    testLogging {
        // No log level specified so the
        // property is set on LIFECYCLE log level.
        // We can pass arguments to determine
        // which test events we want to see in the
        // command-line output.
        events 'passed'

        // Show logging events for test methods.
        minGranularity = 3

        // All valid values for the stackTrace output.
        stackTraceFilters 'groovy', 'entry_point', 'truncate'

        // Show System.out and System.err output
        // from the tests.
        showStandardStreams = true

        // Configure options for DEBUG log level.
        debug {
            events 'started'
        }
    }

}
```

# Generating test reports

We have already seen the HTML reports that are generated when we run the tests, in the `build/reports/tests` directory. To change the directory name, we can set the `testReportDir` property as part of the `test` task.

Besides the generated HTML report, we have XML files that are generated by the `test` task, with the results of the tests. These XML files are actually the input for the generated HTML report. There are a lot of tools available that can use the XML files generated by JUnit or TestNG and perform an analysis on them. We can find the files in the `build/test-results` directory. To change this directory, we must change the `testResultDir` property of the `test` task.

To disable the generation of the test reports, we set the property `testReport` to `false`.

The following build file shows how we can change the report directories and disable the generation of the test reports:

```
apply plugin: 'java'

repositories {
    mavenCentral()
}

dependencies {
    testCompile 'junit:junit:[4.8,)'
}

test.testReportDir = file("$buildDir/test-reports")
test.testResultsDir = file("$buildDir/test-results")
test.testReport = false
```

# Running Java applications

If we want to execute a Java executable from a Gradle build, we have several options. Before we explore these options, we will first create a new Java class with a `main()` method in our project. We will execute this Java class from our build file.

In the directory `src/main/java/gradle/sample`, we need to create a new file `SampleApp.java`. The following code listing shows the contents of the file. We use our `Sample` class to print the value of the `getWelcomeMessage()` method to `System.out`:

```
// File: src/main/java/gradle/sample/SampleApp.java
package gradle.sample;
```

```
import java.util.ResourceBundle;

public class SampleApp {

    public SampleApp() {
    }

    public static void main(final String[] arguments) {
        final SampleApp app = new SampleApp();
        app.welcomeMessage();
    }

    public void welcomeMessage() {
        final String welcomeMessage = readMessage();
        showMessage(welcomeMessage);
    }

    private String readMessage() {
        final Sample sample = new Sample();
        final String message = sample.getWelcomeMessage();
        return message;
    }

    private void showMessage(final String message) {
        System.out.println(message);
    }
}
```

To run our `SampleApp` class we can use the `javaexec()` method that is part of Gradle's `Project` class. We could also use the `JavaExec` task in our build file. Finally, we could use the application plugin to run our `SampleApp` class.

# Running an application from a project

The `Project` class that is always available in our build file has the `javaexec()` method. With this method we can execute a Java class. The method accepts a closure that is used to configure the `org.gradle.process.JavaExecSpec` object. `JavaExecSpec` has several methods and properties we can use to configure the `main` class that needs to be executed, optional arguments, and system properties. A lot of the options are the same as for running tests.

We create a new build file and use the `javaexec()` method to run our `SampleApp` class with some extra options:

```
apply plugin: 'java'

task runJava(dependsOn: classes) << {
    javaexec {
        // Java main class to execute.
        main = 'gradle.sample.SampleApp'

        // We need to set the classpath.
        classpath sourceSets.main.runtimeClasspath

        // Extra options can be set.
        maxHeapSize = '128m'
        systemProperty 'sysProp', 'notUsed'
        jvmArgs '-client'
    }
}
runJava.description = 'Run gradle.sample.SampleApp'
```

To run our Java class, we execute the `runJava` task from the command line and get the following output:

```
$ gradle runJava
:compileJava UP-TO-DATE
:processResources UP-TO-DATE
:classes UP-TO-DATE
:runJava
Welcome to Gradle.

BUILD SUCCESSFUL

Total time: 1.465 secs
```

# Running an application as task

Besides the `javaexec()` method, we can define a new task of type `org.gradle.api.tasks.JavaExec`. To configure the task, we can use the same methods and properties as with the `javaexec()` method.

In the following sample build file, we create the task `runJava` of type `JavaExec`. We configure the task to set the `classpath` and `main` class. Also, we see how we can add other properties and invoke other methods to further configure the execution of the Java class:

```
apply plugin: 'java'

task runJava(type: JavaExec) {
    dependsOn classes
    description = 'Run gradle.sample.SampleApp'

    // Java main class to execute.
    main = 'gradle.sample.SampleApp'

    // We need to set the classpath.
    classpath sourceSets.main.runtimeClasspath

    // Extra options can be set.
    systemProperty 'sysProp', 'notUsed'
    jvmArgs '-client'

    // We can pass arguments to the main() method
    // of gradle.sample.SampleApp.
    args 'mainMethodArgument', 'notUsed'
}
```

If we run the task we get the following output:

```
$ gradle runJava
:compileJava UP-TO-DATE
:processResources UP-TO-DATE
:classes UP-TO-DATE
:runJava
Welcome to Gradle.

BUILD SUCCESSFUL

Total time: 0.932 secs
```

# Running an application with the application plugin

Another way to run a Java application is with the application plugin. The application plugin adds functionality to our build file to run Java applications and also to bundle the Java application for distribution.

To use the application plugin, we must add the plugin to our build file with the apply() method. Once we have added the plugin, we can set the main class to be executed with the property mainClassName. This time, we don't have to create a new task ourselves. The plugin has added the run task that we can invoke to run the Java application.

The sample build file uses the application plugin to run our SampleApp class:

```
apply plugin: 'java'
apply plugin: 'application'

mainClassName = 'gradle.sample.SampleApp'

// Extra configuration for run task if needed.
run {
    // Extra options can be set.
    systemProperty 'sysProp', 'notUsed'
    jvmArgs '-client'

    // We can pass arguments to the main() method
    // of gradle.sample.SampleApp.
    args 'mainMethodArgument', 'notUsed'
}
```

We can invoke the run task and see the output of the SampleApp class:

```
$ gradle run
:compileJava UP-TO-DATE
:processResources UP-TO-DATE
:classes UP-TO-DATE
:run
Welcome to Gradle.

BUILD SUCCESSFUL

Total time: 1.423 secs
```

Note that we don't have to set the `classpath` property anymore. The plugin automatically includes the `runtimeClasspath` object of the project to execute the Java class.

# Creating a distributable application archive

With the application plugin we can also build a distribution with our Java application. This means we can distribute the application and people can run the Java application without Gradle. The plugin will create the necessary operating system-specific start scripts and package all necessary classes and dependencies.

The following table shows the extra tasks we can use with the application plugin to build a distribution:

| Task | Depends on | Type | Description |
| --- | --- | --- | --- |
| startScripts | jar | CreateStart Scripts | Creates operating system-specific scripts to run the Java application. |
| installApp | jar, startScripts | Sync | Installs the application into a directory. |
| distZip | jar, startScripts | Zip | Creates a full distribution ZIP archive including all necessary files to run the Java application. |

All tasks depend on the `jar` task. In order to get a meaningful JAR filename, we set the properties `archivesBaseName` and `version` in our build file:

```
apply plugin: 'java'
apply plugin: 'application'

archivesBaseName = 'gradle-sample'
version = '1.0'

mainClassName = 'gradle.sample.SampleApp'
```

To create the start scripts, we invoke the `createScript` task. After we have executed the task, we have two files, `sample` and `sample.bat`, in the directory `build/scripts`. The `sample.bat` file is for the Windows operating system and `sample` is for other operating systems, such as Linux or OS X.

To have all files that are needed for running the application in a separate directory, we must run the `installApp` task. When we execute the task, we get a sample directory in the `build/install` directory. The `sample` directory has a `bin` directory with the start scripts and a `lib` directory with the JAR file containing the `SampleApp` application. We can change to the `build/install/sample` directory and then invoke `bin/sample` or `bin/sample.bat` to run our application:

```
$ gradle installApp
:compileJava UP-TO-DATE
:processResources UP-TO-DATE
:classes UP-TO-DATE
:jar UP-TO-DATE
:startScripts UP-TO-DATE
:installApp


BUILD SUCCESSFUL


Total time: 1.511 secs
$ cd build/install/sample
$ bin/sample
Welcome to Gradle.
```

To create a ZIP archive with all necessary files, which would enable others to run the application, we run the `distZip` task. The resulting ZIP archive can be found in the directory `build/distributions`. We can distribute this ZIP file and people can unzip the archive on their computers to run the Java application:

```
$ gradle distZip
:compileJava UP-TO-DATE
:processResources UP-TO-DATE
:classes UP-TO-DATE
:jar UP-TO-DATE
:startScripts UP-TO-DATE
```

```
:distZip

BUILD SUCCESSFUL

Total time: 1.089 secs
$ jar tvf build/distributions/sample-1.0.zip
     0 Mon Apr 30 08:08:10 CEST 2012 sample-1.0/
     0 Mon Apr 30 08:08:10 CEST 2012 sample-1.0/lib/
  1890 Mon Apr 30 08:01:12 CEST 2012 sample-1.0/lib/gradle-sample-1.0.jar
     0 Mon Apr 30 08:08:10 CEST 2012 sample-1.0/bin/
  4997 Mon Apr 30 08:01:14 CEST 2012 sample-1.0/bin/sample
  2347 Mon Apr 30 08:01:14 CEST 2012 sample-1.0/bin/sample.bat
```

If we want to add other files to the distribution, we can create the directory `src/dist` and place files in there. Any files in the `src/dist` directory are included in the distribution ZIP archive. To include files from another directory, we can use the `applicationDistribution` copy specification.

The following sample build file uses the `applicationDistribution` copy specification to include the output of the `docs` task. Gradle will automatically execute the `docs` task before invoking the `distZip` task:

```
apply plugin: 'java'
apply plugin: 'application'
apply plugin: 'idea'

archivesBaseName = 'gradle-sample'
version = '1.0'

mainClassName = 'gradle.sample.SampleApp'

task docs {
    def docsDir = 'docs'
    def docsResultDir = file("$buildDir/$docsDir")

    // Assign directory to task outputs.
    outputs.dir docResultDir

    doLast {
        docsResultDir.mkdirs()
        new File(docsResultDir, 'README').write('Please read me.')
    }
```

```
}

applicationDistribution.from(docs) {
    // Directory in distribution ZIP archive.
    into 'docs'
}
```

# Publishing artifacts

A software project can contain artifacts that we want to publish. An artifact can be a ZIP or JAR archive file or any other file. In Gradle, we can define more than one artifact for a project. We can publish these artifacts to a central repository so other developers can use our artifacts in their projects. These central repositories can be available on a company intranet, a network drive, or via the Internet.

In Gradle, we group artifacts through configurations, just like dependencies. A configuration can contain both dependencies and artifacts. If we add the Java plugin to our project, we also get two extra tasks per configuration to build and upload the artifacts belonging to the configuration. The task to build the artifacts is called `build<configurationName>`, and the task to upload the artifacts is named `upload<configurationName>`.

The Java plugin also adds the configuration `archives` that can be used to assign artifacts. The default JAR artifact for a Java project is already assigned to this configuration. We can assign more artifacts to this configuration for our project. We can also add new configurations to assign artifacts in a project.

For our Java project we will define the following sample build file:

```
apply plugin: 'java'

archivesBaseName = 'gradle-sample'
version = '1.0'
```

Because we use the Java plugin we have the `archives` configuration available. When we execute the task `buildArchives`, our Java code gets compiled and a JAR file is created in the directory `build/libs`, with the name `gradle-sample-1.0.jar`.

To publish our JAR file, we can execute the task `uploadArchives`, but we must first configure where to publish the artifact. The repositories we have defined for dependencies are not used to upload the artifacts. We have to define the upload repository in the `uploadArchives` task. We can reference a repository already defined in our project or define the repositories in the task.

The following sample build file defines an upload repository at project level and at the task level:

```
apply plugin: 'java'

archivesBaseName = 'gradle-sample'
version = '1.0'

repositories {
    flatDir {
        name 'uploadRepository'
        dirs 'upload'
    }
}

uploadArchives {
    repositories {
        // Use repository defined in project
        // for uploading the JAR file.
        add project.repositories.uploadRepository

        // Extra upload repository defined in
        // the upload task.
        flatDir {
            dirs 'libs'
        }
    }
}
```

If we invoke the task `uploadArchives`, the JAR file is created and copied to the `libs` and `upload` directories. An `ivy.xml` configuration file is also created and copied to the directories:

```
$ gradle uploadArchives
:compileJava
:processResources
:classes
:jar
:uploadArchives

BUILD SUCCESSFUL

Total time: 0.8 secs
```

```
$ ls upload
ivy-1.0.xml   sample-1.0.jar
sample mrhaki$ ls libs
ivy-1.0.xml   sample-1.0.jar
```

We can use all Ivy resolvers to define upload repositories.

# Uploading to a Maven repository

If we want to upload to a Maven repository, we must create a **Maven POM (Project Object Model)** file. The Maven POM file contains all necessary information about our artifact. Gradle can generate the POM file for us. We must add the Maven plugin to our project in order to make this work.

We must configure the repository for our `uploadArchives` task via a closure argument of the `mavenDeployer()` method. In the following sample build file, we will define a Maven repository with the `file` protocol:

```
apply plugin: 'java'
apply plugin: 'maven'

archivesBaseName = 'gradle-sample'
group = 'gradle.sample'
version = '1.0'

uploadArchives {
    repositories {
        mavenDeployer {
            repository(url: 'file:./maven')
        }
    }
}
```

Note that we set the `group` property of our project so it can be used as the `groupId` of the Maven POM. The `version` property is used as the version and the `archivesBaseName` property is used as the artifact ID. We can invoke the `uploadArchives` task to deploy our artifact:

```
$ gradle uploadArchives
:compileJava UP-TO-DATE
:processResources UP-TO-DATE
:classes UP-TO-DATE
:jar UP-TO-DATE
```

```
:uploadArchives
```

```
Uploading: gradle/sample/gradle-sample/1.0/gradle-sample-1.0.jar to
repository remote at file:./maven
```

```
Transferring 2K from remote
```

```
Uploaded 2K
```

```
BUILD SUCCESSFUL
```

```
Total time: 1.196 secs
$ ls maven/gradle/sample/gradle-sample/1.0/
```

```
gradle-sample-1.0.jar
```

```
gradle-sample-1.0.jar.sha1
```

```
gradle-sample-1.0.pom.md5
```

```
gradle-sample-1.0.jar.md5
```

```
gradle-sample-1.0.pom
```

```
gradle-sample-1.0.pom.sha1
```

The contents of the generated POM file `gradle-sample-1.0.pom` are as follows:

```
<?xml version="1.0" encoding="UTF-8"?>
<project xsi:schemaLocation="http://maven.apache.org/POM/4.0.0 http://
maven.apache.org/xsd/maven-4.0.0.xsd" xmlns="http://maven.apache.org/
POM/4.0.0"
    xmlns:xsi="http://www.w3.org/2001/XMLSchema-instance">
  <modelVersion>4.0.0</modelVersion>
  <groupId>gradle.sample</groupId>
  <artifactId>gradle-sample</artifactId>
  <version>1.0</version>
</project>
```

Gradle uses the native Maven ANT tasks to deploy the artifacts to a Maven repository. The `file` protocol is supported without any extra configuration, but if we want to use other protocols we must configure the libraries those protocols depend on.

| Protocol | Library |
| --- | --- |
| http | org.apache.maven.wagon:<br>wagon-http:1.0-beta-2 |
| ssh | org.apache.maven.wagon:<br>wagon-ssh:1.0-beta-2 |
| ssh-external | org.apache.maven.wagon:<br>wagon-ssh-external:1.0-beta-2 |

| Protocol | Library |
|----------|---------|
| scp | org.apache.maven.wagon: wagon-scp:1.0-beta-2 |
| ftp | org.apache.maven.wagon: wagon-ftp:1.0-beta-2 |
| webdav | org.apache.maven.wagon: wagon-webdav-jackrabbit: 1.0-beta-6 |
| file | - |

In the following sample build file, we use the scp protocol to define a Maven repository and use it to upload the project's artifact:

```
apply plugin: 'java'
apply plugin: 'maven'

archivesBaseName = 'gradle-sample'
group = 'gradle.sample'
version = '1.0'

configurations {
    mavenScp
}

repositories {
    mavenCentral()
}

dependencies {
    mavenScp 'org.apache.maven.wagon:wagon-scp:1.0-beta-2'
}

uploadArchives {
    repositories {
        mavenDeployer {
            configuration = configurations.mavenScp
            repository(url: 'scp://localhost/mavenRepo') {
                authentication(username: 'user', privateKey: 'id_sha')
            }
        }
    }
}
```

The Maven plugin also adds the `install` task to our project. With the `install` task, we can install the artifact to our local Maven repository. Gradle will use the default location of the local Maven repository or the location that is defined in a Maven `settings.xml` file.

# Multiple artifacts

Until now, we have uploaded a single artifact to a repository. In a Gradle project, we can define multiple artifacts and deploy them. We need to define an `archive` task and assign it to a configuration. We use the `artifacts{}` script block to define a configuration closure, to assign an artifact to a configuration. The artifact is then deployed to a repository when we execute the upload task.

In the following sample build, we create JAR files with the source code and Javadoc documentation. We assign both JAR files as artifacts to the `archives` configuration:

```
apply plugin: 'java'

archivesBaseName = 'gradle-sample'
version = '1.0'

task sourcesJar(type: Jar) {
    classifier = 'sources'
    from sourceSets.main.allSource
}

task docJar(type: Jar, dependsOn: javadoc) {
    classifier = 'docs'
    from javadoc.destinationDir
}

artifacts {
    archives sourcesJar
    archives docJar
}

uploadArchives {
    repositories {
        flatDir {
            dirs 'upload'
        }
    }
}
```

# Signing artifacts

We can digitally sign artifacts in Gradle with the signing plugin. The plugin only has support for generating **Pretty Good Privacy (PGP)** signatures, which is the signature format required for publication to the Maven Central Repository. To create a PGP signature we must install some PGP tools on our computers. Installation of the tools is different for each operating system. With the PGP software we need to create a key pair that we can use to sign our artifacts.

We need to configure the signing plugin with the information about our key pair. We need the hexadecimal representation of the public key, the path to the secret key ring file with our private key, and the passphrase used to protect the private key. The values of these properties are assigned to the Gradle project properties `signing.keyId`, `signing.secretKeyRingFile`, and `signing.password`. The values of these properties are best kept secret, so it is better to store them in our `gradle.properties` file in the Gradle user directory and apply secure file permissions to
the file. It is best to make the file read-only for a single user.

The following sample `gradle.properties` file has the `signing` properties set. The values of the properties shown are sample values. These will be different for other users:

```
signing.keyId=4E12C354
signing.secretKeyRingFile=/Users/current/.gnupg/secring.gpg
signing.password=secret phassphrase
```

We are ready to sign our artifacts. We need to configure which artifacts we want signed. The signing plugin has a DSL we can use to define which tasks or configurations we want signed.

In our sample Java project, we have the `archives` configuration with artifacts of our project. To sign the artifacts, we can use the `signing()` method and a closure to configure that all artifacts of the `archives` configuration need to be signed. The following sample build file shows how we can do this:

```
apply plugin: 'java'
apply plugin: 'signing'

archivesBaseName = 'gradle-sample'
version = '1.0'

signing {
    sign configurations.archives
}
```

The signing plugin adds a new task, named `signArchives`, to our project, because we have configured that we want the `archives` configuration to be signed. The signing plugin adds tasks with the pattern `sign<configurationName>` to our project, for each configuration we configure to be signed.

We can invoke the `signArchives` task to sign our JAR artifact or use the `jar` task, which is automatically dependent on the `signArchives` task:

```
$ gradle signArchives
:compileJava UP-TO-DATE
:processResources UP-TO-DATE
:classes UP-TO-DATE
:jar UP-TO-DATE
:signArchives

BUILD SUCCESSFUL

Total time: 1.649 secs
$ ls build/libs/gradle-sample-1.0.jar*
build/libs/gradle-sample-1.0.jar
build/libs/gradle-sample-1.0.jar.asc
```

Note that the signature file `gradle-sample-1.0.jar.asc` is placed next to the artifact.

If the artifact we want to sign is not part of a configuration, we can use the signing DSL to configure a task to be signed. The task must create an archive file in order to be used for signing. After we have configured the task to be signed, the signing plugin adds a new task with the naming pattern `sign<taskName>`. We can execute that task to sign the output of the configured task.

The following build file has the task `sourcesJar`, to create a new archive with the source files of our project. We use the signing DSL to configure our task for signing:

```
apply plugin: 'java'
apply plugin: 'signing'

archivesBaseName = 'gradle-sample'
version = '1.0'

task sourcesJar(type: Jar) {
    classifier = 'sources'
```

```
        from sourceSets.main.allSource
    }

    signing {
        sign sourcesJar
    }
```

We can invoke the task `signSourcesJar` to digitally sign our JAR file with the sources of our project. The generated signature file is placed next to the JAR file in the `build/libs` directory. We can also invoke the `assemble` task to create the digitally signed JAR file, because this task is made dependent on all our archive tasks, including the signing tasks:

```
$ gradle signSourcesJar
:sourcesJar
:signSourcesJar


BUILD SUCCESSFUL


Total time: 0.87 secs
sample mrhaki$ ls build/libs/gradle-sample-1.0-sources.jar*
build/libs/gradle-sample-1.0-sources.jar
build/libs/gradle-sample-1.0-sources.jar.asc
```

# Publishing signature files

To publish our signatures to a repository, we don't have to do anything special. Gradle automatically adds the generated signature files to our `archives` configuration. So, if we configure the `uploadArchives` task with a valid repository, we only have to run the `uploadArchives` task to upload both our artifacts with their signature files.

The following code adds the task `sourcesJar` to the build file, and we assign it to the `archives` configuration. We configure the signing plugin to use the `archives` configuration to find the artifacts to sign. Finally, we configure a simple file-based repository to store the artifacts with their signature files:

```
apply plugin: 'java'
apply plugin: 'signing'

archivesBaseName = 'gradle-sample'
version = '1.0'
```

```
task sourcesJar(type: Jar) {
    classifier = 'sources'
    from sourceSets.main.allSource
}

artifacts {
    archives sourcesJar
}

signing {
    sign configurations.archives
}

uploadArchives {
    repositories {
        flatDir {
            dirs 'upload'
        }
    }
}
```

We can execute the task `uploadArchives` and look in the `upload` directory to see all the files that are created:

```
$ gradle uploadArchives
:compileJava UP-TO-DATE
:processResources UP-TO-DATE
:classes UP-TO-DATE
:jar UP-TO-DATE
:sourcesJar UP-TO-DATE
:signArchives UP-TO-DATE
:uploadArchives

BUILD SUCCESSFUL

Total time: 0.816 secs
sample mrhaki$ ls upload/
gradle-sample-1.0-sources.asc
gradle-sample-1.0.asc
ivy-1.0.xml
gradle-sample-1.0-sources.jar
gradle-sample-1.0.jar
```

## Configuring conditional signing

With the signing DSL, we can also configure a condition to determine whether signing is required, for example, defining a condition to only sign the artifacts when the project is ready to be released.

In the sample build file, we only want to sign the artifacts if the `uploadArchives` task is part of the Gradle task graph to be executed and if the version of the project doesn't end with the `String` value `DEV`:

```
apply plugin: 'java'
apply plugin: 'signing'

archivesBaseName = 'gradle-sample'
version = '1.0-DEV'

signing {
    required {
        !version.endsWith('DEV') &&
        gradle.taskGraph.hasTask('uploadArchives')
    }
    sign configurations.archives
}
```

# Packaging Java Enterprise Edition applications

We have learned how to create ZIP, TAR, and JAR archives with Gradle in this chapter and the previous one. In a Java project we can also package our applications as **Web application Archive (WAR)** or **Enterprise Archive (EAR)** files. For a web application we would like to package our application as a WAR file, while a **Java Enterprise Edition** application can be packaged as an EAR file. Gradle also supports these types of archives with plugins and tasks.

## Creating a WAR file

To create a WAR file we can add a new task of type `War` to our Java project. The properties and methods of the `War` task are the same as for the other archive tasks such as `Jar`. In fact, the `War` task extends the `Jar` task.

The War task has an extra method, webInf(), to define a source directory for the WEB-INF directory in a WAR file. The webXml property can be used to reference a web.xml file that needs to be copied into the WAR file. This is just another way to include a web.xml file; we can also place the web.xml file in the WEB-INF directory of the root source directory we defined for the WAR file.

With the classpath() method, we can define a dependency configuration or directory with libraries or class files we want copied to our WAR file. If the file is a JAR or ZIP file, it is copied to the WEB-INF/lib directory and other files are copied into the WEB-INF/classes directory.

In the following sample build file we define a new task war. We set the root of the WAR file contents to the directory src/main/webapp. We use the webInf() and classpath() methods to customize the contents of the WEB-INF, WEB-INF/classes, and WEB-INF/lib folders. And, we set a custom web.xml file with the webXml property of the task:

```
apply plugin: 'java'

version = '1.0'

task war(type: War) {
    dependsOn classes

    from 'src/main/webapp'

    // Files copied to WEB-INF.
    webInf {
        from 'src/main/webInf'
    }

    // Copied to WEB-INF/classes.
    classpath sourceSets.main.runtimeClasspath

    // Copied to WEB-INF/lib.
    classpath fileTree('libs')

    // Custom web.xml.
    webXml = file('src/main/webXml/web-dev.xml')

    baseName = 'gradle-webapp'
}

assemble.dependsOn war
```

To create the WAR file we can execute the `war` or `assemble` task. The `war` task is added to the `assemble` task as a task dependency. That is why, if we invoke the `assemble` task, Gradle will execute the `war` task. Once we have executed the task, the WAR file `gradle-webapp-1.0.war` is created in the directory `build/libs`:

```
$ gradle war
:compileJava
:processResources
:classes
:war

BUILD SUCCESSFUL

Total time: 0.727 secs
web mrhaki$ ls build/libs
gradle-webapp-1.0.war
```

# Using the War plugin

Instead of creating a `War` task ourselves, we can apply the War plugin in our project. This plugin adds a `war` task for us that we can invoke. Also, the default JAR archive is not created for our project any more, as part of the `assemble` task.

The plugin also adds two dependency configurations to our project, with the names `providedCompile` and `providedRuntime`. Any dependencies added to these configurations are not copied to the `WEB-INF/lib` directory of our WAR file. If a dependency exists both in the `runtime` and `providedRuntime` configuration, it is not copied to the `WEB-INF/lib` folder. This also works for transitive dependencies.

The default source directory for the contents of the WAR file is `src/main/webapp`. We can change this with the property `webAppDirName`, if we want to use another directory. This property is a convention property provided by the War plugin.

To customize the added `war` task, we still use the same methods and properties we have used for the `war` task we created ourselves.

In the sample build file, we now apply the War plugin. We assign some dependencies to the extra dependency configurations and customize the `war` task:

```
apply plugin: 'war'

version = '1.0'
```

```
repositories {
    mavenCentral()
}

configurations {
    extraLibs
}

dependencies {
    providedCompile 'javax.servlet:servlet-api:3.0'
    providedRuntime 'webcontainer:logging:1.0'
    extraLibs 'sample:lib:2.1'
}

war {
    classpath configuration.extraLibs

    // Custom web.xml.
    webXml = file('src/main/webXml/web-dev.xml')

    baseName = 'gradle-webapp'
}
```

# Creating an EAR file

To create an EAR file we can create a new task of type `Ear`. This task has the same properties and methods as the `Jar` task. The `Ear` task extends the `Jar` task.

With the `lib()` method, we can define which files need to be copied to the `lib` directory in the EAR file.

The following build file has a simple `ear` task:

```
import org.gradle.plugins.ear.Ear

apply plugin: 'java'

version = '1.0'

task ear(type: Ear) {
    from 'src/main/application'
    lib {
        from fileTree('earLibs')
    }
```

```
        baseName = 'gradle-enterprise-app'
    }

    assemble.dependsOn ear
```

We can execute the `ear` task and look in the `build/libs` directory to see the resulting `gradle-enterprise-app-1.0.ear` file:

```
$gradle ear
:ear

BUILD SUCCESSFUL

Total time: 0.694 secs
web mrhaki$ ls build/libs
gradle-enterprise-app-1.0.ear
```

# Using the Ear plugin

The best way to create an EAR file is by applying the Ear plugin to our project. The plugin adds an `ear` task to our project and makes sure the `assemble` task will build the EAR file instead of the JAR file of the project.

The plugin also adds two new dependency configurations: `deploy` and `earlib`. Dependencies assigned to the `deploy` configuration are copied to the root of the EAR file. The dependencies are not transitive. The dependencies assigned to the `earlib` configuration are transitive and are copied to the `lib` directory in the EAR file. We can customize the name of the `lib` directory in the EAR file with the project or `ear` task property `libDirName`.

Any files in the `src/main/application` directory are also added to the EAR file. We can change this directory location with the property `appDirName`, which is added by the plugin. Here, we can place the file `application.xml` in the directory `META-INF`, as an EAR descriptor file.

In the sample build file, we apply the Ear plugin and customize the `ear` task:

```
apply plugin: 'java'
apply plugin: 'ear'

version = '1.0'

repositories {
    flatDir {
```

```
            dirs 'lib'
        }
        mavenCentral()
    }

    dependencies {
        deploy 'sample:gradle-web:1.0'
        earlib 'org.slf4j:slfj4-impl:1.6.2'
    }

    ear.baseName = 'gradle-enterprise-app'
```

We can run the `assemble` or `ear` task to create the EAR file `gradle-enterprise-app-1.0.ear` in the directory `build/libs`:

```
$ gradle clean assemble
:clean
:compileJava
:processResources
:classes
:ear
:assemble

BUILD SUCCESSFUL

Total time: 0.741 secs
web mrhaki$ ls build/libs
gradle-enterprise-app-1.0.ear
```

# Summary

In this chapter, we have learned how we can run JUnit or TestNG tests from a Gradle build. We have seen how to get the test results and reports that are generated by executing the tests.

With the application plugin, we have learned how to create a distributable ZIP file with all the code and scripts necessary to run the Java application we have built.

We have learned how to upload our project artifacts to a repository so other projects can use our code. We have seen that we can use Gradle to create an artifact that is ready to be uploaded to a Maven repository.

To digitally sign our artifacts, we have seen how to use the signing plugin together with locally installed PGP tools.

Also, we have seen how we can use the War and Ear plugins to create web and enterprise applications with Gradle. We can use tasks, methods, and configuration properties to configure the packaging output.

In the next chapter, we will look at how we can run and create a multi-module project with Gradle. We will also learn how to create dependencies between projects and how to apply a common configuration to multiple projects at once.

# 7
# Multi-project Builds

When applications and projects get bigger, we usually split up several parts of the application into separate projects. Gradle has great support for multi-project builds. We can configure multiple projects in an easy way. Gradle is also able to resolve dependencies between projects and will build the necessary projects in the right order. So, we don't have to switch to a specific directory to build the code; Gradle will resolve the correct project order for us.

In this chapter we will learn about multi-project configuration and dependencies. First, we will look at how we can configure projects and tasks. Then we will use a multi-project Java application to learn how we can have inter-project dependencies and how Gradle resolves these for us.

## Working with multi-project builds

Let's start with a simple multi-project structure. We have a root project called `garden` with two other projects, `tree` and `flower`. The project structure is as follows:

```
garden/
    tree/
    flower/
```

We will add a new task `printInfo` to each of these projects. The task will print out the name of the project to `System.out`. We must add a file `build.gradle` to each project, with the following contents:

```
task printInfo << {
    println "This is ${project.name}"
}
```

To execute the task for each project, we must first enter the correct directory and then invoke the task with Gradle. Or, we run `build.gradle` for a specific project with the `-b` argument of Gradle. We get the following output, if we run the task for each project:

```
garden $ gradle -q printInfo
This is garden
garden $ cd tree
tree $ gradle -q printInfo
This is tree
tree $ cd ..
garden $ gradle -b flower/build.gradle printInfo
This is flower
```

We have multiple projects, but we haven't used Gradle's support for multi-project builds yet. Let's reconfigure our projects and use Gradle multi-project support. We need to add a new file, `settings.gradle`, in the `garden` directory. In this file, we define the projects that are part of our multi-project build. We use the `include()` method to set the projects that are part of our multi-project build. The project with the file `settings.gradle` is automatically part of the build. We will use the following line in the `settings.gradle` file to define our multi-project build:

```
include 'tree', 'flower'
```

Now, we can execute the `printInfo` task for each project with a single command. We get the following output if we execute the task:

```
garden $ gradle printInfo
:printInfo
This is garden
:flower:printInfo
This is flower
:tree:printInfo
This is tree


BUILD SUCCESSFUL


Total time: 1.778 secs
```

# Executing tasks by project path

We see the output of each invocation of the task `printInfo`. The path of the project task is also displayed. The root project is denoted by a colon (`:`) and has no explicit name. The `flower` project is referenced as `:flower`, and the task `printInfo` of the `flower` project is referenced as `:flower:printInfo`. The path of a task is the name of the project and a colon (`:`) followed by the task name. The colon separates the project and task name. We can reference a specific task in a project using this syntax as well, from the command line. If we want to invoke the `printInfo` task of the `flower` project, we can run the following command:

```
graden $ gradle :flower:printInfo
:flower:printInfo
This is flower


BUILD SUCCESSFUL


Total time: 2.335 secs
```

This also works for executing tasks in a root project from another project directory. If we first go to the `flower` project directory and want to execute the `printInfo` task of the root project, we must use the syntax `:printInfo`. We get the following output, if we execute the `printInfo` task of the root project, the current project, and the `flower` project, from the `tree` project directory:

```
garden $ cd tree
tree $ gradle :printInfo printInfo :flower:printInfo
:printInfo
This is garden
:tree:printInfo
This is tree
:flower:printInfo
This is flower


BUILD SUCCESSFUL


Total time: 1.707 secs
```

Gradle takes a couple of steps to determine whether a project must be executed as a single or multi-project build:

1.  First, Gradle looks for a file `settings.gradle` in a directory with the name `master`, at the same level as the current directory.

2.  If `settings.gradle` is not found, the parent directories of the current directory are searched for a `settings.gradle` file.

3.  If `settings.gradle` is found, the project is executed as a single project build.

4.  If a `settings.gradle` file is found, and the current project is part of the multi-project definition, the project is executed as part of the multi-project build. Otherwise, the project is executed as a single project build.

We can force Gradle to not look for a `settings.gradle` file in parent directories, with the command-line argument `--no-search-upward` (or `-u`).

# Using a flat layout

In our current project setup, we have defined a hierarchical layout of the projects. We placed the `settings.gradle` file in the parent directory, and with the `include()` method, we added the `tree` and `flower` projects to our multi-project build.

We can also use a flat layout to set up our multi-project build. We must first create a `master` directory in the `garden` directory. We move our `build.gradle` and `settings.gradle` file from the `garden` directory to the `master` directory. Because we don't have a hierarchical layout any more, we must replace the `include()` method with the `includeFlat()` method. Our `settings.gradle` file now looks like this:

```
includeFlat 'tree', 'flower'
```

The projects are referenced via the parent directory of the `master` directory. So, if we define `tree` as an argument for the `include()` method, the actual path that is used to resolve the project directory is `master/../tree`.

To invoke the `printInfo` task for each project, we run Gradle from the `master` directory with the following command:

```
master $ gradle printInfo
:printInfo
This is master
:flower:printInfo
This is flower
```

```
:tree:printInfo
This is tree


BUILD SUCCESSFUL


Total time: 2.373 secs
```

# Defining projects

We have added a `build.gradle` file to the `tree` and `flower` projects, with an implementation of the `printInfo` task. But, with the multi-project support of Gradle, we don't have to do that. We can define all project tasks and properties in the root `build.gradle` file. We can use this to define common functionality for all projects, in a single place.

We can reference a project with the `project()` method and use the complete name of the project as an argument. We must use a closure to define the tasks and properties of the project.

For our example project, we first remove the `build.gradle` files from the `tree` and `flower` directories. Next, we change the `build.gradle` file in the `master` directory. Here, we define the `printInfo` tasks with the `project()` method for the `tree` and `flower` projects:

```
task printInfo << {
    println "This is ${project.name}"
}

project(':flower') {
    task printInfo << {
        println "This is ${project.name}"
    }
}

project(':tree') {
    task printInfo << {
        println "This is ${project.name}"
    }
}
```

If we execute the `printInfo` task from the `master` directory, we see that all `printInfo` tasks of the projects are invoked:

```
master $ gradle printInfo
:printInfo
This is master
:flower:printInfo
This is flower
:tree:printInfo
This is tree

BUILD SUCCESSFUL

Total time: 2.434 secs
```

Gradle also has the `allprojects{}` script block to apply project tasks and properties to all projects that are part of the multi-project build. We can rewrite our `build.gradle` file and use the `allprojects{}` script block to get a clean definition of the task without repeating ourselves:

```
allprojects {
    task printInfo << {
        println "This is ${project.name}"
    }
}
```

If we invoke the `printInfo` task from the `master` directory, we see that each project has the newly added task:

```
master $ gradle -q printInfo
This is master
This is flower
This is tree
```

If we only want to configure the subprojects `tree` and `flower`, we must use the `subprojects{}` script block. With this script block, only tasks and properties of the subprojects of a multi-project build are configured. In the following example build file, we only configure the subprojects:

```
subprojects {
    task printInfo << {
        println "This is ${project.name}"
    }
}
```

If we invoke the `printInfo` task, we see that our `master` project no longer has the `printInfo` task:

```
master mrhaki$ gradle -q printInfo
This is flower
This is tree
```

Gradle will not throw an exception if the `printInfo` task is not defined for a single project. Gradle will first build a complete task graph for all the projects that are part of the multi-project build. If any of the projects contains the task we want to run, the task for that project is executed. Only when none of the projects has the task, will Gradle fail the build.

We can combine the `allprojects{}` and `subprojects{}` script blocks, and the `project()` method, to define common behavior and apply specific behavior for specific projects. In the following sample build file, we add extra functionality to the `printInfo` task, at different levels:

```
allprojects {
    task printInfo << {
        println "This is ${project.name}"
    }
}

subprojects {
    printInfo << {
        println "Can be planted"
    }
}

project(':tree').printInfo << {
    println "Has leaves"
}

project(':flower') {
    printInfo.doLast {
        println 'Smells nice'
    }
}
```

Now when we execute the `printInfo` task, we get the following output:

```
$ gradle printInfo
:printInfo
This is master
```

```
:flower:printInfo
This is flower
Can be planted
Smells nice
:tree:printInfo
This is tree
Can be planted
Has leaves

BUILD SUCCESSFUL

Total time: 1.692 secs
```

We have added specific behavior to the `tree` and `flower` projects, with the `project()` method. But, we could also have added a `build.gradle` file to the `tree` and `flower` projects and added the extra functionality there.

# Filtering projects

To apply specific configuration to more than one project, we can also use project filtering. In our `build.gradle` file, we must use the `configure()` method. We define a filter based on the project names as argument of the method. In a closure, we define the configuration for each found project.

In the following sample build file, we use a project filter to find the projects that have names that start with an `f` and then apply a configuration to the project:

```
allprojects {
    task printInfo << {
        println "This is ${project.name}"
    }
}

configure(allprojects.findAll { it.name.startsWith('f') }) {
    printInfo << {
        println 'Smells nice'
    }
}
```

We have used the project name as a filter. We can also use project properties to define a filter. Because project properties are only set after the build is defined, either with a `build.gradle` file or with the `project()` method, we must use the `afterEvaluate()` method. This method is invoked once all projects are configured and project properties are set. We pass our custom configuration as a closure to the `afterEvaluate()` method.

In the following example build file, we read the project property `hasLeaves` for the projects `tree` and `flower`. If the property is `true`, we customize the `printInfo` task for that project:

```
allprojects {
    task printInfo << {
        println "This is ${project.name}"
    }
}

subprojects {
    afterEvaluate { project ->
        if (project.hasLeaves) {
            project.printInfo << {
                println 'Has leaves'
            }
        }
    }
}

project(':flower') {
    ext.hasLeaves = false
}

project(':tree') {
    ext.hasLeaves = true
}
```

When we execute the `printInfo` task from the master directory, we get the following output:

```
master $ gradle printInfo
:printInfo
This is master
:flower:printInfo
This is flower
```

```
:tree:printInfo
This is tree
Has leaves


BUILD SUCCESSFUL


Total time: 2.386 secs
```

# Defining task dependencies between projects

If we invoke the print Info task, we see that the printInfo task of the flower project is executed before the tree project. Gradle uses the alphabetical order of the projects, by default, to determine the execution order of the tasks. We can change this execution order by defining explicit dependencies between tasks in different projects.

If we first want to execute the printInfo task of the tree project before the flower project, we can define that the printInfo task of the flower project depends on the printInfo task of the tree project. In the following example build file, we will change the dependency of the printInfo task in the flower project. We will use the dependsOn() method to reference the printInfo task of the tree project:

```
allprojects {
    task printInfo << {
        println "This is ${project.name}"
    }
}

project(':flower') {
    printInfo.dependsOn ':tree:printInfo'
}
```

If we execute the printInfo task, we see in the output that the printInfo task of the tree project is executed before the printInfo task of the flower project:

```
master $ gradle printInfo
:printInfo
This is master
:tree:printInfo
This is tree
:flower:printInfo
```

```
This is flower


BUILD SUCCESSFUL


Total time: 2.188 secs
```

# Defining configuration dependencies

Besides task dependencies between projects, we can also include other configuration dependencies. For example, we could have a project property, set by one project, that is used by another project. Gradle will evaluate the projects in alphabetical order. In the next example, we create a new `build.gradle` file in the `tree` directory and set a property on the root project:

```
rootProject.ext.treeMessage = 'I am a tree'
```

We also create a `build.gradle` file in the `flower` project and set a project property with a value based on the root project property set by the `tree` project:

```
ext.message = rootProject.hasProperty('treeMessage') ?
    rootProject.treeMessage : 'is not set'

printInfo.doLast {
    println "Tree say ${message}"
}
```

When we execute the `printInfo` task, we get the following output:

```
master $ gradle printInfo
:printInfo
This is master
:flower:printInfo
This is flower
Tree say is not set
:tree:printInfo
This is tree


BUILD SUCCESSFUL


Total time: 2.254 secs
```

Note that the `printInfo` task in the `flower` project cannot display the value of the root project property, because the value is not yet set by the `tree` project. To change the evaluation order of the project, we can explicitly define that the `flower` project depends on the `tree` project, with the `evaluationDependsOn()` method. We change the `build.gradle` file in the `flower` directory and add `evaluationDependsOn(':tree')` to the top of the file:

```
evaluationDependsOn ':tree'

ext.message = rootProject.hasProperty('treeMessage') ?
    rootProject.treeMessage : 'is not set'

printInfo.doLast {
    println "Tree say ${message}"
}
```

When we execute the `printInfo` task again, we see in the output that the value of the root project property is available in the `flower` project:

```
master $ gradle printInfo
:printInfo
This is master
:flower:printInfo
This is flower
Tree say I am a tree
:tree:printInfo
This is tree

BUILD SUCCESSFUL

Total time: 2.303 secs
```

# Working with Java multi-project builds

In a Java project, we usually have compile or runtime dependencies between projects. The output of one project is a compile dependency for another project, for example. This is very common in Java projects. Let's create a Java project with a common project that contains a Java class used by other projects. We will add a services project that references the class in the common project. Finally, we will add a web project with a Java servlet class that uses classes from the services project.

We have the following directory structure for our project:

```
root/
build.gradle
settings.gradle
common/
    src/main/java/sample/gradle/util/
        Logger.java
services/sample
    src/main/java/sample/gradle/
        api/
            SampleService.java
        impl/
            SampleImpl.java
    src/test/java/sample/gradle/impl/
        SampleTest.java
web/
    src/main/java/sample/gradle/web/
        SampleServlet.java
    src/main/webapp/WEB-INF/
        web.xml
```

In the root directory, we create a `settings.gradle` file. We will use the `include()` method to add the `common`, `web`, and `services/sample` projects to the build:

```
include 'common', 'services:sample', 'web'
```

Next, we create a `build.gradle` file in the root directory. We apply the Java plugin to each subproject and add a `testCompile` dependency on the JUnit libraries. This configuration is applied to each subproject in our build. Our `:services:sample` project has a dependency on the `common` project. We will configure this dependency in the project configuration of `:services:sample`. We will use the `project()` method to define this inter-project dependency. Our web project uses classes from both the `:common` and the `:services:sample` projects. We only have to define the dependency on the `:services:sample` project. Gradle will automatically add the dependencies for that project to the `:web` project. In our project, this means the `:common` project is also added as a transitive project dependency, and we can use the `Logger` class from that project in our `SampleServlet` class. We will add another external dependency for the **Servlet API** to our `:web` project and also apply the War plugin to our `:web` project:

```
subprojects {
    apply plugin: 'java'

    repositories {
```

```
            mavenCentral()
        }

        dependencies {
            testCompile 'junit:junit:4.8.2'
        }
    }

    project(':services:sample') {
        dependencies {
            compile project(':common')
        }
    }

    project(':web') {
        apply plugin: 'war'

        dependencies {
            compile project(':services:sample')
            compile 'javax.servlet:servlet-api:2.5'
        }
    }
```

The project dependencies are also called **lib** dependencies. These dependencies are used to evaluate the execution order of the projects. Gradle will analyze the dependencies and then decide which project needs to be built first, so the resulting classes can be used by dependent projects.

Let's build our project with the following command from the root directory:

```
root $ gradle build
:common:compileJava
:common:processResources UP-TO-DATE
:common:classes
:common:jar
:common:assemble
:common:compileTestJava UP-TO-DATE
:common:processTestResources UP-TO-DATE
:common:testClasses UP-TO-DATE
:common:test
:common:check
:common:build
:services:compileJava UP-TO-DATE
```

```
:services:processResources UP-TO-DATE

:services:classes UP-TO-DATE

:services:jar

:services:assemble

:services:compileTestJava UP-TO-DATE

:services:processTestResources UP-TO-DATE

:services:testClasses UP-TO-DATE

:services:test

:services:check

:services:build

:services:sample:compileJava

:services:sample:processResources UP-TO-DATE

:services:sample:classes

:services:sample:jar

:web:compileJava

:web:processResources UP-TO-DATE

:web:classes

:web:war

:web:assemble

:web:compileTestJava UP-TO-DATE

:web:processTestResources UP-TO-DATE

:web:testClasses UP-TO-DATE

:web:test

:web:check

:web:build

:services:sample:assemble

:services:sample:compileTestJava

:services:sample:processTestResources UP-TO-DATE

:services:sample:testClasses

:services:sample:test

:services:sample:check

:services:sample:build


BUILD SUCCESSFUL


Total time: 5.19 secs
```

A lot of tasks are executed, but we don't have to worry about their dependencies. Gradle will make sure the correct order of tasks is executed.

We can also have project dependencies based on a configuration in a project. Suppose we define a separate JAR artifact with only the SampleService class in the :services:sample project. We can add this as a separate dependency to our :web project. In the following example build file, we create a new JAR file with the SampleService class and then use that as a lib dependency in the :web project:

```
subprojects {
    apply plugin: 'java'

    repositories {
        mavenCentral()
    }

    dependencies {
        testCompile 'junit:junit:4.8.2'
    }
}

project(':services:sample') {
    configurations {
        api
    }

    task apiJar(type: Jar) {
        baseName = 'api'
        dependsOn classes
        from sourceSets.main.output
        include 'sample/gradle/api/SampleService.class'
    }

    artifacts {
        // Add output of apiJar task to api configuration.
        // so we can reference it from the :web project.
        api apiJar
    }

    dependencies {
        compile project(':common')
    }
}
```

```
project(':web') {
    apply plugin: 'war'

    dependencies {
        compile project(path: ':services:sample', configuration:
'api')
        compile project(':services:sample')
        compile 'javax.servlet:servlet-api:2.5'
    }
}
```

# Using partial builds

Because of the lib dependencies between the projects, we can execute partial builds in
Gradle. This means we don't have to be in the root directory of our project to build the
necessary projects. We can change to a project directory and invoke the build task from
there, and Gradle will build all necessary projects first and then the current project.

Let's change to the services/sample directory and invoke the build task from there
and look at the output:

```
root $ cd services/sample
sample $ gradle build
:common:compileJava UP-TO-DATE
:common:processResources UP-TO-DATE
:common:classes UP-TO-DATE
:common:jar UP-TO-DATE
:services:sample:compileJava UP-TO-DATE
:services:sample:processResources UP-TO-DATE
:services:sample:classes UP-TO-DATE
:services:sample:jar UP-TO-DATE
:services:sample:assemble UP-TO-DATE
:services:sample:compileTestJava UP-TO-DATE
:services:sample:processTestResources UP-TO-DATE
:services:sample:testClasses UP-TO-DATE
:services:sample:test UP-TO-DATE
:services:sample:check UP-TO-DATE
:services:sample:build UP-TO-DATE

BUILD SUCCESSFUL

Total time: 3.201 secs
```

The :common project is built before our :services:sample project. If we don't want the projects we are dependent on to be built, we must use the --no-rebuild (or -a) command-line argument. Gradle will now skip the building of projects that our project depends on and will use cached versions of the dependencies.

When we use the -a argument, while invoking the build task, we get the following output:

```
sample $ gradle -a build
:services:sample:compileJava UP-TO-DATE
:services:sample:processResources UP-TO-DATE
:services:sample:classes UP-TO-DATE
:services:sample:jar UP-TO-DATE
:services:sample:assemble UP-TO-DATE
:services:sample:compileTestJava UP-TO-DATE
:services:sample:processTestResources UP-TO-DATE
:services:sample:testClasses UP-TO-DATE
:services:sample:test UP-TO-DATE
:services:sample:check UP-TO-DATE
:services:sample:build UP-TO-DATE


BUILD SUCCESSFUL


Total time: 3.237 secs
```

If we invoke the build task on our :services:sample project, the :common project is also built. But there is a catch, as only the jar task of the :common project is executed. Normally, the build task also runs tests and executes the check task. Gradle will skip those tasks only if the project is built as a lib dependency.

If we want to execute the tests and checks for the dependency projects, we must execute the buildNeeded task. Gradle will then do a complete build of all dependent projects. Let's execute the buildNeeded task from the services/sample directory and look at the output:

```
sample $ gradle buildNeeded
:common:compileJava UP-TO-DATE
:common:processResources UP-TO-DATE
:common:classes UP-TO-DATE
:common:jar UP-TO-DATE
:common:assemble UP-TO-DATE
```

```
:common:compileTestJava UP-TO-DATE

:common:processTestResources UP-TO-DATE

:common:testClasses UP-TO-DATE

:common:test UP-TO-DATE

:common:check UP-TO-DATE

:common:build UP-TO-DATE

:common:buildNeeded UP-TO-DATE

:services:sample:compileJava UP-TO-DATE

:services:sample:processResources UP-TO-DATE

:services:sample:classes UP-TO-DATE

:services:sample:jar UP-TO-DATE

:services:sample:assemble UP-TO-DATE

:services:sample:compileTestJava UP-TO-DATE

:services:sample:processTestResources UP-TO-DATE

:services:sample:testClasses UP-TO-DATE

:services:sample:test UP-TO-DATE

:services:sample:check UP-TO-DATE

:services:sample:build UP-TO-DATE

:services:sample:buildNeeded UP-TO-DATE


BUILD SUCCESSFUL


Total time: 3.335 secs
```

If we have made changes to our `:services:sample` project, we might also want projects that are dependent on the sample project to be built. We can use this to make sure we have not broken any code that depends on our project. Gradle has a `buildDependents` task to do this. For example, let's execute this task from our `:services:sample` project; our `:web` project is also built because it has a dependency on the `:services:sample` project. We get the following output when we execute the `buildDependents` task:

```
sample $ gradle buildDependents

:common:compileJava UP-TO-DATE

:common:processResources UP-TO-DATE

:common:classes UP-TO-DATE

:common:jar UP-TO-DATE

:services:sample:compileJava UP-TO-DATE
```

```
:services:sample:processResources UP-TO-DATE
:services:sample:classes UP-TO-DATE
:services:sample:apiJar
:services:sample:jar UP-TO-DATE
:web:compileJava
:web:processResources UP-TO-DATE
:web:classes
:web:war
:web:assemble
:web:compileTestJava UP-TO-DATE
:web:processTestResources UP-TO-DATE
:web:testClasses UP-TO-DATE
:web:test
:web:check
:web:build
:web:buildDependents
:services:sample:assemble UP-TO-DATE
:services:sample:compileTestJava UP-TO-DATE
:services:sample:processTestResources UP-TO-DATE
:services:sample:testClasses UP-TO-DATE
:services:sample:test UP-TO-DATE
:services:sample:check UP-TO-DATE
:services:sample:build UP-TO-DATE
:services:sample:buildDependents

BUILD SUCCESSFUL

Total time: 3.896 secs
```

# Using the Jetty plugin

In the previous section, we created a Java project with a web subproject.
The web project has a simple servlet. To execute the servlet, we must create a
WAR file and deploy the WAR file to a servlet container such as Tomcat or Jetty.

With the Jetty plugin, we can run our web project from the command line in a Jetty web container. We don't have to install Jetty on our computer; we only need to apply the Jetty plugin to our project. The plugin will take care of configuring Jetty and starting the web container. If everything is okay, we can open a web browser and access our servlet.

To add the Jetty plugin to our web project, let's create a new file, `build.gradle`, in the `web` directory. Here, we use the `apply()` method to add the Jetty plugin to the project:

```
apply plugin: 'jetty'
```

The plugin adds the following tasks to our project: `jettyRun`, `jettyRunWar`, and `jettyStop`. The following table shows the different tasks:

| Task | Depends on | Type | Description |
| --- | --- | --- | --- |
| jettyRun | classes | JettyRun | Start a Jetty web container and deploy the exploded web application. |
| jettyRunWar | war | JettyRunWar | Start a Jetty web container and deploy the WAR file. |
| jettyStop | – | JettyStop | Stop a running Jetty web container. |

We can test our servlet in a web browser after we execute the `jettyRun` or `jettyWar` task. We get the following output when we execute the `jettyRun` task from the root of the multi-project build:

```
root $ gradle :web:jettyRun
:common:compileJava UP-TO-DATE
:common:processResources UP-TO-DATE
:common:classes UP-TO-DATE
:common:jar UP-TO-DATE
:services:sample:compileJava UP-TO-DATE
:services:sample:processResources UP-TO-DATE
:services:sample:classes UP-TO-DATE
:services:sample:jar UP-TO-DATE
:web:compileJava UP-TO-DATE
:web:processResources UP-TO-DATE
:web:classes UP-TO-DATE
> Building > :web:jettyRun > Running at http://localhost:8080/web
```

Gradle will keep running, and at the end, we see that the application is running at `http://localhost:8080/web`. We can open a web browser and access our web application. In the following screenshot, we see the output of the servlet:

To stop the Jetty web container, we press *Ctrl* + *C* at the command line, to return to our prompt.

We can change the port number via the `Project` convention property, `httpPort`, added by the Jetty plugin or the task property, `httpPort`, of the `jettyRun` and `jettyRunWar` tasks. To change the context path, we can set the `contextPath` property of the `jettyRun` and `jettyRunWar` tasks.

If we want the Jetty container to automatically scan for changes, we can set the `reload` property to `automatic`. If the property is set to `manual`, we must press *Enter* on the command line, to reload changes. We can set the scan interval in seconds, with the property `scanIntervalSeconds`.

In the following sample build file, we customize the Jetty web container with another HTTP port, context path, and automatic reloading:

```
apply plugin: 'jetty'
```

```
httpPort = 8090

jettyRun {
    contextPath = 'sample'
    reload = 'automatic'
    scanIntervalSeconds = 10
}
```

We can even customize the Jetty container further with custom Jetty configuration files. We could use the `jettyRun` task property, `jettyConfig`, to use configuration files. Or, we can add extra runtime libraries with the `additionalRuntimeJars` property.

If we want to use the `jettyStop` task, we must also define the `stopPort` and `stopKey` properties in either our `Project` or task. If we have defined these properties, we can open a new command-line prompt and invoke the `jettyStop` task to stop a running Jetty web container.

In the following example build file, we apply some of these properties and methods to customize the Jetty configuration:

```
apply plugin: 'jetty'

configurations {
    jettyAdditionalLibs
}

dependencies {
    jettyAdditionalLibs 'org.slf4j:slf4j-simple:1.6.6'
}

// Properties for stopping Jetty with jettyStop
stopPort = 8109
stopKey = 'JettyStop'

jettyRun {
    // External Jetty configuration file.
    jettyConfig = file('src/jetty/jetty.xml')

    // Extra libraries for Jetty runtime.
    additionalRuntimeJars configurations.jettyAdditionalLibs
}
```

# Summary

Multi-project builds are very common in software projects. Gradle has great support for multi-project builds. We can use a hierarchical layout as project structure, but we can easily customize this and use other layouts.

Configuring projects is easy and can be done in one place, at the root of the projects. We can also add project configurations at the project level itself. Not only can we define dependencies between projects on a project library level, but we can also do so via configuration or task dependencies. Gradle will resolve the correct way to build the complete project, so we don't have to worry too much about that.

Because Gradle knows which projects will be involved before a task is executed, we can do partial multi-project builds. Gradle will automatically build project dependencies, which are necessary for our current project. And we can use a single task to build the projects that depend on our current project.

Finally, we saw how we can run our web application code in a Jetty web container, with the Jetty plugin. We apply the plugin and execute the `jettyRun` or `jettyRunWar` tasks to run our code as a web application. We can open a web browser and execute our code.

In the next chapter, we will look at how we can use other languages besides Java, with Gradle.

# 8
# Mixed Languages

We have seen how to use Gradle for projects with Java code. Gradle has support for other languages as well. In the last couple of years, other languages for Java Virtual Machine have emerged. In this chapter, we will take a look at Gradle's support for the Groovy and Scala languages. Both languages are supported by Java Virtual Machine.

We will see how we can apply the correct plugin and configuration to our Gradle build files to work with the different languages.

Gradle also supports C++. The C++ plugin adds support to compile source files. Javascript and Closure plugins are available as third-party plugins, which add support for those languages. We will not cover this support in this book. We will focus on the JVM languages—Groovy and Scala.

## Using the Groovy plugin

To use Groovy sources in our project, we can apply the Groovy plugin. The Groovy plugin makes it possible to compile Groovy source files to class files. The project can contain both Java and Groovy source files. The compiler that Gradle uses is a joint compiler that can compile Java and Groovy source files.

The plugin also adds new tasks to our build. To compile the Groovy source files we can invoke the `compileGroovy` task. Test sources written in Groovy can be compiled with the `compileTestGroovy` task. Also, a `compile<SourceSet>Groovy` task is added for each extra source set in our build definition. So, if we create a new source set with the name `api`, there will be a `compileApiGroovy` task.

In the following example build file, we apply the Groovy plugin:

```
apply plugin: 'groovy'
```

If we invoke the `tasks` task to see what is available, we get the following output:

```
$ gradle tasks --all
:tasks


------------------------------------------------------------

All tasks runnable from root project

------------------------------------------------------------


Build tasks
-----------

assemble - Assembles all Jar, War, Zip, and Tar archives. [jar]

build - Assembles and tests this project. [assemble, check]

buildDependents - Assembles and tests this project and all projects that
depend on it. [build]

buildNeeded - Assembles and tests this project and all projects it
depends on. [build]

classes - Assembles the main classes.

    compileGroovy - Compiles the main Groovy source.

    compileJava - Compiles the main Java source.

    processResources - Processes the main resources.

clean - Deletes the build directory.

jar - Assembles a jar archive containing the main classes. [classes]

testClasses - Assembles the test classes. [classes]

    compileTestGroovy - Compiles the test Groovy source.

    compileTestJava - Compiles the test Java source.

    processTestResources - Processes the test resources.


Documentation tasks
--------------------

groovydoc - Generates Groovydoc API documentation for the main source
code. [classes]

javadoc - Generates Javadoc API documentation for the main source code.
[classes]
```

```
Help tasks
----------

dependencies - Displays the dependencies of root project 'groovy'.

help - Displays a help message

projects - Displays the sub-projects of root project 'groovy'.

properties - Displays the properties of root project 'groovy'.

tasks - Displays the tasks runnable from root project 'groovy' (some of
the displayed tasks may belong to subprojects).


Verification tasks
------------------

check - Runs all checks. [test]

test - Runs the unit tests. [classes, testClasses]


Rules
-----

Pattern: build<ConfigurationName>: Assembles the artifacts of a
configuration.

Pattern: upload<ConfigurationName>: Assembles and uploads the artifacts
belonging to a configuration.

Pattern: clean<TaskName>: Cleans the output files of a task.


BUILD SUCCESSFUL


Total time: 5.175 secs
```

Note that we also got all the tasks from the Java plugin. This is because the Groovy plugin automatically includes the Java plugin. So, even though we only defined the Groovy plugin in our build file, the Java plugin is applied as well.

The extra `compileGroovy` and `compileTestGroovy` tasks are visible in the command output. The new tasks are dependency tasks for the `classes` and `testClasses` tasks. If we invoke the `classes` task, the `compileGroovy` task is also executed.

The plugin adds the `groovy` configuration. The Groovy compiler uses this configuration. So, to compile Groovy source files in our project, we must set a dependency on the `groovy` configuration.

To compile Groovy source files, we must add a dependency, with the Groovy library we want to use, to the groovy configuration. We might expect that Gradle will use the Groovy version that is used by Gradle, but the compilation task is independent of the Groovy version used by Gradle. We have to define the Groovy library ourselves.

It is good to be independent of the Groovy libraries shipped with Gradle, because we can now use the Groovy version we really need. When we do want to use the Groovy libraries shipped with Gradle, we can use the special dependency localGroovy(). For a normal Groovy project this is not advised, but for plugin development it is useful.

First, we create a Groovy source file so we can compile it with Gradle. The default source directory for Groovy source files is src/main/groovy. Let's create a new file, in the directory src/main/groovy/gradle/sample, with the name Sample.groovy. The following code shows the contents of this file:

```groovy
package gradle.sample

import groovy.transform.ToString

@ToString
class Sample {
    String name
}
```

Next, we create a Gradle build file and apply the Groovy plugin. We add the Maven central repository and a Groovy dependency to the groovy configuration:

```groovy
apply plugin: 'groovy'

repositories {
    mavenCentral()
}

dependencies {
    groovy group: 'org.codehaus.groovy', name: 'groovy', version:
'1.8.6'
}
```

When we run the build task, we get the following output:

```
$ gradle build
:compileJava UP-TO-DATE
```

```
:compileGroovy
```

```
Download http://repo1.maven.org/maven2/org/codehaus/groovy/groovy/1.8.6/
groovy-1.8.6.pom
```

```
Download http://repo1.maven.org/maven2/org/codehaus/groovy/groovy/1.8.6/
groovy-1.8.6.jar
```

```
:processResources UP-TO-DATE
```

```
:classes
```

```
:jar
```

```
:assemble
```

```
:compileTestJava UP-TO-DATE
```

```
:compileTestGroovy UP-TO-DATE
```

```
:processTestResources UP-TO-DATE
```

```
:testClasses UP-TO-DATE
```

```
:test
```

```
:check
```

```
:build
```

```
BUILD SUCCESSFUL
```

```
Total time: 9.595 secs
```

When we don't have the specified Groovy library in our cache, it is downloaded from the Maven repository, by Gradle. The source code file is compiled, and if we look in the `build/classes` directory, we see the compiled class file.

The Groovy plugin also adds new source set properties. The following table shows the extra properties:

| Property name | Type | Description |
| --- | --- | --- |
| groovy | org.gradle.api.file. SourceDirectorySet | The Groovy source files for this project. Contains both .java and .groovy source files if they are in the groovy directory. |
| groovy.srcDirs | java.util.Set <java.io.File> | Directories with the Groovy source files. Can also contain Java source files for joint compilation. |
| allGroovy | org.gradle.api. file.FileTree | Only the Groovy source files. All files with extension .groovy are part of this collection. |

We extend our previous build file and add the task groovySourceSetsProperties. We print out the extra properties and their values with this task. The build now looks like this:

```
apply plugin: 'groovy'

repositories {
    mavenCentral()
}

dependencies {
    groovy group: 'org.codehaus.groovy', name: 'groovy', version:
'1.8.6'
}

task groovySourceSetProperties << {
    sourceSets {
        main {
            println "groovy.srcDirs = ${groovy.srcDirs}"
            println "groovy.files = ${groovy.files.name}"
            println "allGroovy.files = ${allGroovy.files.name}"
        }
    }
}
```

When we run the task groovySourceSetProperties on the command line, we see the following output:

```
$ gradle groovySourceSetProperties
:groovySourceSetProperties
groovy.srcDirs = [/gradle-book/samples/chapter8/groovy/src/main/groovy]
groovy.files = [Sample.groovy]
allGroovy.files = [Sample.groovy]

BUILD SUCCESSFUL

Total time: 2.997 secs
```

When our Java code uses Groovy classes, and vice versa, we can use the joint compilation feature. We must make sure both the Java and Groovy source files are in the src/main/groovy directory.

# Creating documentation with the Groovy plugin

The Groovy plugin also adds the groovydoc task. The groovydoc task is like the javadoc task from the Java plugin. Gradle uses the **Groovydoc** tool, which is available from the Groovy version that we have defined as a dependency to the groovy configuration.

The task has several properties we can change. For example, we can set the header and footer to be used in the generated documentation.

In the following build file, we configure the groovydoc task:

```
apply plugin: 'groovy'

version = 1.0

repositories {
    mavenCentral()
}

dependencies {
    groovy group: 'org.codehaus.groovy', name: 'groovy', version:
'1.8.6'
}

groovydoc {
    header = 'GroovyDoc for sample project'
    footer = "Generated documentation - $version"
    docTitle = 'GroovyDoc Title'
    windowTitle = docTitle
    use = true // Create class and package usage pages

    // Exclude files, use include to include files
    exclude '**/*Doc.groovy'
}
```

When we run the groovydoc task, we can see the generated documentation in the build/docs/groovydoc directory. We must open the index.html file in our web browser to see the result.

# Using the Scala plugin

We can also use Gradle to work with Scala source files. We can have a Scala-only project, or we can have both Java and Scala source files in our project. We must apply the Scala plugin to enable Scala support for our build. The plugin adds new tasks to compile the Scala source files. With the `compileScala` task, we compile our main Scala source files. The source files must be in the `src/main/scala` directory. The `compileTestScala` task compiles all Scala source code files that are in the `src/test/scala` directory. The plugin also adds a `compile<SourceSet>Scala` task for custom-defined source sets in our build.

The compile tasks support both Java and Scala source files with joint compilation. We can place our Java source files in say the `src/main/java` directory of our project and the Scala source files in the `src/main/scala` directory. The compiler will compile both types of files. To be able to compile the files, we must add dependencies to the Scala tools in our build file. The Scala plugin adds the `scalaTools` dependency configuration to our build. We must assign the correct dependencies from a Maven repository to this configuration, so that Gradle can invoke the compiler to compile the source files.

Let's create a simple Scala source file in the directory `src/main/scala/gradle/sample` and save it as `Sample.scala`:

```
package gradle.sample

class Sample(val name: String) {
    def getName() = name
}
```

In the following example build file, we apply the Scala plugin. Also, in the dependencies section we set the correct dependencies for the compiler:

```
apply plugin: 'scala'

repositories.mavenCentral()

ext {
    scala = [version: '2.9.2', group: 'org.scala-lang']
}

dependencies {
    scalaTools "${scala.group}:scala-compiler:${scala.version}"
    scalaTools "${scala.group}:scala-library:${scala.version}"
}
```

To build the project, we invoke the `build` task and get the following output:

```
$ gradle build
:compileJava UP-TO-DATE
:compileScala
Download http://repo1.maven.org/maven2/org/scala-lang/scala-
library/2.9.2/scala-library-2.9.2.pom
Download http://repo1.maven.org/maven2/org/scala-lang/scala-
library/2.9.2/scala-library-2.9.2.jar
Download http://repo1.maven.org/maven2/org/scala-lang/scala-
compiler/2.9.2/scala-compiler-2.9.2.pom
Download http://repo1.maven.org/maven2/org/scala-lang/scala-
compiler/2.9.2/scala-compiler-2.9.2.jar
:processResources UP-TO-DATE
:classes
:jar
:assemble
:compileTestJava UP-TO-DATE
:compileTestScala UP-TO-DATE
:processTestResources UP-TO-DATE
:testClasses UP-TO-DATE
:test
:check
:build


BUILD SUCCESSFUL


Total time: 17.167 secs
```

Note how the `compileScala` and `compileTestScala` tasks are dependency tasks
for the `classes` and `testClasses` tasks respectively. So, the newly added tasks
are automatically part of the normal build tasks we know from our Java projects.
The Scala plugin will even automatically include the Java plugin, if we don't apply
the Java plugin ourselves.

We can define a custom source set in our project. The Scala plugin adds a `compile` task for each source set to our project. In the following Gradle build file, we add a new source set with the name `actors`:

```
apply plugin: 'scala'

repositories.mavenCentral()

ext {
    scala = [version: '2.9.2', group: 'org.scala-lang']
}

dependencies {
    scalaTools "${scala.group}:scala-compiler:${scala.version}"
    scalaTools "${scala.group}:scala-library:${scala.version}"

    compile "${scala.group}:scala-library:${scala.version}"
}

sourceSets {
    actors
}
```

When we invoke the `tasks` command, we see that Gradle added `compileActorsScala` to the list of available tasks:

```
$ gradle tasks --all
:tasks


------------------------------------------------------------
All tasks runnable from root project
------------------------------------------------------------


Build tasks
-----------
actorsClasses - Assembles the actors classes.
    compileActorsJava - Compiles the actors Java source.
    compileActorsScala - Compiles the actors Scala source.
    processActorsResources - Processes the actors resources.
assemble - Assembles all Jar, War, Zip, and Tar archives. [jar]
build - Assembles and tests this project. [assemble, check]
```

```
buildDependents - Assembles and tests this project and all projects that
depend on it. [build]
buildNeeded - Assembles and tests this project and all projects it
depends on. [build]
classes - Assembles the main classes.
    compileJava - Compiles the main Java source.
    compileScala - Compiles the main Scala source.
    processResources - Processes the main resources.
clean - Deletes the build directory.
jar - Assembles a jar archive containing the main classes. [classes]
testClasses - Assembles the test classes. [classes]
    compileTestJava - Compiles the test Java source.
    compileTestScala - Compiles the test Scala source.
    processTestResources - Processes the test resources.
...
```

The task `actorsClasses` is added and has all the compile tasks for the `actors` source set. When we want the `actorsClasses` task to be part of the `build` task, we can assign it as a task dependency to the `jar` task. In the following example build file, we use the `from()` method of the `jar` task to assign the output of the `actors` source set as part of the JAR file contents:

```
apply plugin: 'scala'

repositories.mavenCentral()

ext {
    scala = [version: '2.9.2', group: 'org.scala-lang']
}

dependencies {
    scalaTools "${scala.group}:scala-compiler:${scala.version}"
    scalaTools "${scala.group}:scala-library:${scala.version}"

    compile "${scala.group}:scala-library:${scala.version}"
}

sourceSets {
    actors
}

jar {
    from sourceSets.actors.output
}
```

When we execute the `build` task, our source files in the source set `actors` are compiled and added to the JAR file.

The Scala plugin also adds several new properties to a source set. The following table shows the extra properties:

| Property name | Type | Description |
| --- | --- | --- |
| scala | org.gradle.api.file. SourceDirectorySet | The Scala source files for this project; contains both .java and .scala source files if they are in the scala directory. |
| scala.srcDirs | java.util.Set <java.io.File> | Directories with the Scala source files; can also contain Java source files for joint compilation. |
| allScala | org.gradle.api. file.FileTree | Only the Scala source files. All files with extension .scala are part of this collection. |

Let's create a new task, `scalaSourceSetsProperties`, to see the contents of each of these properties:

```
apply plugin: 'scala'

repositories.mavenCentral()

ext {
    scala = [version: '2.9.2', group: 'org.scala-lang']
}

dependencies {
    scalaTools "${scala.group}:scala-compiler:${scala.version}"
    scalaTools "${scala.group}:scala-library:${scala.version}"

    compile "${scala.group}:scala-library:${scala.version}"
}

task scalaSourceSetsProperties << {
    sourceSets {
        main {
            println "scala.srcDirs = ${scala.srcDirs}"
            println "scala.files = ${scala.files.name}"
            println "allScala.files = ${allScala.files.name}"
        }
    }
}
```

When we invoke the `scalaSourceSetsProperties` task from the command-line, we get the following output:

```
$ gradle scalaSourceSetsProperties
:scalaSourceSetsProperties
scala.srcDirs = [/samples/chapter8/scala/src/main/scala]
scala.files = [Sample.scala]
allScala.files = [Sample.scala]

BUILD SUCCESSFUL

Total time: 3.036 secs
```

# Creating documentation with the Scala plugin

The Scala plugin also adds a `scaladoc` task to our build. We can use this task to generate documentation from the source files. This is like the `javadoc` task from the Java plugin. We can configure the `scaladoc` task to provide extra options.

In the following example build file, we add a title to the generated documentation by configuring the `scaladoc` task:

```
import org.gradle.api.tasks.scala.*

apply plugin: 'scala'

version = 2.1

repositories.mavenCentral()

ext {
    scala = [version: '2.9.2', group: 'org.scala-lang']
}

dependencies {
    scalaTools "${scala.group}:scala-compiler:${scala.version}"
    scalaTools "${scala.group}:scala-library:${scala.version}"

    compile "${scala.group}:scala-library:${scala.version}"
}

scaladoc.title = 'Scala documentation'
```

When we invoke the `scaladoc` task, Gradle will generate the documentation, and the result is in `build/docs/scaladoc`. We can open the file `index.html` in our web browser to see the generated documentation.

# Summary

In this chapter, we learned how we can work with Groovy and Scala source files in a Gradle project. We applied the Groovy or Scala plugins to our project and saw that Gradle added the tasks to compile the source files, to the project. We learned that we must add a dependency to the correct Groovy or Scala version to the dependency configuration added by the plugin. Both plugins will include the Java plugin as well.

We also learned that the plugins also provide some new properties for source sets so we can, for example, find all Groovy or Scala source files in a source set.

In the next chapter, we take a look at how we can add code quality tools to our Gradle builds.

# Maintaining Code Quality

*9*

While working on a project, we want to have some kind of tooling or process in place that we can use to see if our code follows certain standards; either our code has no common coding problems or calculates the complexity of the code.

We need these tools to write better code. Better code means it will be easier to maintain, and this lowers the cost of maintaining the code. In a project team, we want to make sure that the code follows the same standards defined by the project team. A company could define a set of standards that developers need to follow, as a condition for the project to be started.

There are tools already available for Java and Groovy projects to analyze and check source code, such as **Checkstyle, JDepend, PMD, FindBugs, CodeNarc**, and **Sonar**. Gradle has plugins for each of these tools. In this chapter, we will take a look at the plugins and learn how to use them in our projects.

## Using the Checkstyle plugin

If we are working on a Java project, and apply the Java plugin to our project, we get an empty task with the name check. This is a dependency task for the build task. This means that when we execute the build task, the check task is executed as well. We can write our own tasks to check something in our project and make it a dependency task for the check task. So if the check task is executed, our own task is executed as well. And not only the tasks we write ourselves, but the plugins also, can add new dependency tasks to the check task.

We will see in this chapter that most plugins will add one or more tasks as a dependency task to the check task. This means that we can apply a plugin to our project, and when we invoke the check or build task, the extra tasks of the plugin are executed automatically.

Also, the `check` task is dependent on the `test` task. Gradle will always make sure the `test` task is executed before the `check` task, so we know that all source files and test source files are compiled, and tests are run before the code is checked. To add the Checkstyle analysis to our project, we simply have to apply the Checkstyle plugin:

```
apply plugin: 'checkstyle'
```

If we invoke the `tasks` task from the command line, we can see that new tasks have been added by the plugin:

```
$ gradle tasks --all

...


Verification tasks
------------------
check - Runs all checks. [classes, test, testClasses]
  checkstyleMain - Run Checkstyle analysis for main classes
  checkstyleTest - Run Checkstyle analysis for test classes
test - Runs the unit tests. [classes, testClasses]


...
```

The tasks `checkstyleMain` and `checkstyleTest` are added as a dependency for the `check` task. The tasks run the Checkstyle analysis for the main and test classes.

We cannot execute these tasks yet, because we have to add a Checkstyle configuration file to our project. This file contains the rules that we want applied for our code. The plugin will look for a file `checkstyle.xml` in the directory `config/checkstyle` in our project. This is the default location and filename, but we can change it. Let's create a configuration file with the following content:

```
<?xml version="1.0"?>
<!DOCTYPE module PUBLIC
   "-//Puppy Crawl//DTD Check Configuration 1.3//EN"
   "http://www.puppycrawl.com/dtds/configuration_1_3.dtd">
<module name="Checker">
  <module name="JavadocPackage"/>
  <module name="NewlineAtEndOfFile"/>
  <module name="RegexpSingleline">
  <property name="format" value="\s+$"/>
  <property name="minimum" value="0"/>
  <property name="maximum" value="0"/>
  <property name="message" value="Line has trailing spaces."/>
```

```
    </module>

    <module name="TreeWalker">
      <module name="IllegalImport"/>
      <module name="RedundantImport"/>
      <module name="UnusedImports"/>
      <module name="AvoidNestedBlocks"/>
      <module name="EmptyBlock"/>
      <module name="LeftCurly"/>
      <module name="NeedBraces"/>
      <module name="RightCurly"/>
      <module name="DesignForExtension"/>
      <module name="FinalClass"/>
      <module name="HideUtilityClassConstructor"/>
      <module name="InterfaceIsType"/>
      <module name="VisibilityModifier"/>
    </module>

  </module>
```

The Checkstyle plugin does not add the required library dependencies to our project automatically. We need to add an appropriate repository to our project so that the Checkstyle plugin can download all the dependencies.

Let's create the following example build file and add the repository definition:

```
apply {
  plugin 'java'
  plugin 'checkstyle'
}

repositories.mavenCentral()
```

Now we can run the check task and see the output:

```
:compileJava

:processResources UP-TO-DATE

:classes

:checkstyleMain

[ant:checkstyle] /samples/chapter9/sample/src/main/java/gradle/sample/
JavaSample.java:0: File does not end with a newline.

[ant:checkstyle] /samples/chapter9/sample/src/main/java/gradle/sample/
JavaSample.java:0: Missing package-info.java file.

[ant:checkstyle] /samples/chapter9/sample/src/main/java/gradle/sample/
JavaSample.java:8:5: Missing a Javadoc comment.
```

[ant:checkstyle] /samples/chapter9/sample/src/main/java/gradle/sample/
JavaSample.java:9: Line has trailing spaces.

[ant:checkstyle] /samples/chapter9/sample/src/main/java/gradle/sample/
JavaSample.java:10:5: Missing a Javadoc comment.

[ant:checkstyle] /samples/chapter9/sample/src/main/java/gradle/sample/
JavaSample.java:10:29: Parameter args should be final.

[ant:checkstyle] /samples/chapter9/sample/src/main/java/gradle/sample/
JavaSample.java:14: Line has trailing spaces.

[ant:checkstyle] /samples/chapter9/sample/src/main/java/gradle/sample/
JavaSample.java:15: Line has trailing spaces.

[ant:checkstyle] /samples/chapter9/sample/src/main/java/gradle/sample/
JavaSample.java:17:5: Method 'setGreeting' is not designed for extension
- needs to be abstract, final or empty.

[ant:checkstyle] /samples/chapter9/sample/src/main/java/gradle/sample/
JavaSample.java:17:5: Missing a Javadoc comment.

[ant:checkstyle] /samples/chapter9/sample/src/main/java/gradle/sample/
JavaSample.java:17:42: 'greeting' hides a field.

[ant:checkstyle] /samples/chapter9/sample/src/main/java/gradle/sample/
JavaSample.java:21:5: Method 'greet' is not designed for extension -
needs to be abstract, final or empty.

[ant:checkstyle] /samples/chapter9/sample/src/main/java/gradle/sample/
JavaSample.java:21:5: Missing a Javadoc comment.

FAILURE: Build failed with an exception.

* What went wrong:

Execution failed for task ':checkstyleMain'.

> Checkstyle rule violations were found. See the report at / samples/
chapter9/sample/build/reports/checkstyle/main.xml.

* Try:

Run with --stacktrace option to get the stack trace. Run with --info or
--debug option to get more log output.

BUILD FAILED

Total time: 4.889 secs

The `checkstyleMain` task has been executed and the build has failed, because our code doesn't follow our Checkstyle rules. In the output, we can see all the violations of the rules. Gradle will also create an XML file with the violations in the `build/reports/checkstyle` directory.

If we don't want the build to fail, we can use the property `ignoreFailures` of the `checkstyle` tasks. The checks are still executed and the report file is generated, but the build will not fail.

We can configure the Checkstyle plugin with the `checkstyle{}` script block or the `checkstyle` property in a Gradle build. The script block accepts a configuration closure where we can change the properties. In the following build file, we set the `ignoreFailures` property to `true`, so the build will not fail even after Checkstyle finds errors:

```
apply {
    plugin 'java'
    plugin 'checkstyle'
}

repositories.mavenCentral()

checkstyle {
    ignoreFailures = true
}
```

While this book was being written, Gradle used Checkstyle 5.5. To change the version, we can set the `toolVersion` property to another version. For example, if, in the future, Checkstyle 5.6 is released, then we simply have to change the `toolVersion` property and don't need a new Gradle version.

In the following example build file, we set the Checkstyle version to `5.4` by changing the `toolVersion` property. We might need to do this for legacy projects too:

```
apply {
    plugin 'java'
    plugin 'checkstyle'
}

repositories.mavenCentral()

checkstyle {
    toolVersion = 5.4
}
```

To change the Checkstyle configuration file, we can set the property `configFile` to a different value. The default value is `config/checkstyle/checkstyle.xml`. We can, for example, copy the `sun_checks.xml` configuration file from a Checkstyle distribution to the `config/checkstyle` directory. We set the `configFile` property with the value of this new file, and our code is checked using the rules from the `sun_checks.xml` configuration file.

This sample build file shows that we have referenced another Checkstyle configuration file:

```
apply {
  plugin 'java'
  plugin 'checkstyle'
}

repositories.mavenCentral()

checkstyle {
    configFile = file('config/checkstyle/sun_checks.xml')
}
```

A Checkstyle configuration supports property expansion. This means that the configuration file has variable property values with the syntax `${propertyName}`. We can set the value for such a property by using the `configProperties` property of the Checkstyle configuration closure. This property accepts a map, where the keys are the property names from the Checkstyle configuration file and the values are the property values. If the Checkstyle configuration file has a property with the name `tabWidth`, for example, we can set the value with the following example build file:

```
apply {
  plugin 'java'
  plugin 'checkstyle'
}

repositories.mavenCentral()

// Set checkstyle options, that are used by
// all checkstyle tasks.
checkstyle {
  configProperties = [tabWidth: 10]
}
```

We use the `checkstyle{}` script block to change the properties for all the
`checkstyle` tasks in a project. But we can also configure individual `checkstyle`
tasks in our build file. We have got the `checkstyleMain` and `checkstyleTest` tasks,
and we can alter their configuration just like any other task.

Let's create the following example build file and change the properties of the
`checkstyleTest` task, which will override the properties set in the `checkstyle{}`
script block:

```
apply {
  plugin 'java'
  plugin 'checkstyle'
}

repositories.mavenCentral()

// Set checkstyle options, that are used by
// all checkstyle tasks.
checkstyle {
  configFile = file('config/checkstyle/sun_checks.xml')
}

// Reconfigure the checkstyleTest task.
checkstyleTest {
  configFile = file('config/checkstyle/test.xml')
  ignoreFailures = true
}
```

If we have defined custom source sets in our build, then the Checkstyle plugin
automatically adds a `checkstyle<SourceSet>` task to the project. If our source set
is named `api`, then we can invoke the `checkstyleApi` task to only check this source
set. The `checkstyleApi` task is also added as a dependency task for the `check` task.
So once we run the `check` task, Gradle will invoke the `checkstyleApi` task as well.

In this example build file, we create a new source set with the name `api`:

```
apply {
  plugin 'java'
  plugin 'checkstyle'
}

repositories.mavenCentral()

sourceSets {
  api
}
```

If we invoke the `tasks` task, we can see in the output that a newly created task `checkstyleApi` is added, which is a dependency task for the `check` task:

```
$ gradle tasks --all

...


Verification tasks
-----------------
check - Runs all checks. [apiClasses, classes, test, testClasses]
  checkstyleApi - Run Checkstyle analysis for api classes
  checkstyleMain - Run Checkstyle analysis for main classes
  checkstyleTest - Run Checkstyle analysis for test classes
test - Runs the unit tests. [classes, testClasses]


...
```

The report XML files that are generated are placed in the `build/reports/checkstyle` directory. The name of the files is based on the source set name. So the `checkstyleMain` task will generate the report file `build/reports/checkstyle/main.xml`. We can configure this in our build file. We can change the reports output directory with the `reportsDir` property. We can change the destination file for a specific `checkstyle` task with the `destination` property. We can also disable the report generation with the `enabled` property, for a given task.

The following sample build file changes the reporting directory, the destination file for the `checkstyleMain` task, and disables report generation for the `checkstyleTest` task:

```
apply {
  plugin 'java'
  plugin 'checkstyle'
}

repositories.mavenCentral()

checkstyle {
  reportsDir = file("${buildDir}/checkstyle-output")
}
```

```
checkstyleTest {
  reports.xml.enabled = false
}

checkstyleMain {
  reports {
    xml {
      destination = file("${checkstyle.reportsDir}/checkstyle.xml")
    }
  }
}
```

# Using the PMD plugin

Another tool for analyzing the Java source code is PMD. It finds unused variables, empty catch blocks, unnecessary object creation, and so forth. We can configure our own rule sets and even define our own rules. To use PMD with Gradle, we have to apply the PMD plugin to our build. After we have added the plugin, we have the `pmdMain` and `pmdTest` tasks already installed. These tasks will run PMD rules for the main and test source sets. If we have a custom source set, then the plugin adds a `pmd<SourceSet>` task as well. These tasks are also dependency tasks of the `check` task. So if we invoke the `check` task, all the `pmd` tasks are executed as well.

This plugin only defines a structure to work with PMD, but doesn't contain the actual PMD library dependencies. Gradle will download the PMD dependencies the first time that we invoke the `pmd` tasks. We have to define a repository that contains the PMD libraries, such as the Maven Central repository or a corporate intranet repository.

In the following build file, we apply the PMD plugin and define a custom source set:

```
apply plugin: 'java'
apply plugin: 'pmd'

repositories {
  mavenCentral()
}

sourceSets {
  util
}
```

When we invoke the `check` task, and if there are no rule violations, we get the following output:

```
$ gradle check
:pmdMain
:pmdTest UP-TO-DATE
:pmdUtil UP-TO-DATE
:compileJava UP-TO-DATE
:processResources UP-TO-DATE
:classes UP-TO-DATE
:compileTestJava UP-TO-DATE
:processTestResources UP-TO-DATE
:testClasses UP-TO-DATE
:test
:check

BUILD SUCCESSFUL

Total time: 6.497 secs
```

Note the `pmdMain`, `pmdTest`, and `pmdUtil` tasks that are executed.

If one of the files has a violation, then the build will fail by default. We can set the `ignoreFailures` property for the `pmd` tasks to `true`, so the build will not fail. The following sample build shows how we can set the property `ignoreFailures` to `true`:

```
apply plugin: 'java'
apply plugin: 'pmd'

repositories {
  mavenCentral()
}

sourceSets {
  util
}

pmd {
  // Don't fail the build process when
  // rule violations are found.
  ignoreFailures = true
}
```

Rule violations will be reported in an XML and HTML file in the `build/reports/`
`pmd` directory. The name of the file is the same as the source set name. We can change
the name of the reporting directory and the output filename, or we can also disable
the report generation.

The following example build file changes several properties of the reporting by
the `pmd` tasks:

```
apply plugin: 'java'
apply plugin: 'pmd'

repositories {
  mavenCentral()
}

sourceSets {
  util
}

pmd {
  // Change base reporting dir for PDM reports.
  reportsDir = file("${reporting.baseDir}/pmd-output")
}

configure(tasks.withType(Pmd)) {
  // Disable HTML report generation for all PDM tasks.
  reports.html.enabled = false
}

// Change output file for the single task pmdMain.
pmdMain {
  reports {
    xml.destination = file("${pmd.reportsDir}/pmd.xml")
  }
}
```

Only the basic rule set of PMD is applied if we don't define anything else in the
build file. To change which rules are applied, we can use the `rules` property and
the `rules()` method. With the `rules()` method, we have a convenient way to add
new rules. With the `rules` property, we have to define all the rules we want to use
as a property assignment.

Besides configuring the rules, we can also assign rule set files for the `pmd` tasks. A
rule set file contains several rules and allows customization of the rules. To add a
rule set file, we can use the `ruleSetFiles` property or the `ruleSetFiles()` method.
We need to reference a file to set the property or pass it as a method argument.

The following sample build file shows how we can set rules and rule set files:

```
apply plugin: 'java'
apply plugin: 'pmd'

repositories {
  mavenCentral()
}

pmd {
  // Add rules.
  ruleSets 'design', 'braces'
  // Or use property syntax.
  // ruleSets = ['design', 'braces']

  // Set rule set file.
  ruleSetFiles = [file('config/pmd/customRules.xml')]
  // Or use method.
  //ruleSetFiles file('config/pmd/customRules.xml')
}
```

To change the version of PMD that we want to use, we must set the property `toolVersion` of the PDM plugin. When this book was being written, this was set to version 4.3, but we can change it to other versions if required. In the following example build file, we simply change the version to `4.2` with the `toolVersion` property:

```
apply plugin: 'java'
apply plugin: 'pmd'

pmd.toolVersion = 4.2
```

# Using the FindBugs plugin

FindBugs is another library that we can use to analyze our source code. To use FindBugs in our Gradle builds, we simply have to apply the FindBugs plugin. We can either apply one source code analysis plugin to our project, or we can apply multiple plugins. Each tool has different features. It just depends on what we want to check or what is prescribed per company policy. The plugin will add the tasks `findbugsMain` and `findbugsTest` to analyze the source code from the `main` and `test` source sets. If we have a custom source set, then the task `findbugs<SourceSet>` is also added to the plugin. These tasks are all dependency tasks for the `check` task.

Just as with the other code quality plugins, the FindBugs dependencies are not included with Gradle, but will be downloaded the first time we use the `findbugs` tasks. We must include a repository definition that will enable Gradle to find the FindBugs dependencies. To change the FindBugs version that is being used, we can set the `toolVersion` property with the `findbugs()` method.

In the following build file, we apply the FindBugs plugin and configure an extra source set with the name `webservice`:

```
apply plugin: 'java'
apply plugin: 'findbugs'

repositories {
  mavenCentral()
}

findbugs {
  toolVersion = '2.0.0' // Default version with Gradle 1.1
}

sourceSets {
    webservice
}
```

When we execute the `tasks` task, we see that the `findbugsMain`, `findbugsTest`, and `findbugsWebservice` tasks are dependencies for the `check` task:

```
$ gradle tasks --all

...


Verification tasks
------------------
check - Runs all checks. [classes, test, testClasses, webserviceClasses]
  findbugsMain - Run FindBugs analysis for main classes
  findbugsTest - Run FindBugs analysis for test classes
  findbugsWebservice - Run FindBugs analysis for webservice classes
test - Runs the unit tests. [classes, testClasses]


...
```

If FindBugs finds violations of the rules in our source, then the build will fail. We can set the property `ignoreFailures` to `true`, as shown in the following lines of code, to make sure the build will continue even if violations are found:

```
apply plugin: 'java'
apply plugin: 'findbugs'

repositories.mavenCentral()

// Global setting for all findbugs tasks.
findbugs.ignoreFailures = true

// We can change ignoreFailures property also per task.
findbugsMain.ignoreFailures = false
```

The plugin generates an XML report with the result of the FindBugs analysis in the directory `build/reports/findbugs`. The name of the XML file is the same as the name of the source set that is analyzed. We can also configure the plugin that an HTML report generates. In the following build file, we configure the reporting in the FindBugs plugin:

```
apply plugin: 'java'
apply plugin: 'findbugs'

repositories {
  mavenCentral()
}

findbugs {
  // Change base directory for FindBugs reports.
  reportsDir = file("${reporting.baseDir}/findbugs-output")
}

findbugsMain {
  reports {
    html {
      enabled = true

      // Change output file name.
      destination = "${findbugs.reportsDir}/findbugs.html"
    }
    // Only one report (xml or html) can be active.
    xml.enabled = !html.enabled
  }
}
```

If we want to use FindBugs plugins, we can define them as dependencies. The FindBugs plugin adds a `findbugsPlugins` dependency configuration. We can assign plugin dependencies to this configuration, and the `findbugs` tasks will use these plugins to analyze the code.

# Using the JDepend plugin

To get quality metrics for our code base, we can use JDepend. JDepend traverses the generated class files in our project and generates design quality metrics. To use JDepend, we simply have to apply the JDepend plugin in our project. This will add a `jdependMain` and `jdependTest` task. For each extra source set in our project, a `jdepend<SourceSet>` task is added. These tasks are all dependency tasks of the `check` task.

We must configure a repository so Gradle can fetch the JDepend dependencies. Gradle doesn't provide the JDepend libraries in the Gradle distribution. This means that we can easily use another version of JDepend, independent of the Gradle version we are using. We see this behavior in the other code quality plugins as well. To change a version number, we simply have to set the `toolVersion` property of the JDepend plugin.

In the following example build file, we apply the JDepend plugin and create an extra source set:

```
apply plugin: 'java'
apply plugin: 'jdepend'

// Repository definition to get JDepend libraries.
repositories {
  mavenCentral()
}

// We can change the version of JDepend to be used.
jdepend.toolVersion = '2.9.1'

// Custom source set so jdependRestApi task is created.
sourceSets {
  restApi
}
```

When we invoke the `tasks` task, we will see that three `jdepend` tasks are created as a dependency for the `check` task:

```
$ gradle tasks --all

...


Verification tasks
------------------
check - Runs all checks. [classes, restApiClasses, test, testClasses]
  jdependMain - Run JDepend analysis for main classes
  jdependRestApi - Run JDepend analysis for restApi classes
  jdependTest - Run JDepend analysis for test classes
test - Runs the unit tests. [classes, testClasses]


...
```

The `jdepend` tasks create statistics about our code. The results are stored in an XML file in the `build/reports/jdepend` directory. We can configure the JDepend plugin so the directory that we store the reports in is different. For each `jdepend` task, we can also alter the output format. Instead of XML, we can generate a text file with the statistics about our code. We have to choose between XML and text; we cannot choose both report outputs for a single `jdepend` task.

The following sample build file shows several options on how we can change the reports with information about our source code:

```
apply plugin: 'java'
apply plugin: 'jdepend'

// Repository definition to get JDepend libraries.
repositories {
  mavenCentral()
}

jdepend.reportsDir = file("${reporting.baseDir}/jdepend-output")

jdependMain {
  reports {
    text {
      enabled = 'true'
      destination = file("${jdepend.reportsDir}/jdepend.txt")
    }
```

```
    xml {
      enabled = !text.enabled
    }
  }
}
```

# Using the CodeNarc plugin

To check code written in the Groovy language, we can use CodeNarc. CodeNarc has several rules to do a static analysis of Groovy code. Gradle has a CodeNarc plugin, so we can apply the rules from CodeNarc to our Groovy code base. If we apply the plugin, we automatically get a `codenarcMain` and `codenarcTest` target. Also, for each custom source set, we get a new task named `codenarc<SourceSet>`. All these tasks are dependency tasks of the `check` task.

The CodeNarc library is not included with Gradle. We need to define a repository in our build file that contains CodeNarc. If we invoke a `codenarc` task, then Gradle sets CodeNarc dependencies. We can change the version of CodeNarc that we want to use by setting the `codenarc.toolVersion` property.

The plugin defines that we provide a CodeNarc configuration file with the name `codenarc.xml` in the directory `config/codenarc`. We can change the reference to the configuration file with the `configFile` property of the plugin.

Let's create the following example build file and apply the CodeNarc plugin for a Groovy project. We will change the version of CodeNarc that we want to use. We will also redefine the location of the CodeNarc configuration file to `config/codenarc/custom.xml`:

```
apply plugin: 'groovy'
apply plugin: 'codenarc'

// Repository definition to get CodeNarc libraries.
repositories {
  mavenCentral()
}

codenarc {
  // Change version of CodeNarc.
  toolVersion = 0.17

  // Change name of configuration file. Default value
  // is file('config/codenarc/codenarc.xml')
  configFile = file('config/codenarc/rules.groovy')
}
```

When we run the `check` task and our Groovy code base starts violating the configured CodeNarc rules, the build will fail. If we don't want the build to fail on a violation, we can set the property `ignoreFailures` to `true`. We can set this for all `codenarc` tasks with the `codenarc.ignoreFailures` property. We can also set this property for individual `codenarc` tasks.

The following build file shows that we set the property `ignoreFailures` for all the `codenarc` tasks:

```
apply plugin: 'groovy'
apply plugin: 'codenarc'

repositories {
  mavenCentral()
}


codenarc.ignoreFailures = true
```

The `codenarc` tasks create an HTML report with the found results, and place it in the `build/reports/codenarc` directory. The name of the file is defined by the source set name for which the task is executed. We can also choose different output formats. We can set the output to XML or text file formats. We can change the format of the reports with the `reports()` method of the `codenarc` tasks. To change the output directory, we can set the property `codenarc.reportsDir` in our project:

```
apply plugin: 'groovy'
apply plugin: 'codenarc'

// Repository definition to get CodeNarc libraries.
repositories {
  mavenCentral()
}

codenarc {
  toolVersion = 0.17
  configFile = file('config/codenarc/rules.groovy')

  // Change output directory for reports.
  reportsDir = file("${reporting.baseDir}/codenarc-output")
}

tasks.withType(CodeNarc) { task ->
```

```
reports {
  // Enable text format.
  text.enabled = true

  // Configure XML output.
  xml {
    enabled = true

    // Change destination file.
    destination = file("${codenarc.reportsDir}/${task.name}.xml")
  }
}
}
```

# Using the Sonar plugin

Sonar is a complete platform to monitor code quality in a project. Sonar has a web-based dashboard where code quality can be monitored in due time, so we can see if our code has improved over time by using Sonar. Gradle has a Sonar plugin to work with Sonar. This plugin requires Sonar 2.9 or higher. When we apply the plugin, a new task— sonarAnalyze- is added to our project. This task is not a dependency task for the check task, but is a standalone task. The task can analyze not only class files, but also test results, so we can make sure that the build task is executed before the sonarAnalyze task, to add a dependency on the build task to the sonarAnalyze task.

In the following example build file, we will apply the Sonar plugin, and if Sonar is running locally, we can simply execute the sonarAnalyze task:

```
apply plugin: 'java'
apply plugin: 'sonar'

sonarAnalyze.dependsOn 'build'
```

If we run Sonar locally, we don't have to configure anything. Gradle will use the default settings to access the locally running Sonar server. Usually, a Sonar server runs on a remote machine. We can configure the Sonar plugin to use a different address and database settings with the sonar{} script block. The script block accepts a configuration closure with several sections for the server and its database properties.

The following build file has different settings for the Sonar server URL and database properties:

```
apply plugin: 'java'
apply plugin: 'sonar'

sonarAnalyze.dependsOn 'build'

sonar {
  server.url = 'http://sonar.company'
  database {
    url = 'jdbc:mysql://database.server/sonar'
    driverClassName = 'com.mysql.jdbc.Driver'
    username = 'sonar'
    password = 'sonar'
  }
}
```

We can further customize the Sonar settings with a `project()` method and configuration closure. For example, we can change the directory where the Sonar client library files are stored after being downloaded from the Sonar server. We can define the location of the **Clover** or **Cobertura** coverage XML result file and much more. The plugin already uses a lot of default values from project properties. For example, the `version` and `group` properties of a project are used to identify the project in Sonar. The following table shows all the properties we can set via the `project()` method configuration closure:

| Property | Type | Default value | Description |
| --- | --- | --- | --- |
| baseDir | File | project.<br>projectDir | Base directory to do analysis on. |
| binaryDirs | List<File> | sourceSets.<br>main.output.<br>classesDir | Directory with the compiled source code to analyzed. |
| cloverReport<br>Path | File | null | Path to Clover XML report file. |
| cobertura<br>ReportPath | File | null | Path to Cobertura XML report file. |
| date | String | current date | Date of analysis with the format "yyyy-mm-dd". |
| description | String | project.<br>description | Description of the project used in Sonar. |

| Property | Type | Default value | Description |
|---|---|---|---|
| dynamic Analysis | String | reuseReports | Dynamic analysis includes the analysis of test and coverage results. We can set the value to reuseReports, so reports from testReports, clover ReportPath, and coberturaReport Path are used for analysis. The value can be set to false so no dynamic analysis is performed, or true (which is not supported by Gradle) so that Sonar will produce the test and coverage reports. |
| importSource | boolean | true | Makes the source code available in the Sonar web interface. |
| java | SonarJava Settings | | Specific settings for Java source code, such as source compatibility. |
| key | String | project. group:project. name | Identifier of the project in Sonar. |
| language | String | java | Language that needs to be analyzed by Sonar. Only one language per project can be analyzed. |
| libraries | File Collection | sourceSets.main. compileClasspath + Jvm.current(). runtimeJar | Classpath with libraries that are used by the project. |
| name | String | project.name | Name of the project. |

| Property | Type | Default value | Description |
|---|---|---|---|
| property Processors | List <Closure> | empty | List of post-processors of Sonar properties. See also the methods withGlobal Properites() and withProject Properties(). |
| skip | boolean | false | Skip this project for analysis. |
| skipDesign Analysis | boolean | false | Skip design analysis by Sonar. |
| sourceDirs | List<File> | sourceSets. main.allSource. srcDirs | Directories with source files to be analyzed by Sonar. |
| source Encoding | String | JVM's platform encoding | Character encoding of the project source files. |
| source Exclusions | String | null | Pattern of source files to be excluded from analysis. The pattern can be an ANT matching pattern. For example, **/*Fixture.java. |
| testDirs | List<File> | sourceSets. test.allSource. srcDirs | Directories with test source code to be analyzed. |
| testReport Path | File | test. testResultsDir | Directory with the JUnit XML report. |
| version | String | project. version | Version of the project. |
| workDir | File | project. builDir/sonar | Working directory for analysis. |

The following example build file shows several properties that we need to change:

```
apply plugin: 'java'
apply plugin: 'sonar'

version = '2.0-SNAPSHOT'
```

```
group = 'gradle.sample'

sonarAnalyze.dependsOn 'build'

sonar {
  project {
    // Change directory to store Sonar client library files.
    bootstrapDir = file("${buildDir}/sonarClient")

    // Set Sonar profile to be used.
    profile = 'quality'

    // Set path to Cobertura results.
    coberturaReportPath = file("${reporting.baseDir}/cobertura/
cobertura.xml")
  }
}
```

We can add custom properties with the method `withGlobalProperties()`
for properties that are global for Sonar, or the method `withProjectProperties()`
to define a property specific for a project. Both methods accept a closure as the
parameter. A map of the properties is the argument of the closure. In the following
build file, we will see how we can use this mechanism to further customize the
Sonar plugin:

```
apply plugin: 'java'
apply plugin: 'sonar'

version = '2.0-SNAPSHOT'
group = 'gradle.sample'

sonarAnalyze.dependsOn 'build'

sonar {
  withGlobalProperties { properties ->
    properties['sonar.verbose'] = true
  }
  project {
    withProjectProperties { projectProperties ->
      projectProperties['sonar.showSql'] = true
    }
  }
}
```

# Summary

We learned in this chapter that it is easy to use code analysis tools in a Gradle project. We can use Checkstyle, PMD, JDepend, and FindBugs for Java projects. For Groovy projects, we can use CodeNarc. All the plugins of these tools add new tasks to our project, for each source set to do the analysis. Each of these tasks is a dependency task for the `check` task. So when we apply the plugin in a normal build, the code analysis will take place. Also, we learned that the usage and syntax are mostly identical for each plugin.

With the Sonar plugin, we can send the analysis data of our project to a Sonar server. This task is a standalone task that is not part of a normal build process.

In the next chapter, we will take a look at how we can write our own custom task and plugin. We'll learn how we can make it reusable in other Gradle builds.

# 10
# Writing Custom Tasks and Plugins

In Gradle, we can either write a simple task in a build file where we add actions with a closure, or we can configure an existing task that is included with Gradle. The process of writing our own task is easy. There are different ways in which we can create a custom task, which we will cover in this chapter.

We will see how we can create a new task class in our build file and use it in our project. Next, we will learn how to create custom tasks in a separate source file. We also learn in this chapter how we can make our task reusable in other projects.

We will learn how to write a plugin for Gradle. Similar to writing custom tasks, we will cover the different ways to write a plugin. We will also see how we can publish our plugin and learn how we can use it in a new project.

We can write our tasks and plugins in Groovy, which works very well with the Gradle API, but we can also use other languages, such as Java and Scala. As long as the code is compiled into bytecode, we are fine.

## Creating a custom task

When we create a new task in a build and specify a task with the `type` property, we actually configure an existing task. The existing task is called an **enhanced task** in Gradle. For example, the `Copy` task type is an enhanced task. We configure the task in our build file, but the implementation of the `Copy` task is in a separate class file. It is a good practice to separate the task usage from the task implementation. It improves the maintainability and reusability of the task. In this section, we are creating our own enhanced tasks.

# Creating a custom task in the build file

First, let's see how we can create a task to display the current Gradle version in our build by simply adding a new task with a simple action. We have seen these types of tasks earlier in other sample build files. In the following sample build, we create a new `info` task:

```
task info(description: 'Show Gradle version') << {
    println "Current Gradle version: $project.gradle.gradleVersion"
}
```

When we invoke the `info` task from the command line, we see the following output:

```
gradle info
:info
Current Gradle version: 1.1


BUILD SUCCESSFUL


Total time: 2.061 secs
```

Now, we are going to create a new task definition in our build file and make it an enhanced task. We create a new class in our build file and this class extends `org.gradle.api.DefaultTask`. We write an implementation for the class by adding a new method. To indicate that the method is the action of the class, we use the annotation `@TaskAction`.

After we have defined our task class, we can use it in our build file. We add a task to the project tasks container and use the `type` property to reference our new task class.

In the following sample build file, we have a new task class `InfoTask` and the task `info` that uses this new task class:

```
// Use the InfoTask we defined
task info(type: InfoTask)

defaultTasks 'info'

/**
 * Show current Gradle version.
 */
class InfoTask extends DefaultTask {

    @TaskAction
```

```
    def info() {
        println "Current Gradle version:$project.gradle.gradleVersion"
    }
}
```

When we run our build file, the `info` task is invoked automatically because it is a part of the default tasks for the project. In the following output, we can see our current Gradle version:

```
$ gradle
:info
Current Gradle version: 1.1

BUILD SUCCESSFUL

Total time: 2.116 secs
```

To customize our simple task, we can add properties to our task. We can assign values to these properties when we configure the task in our build file.

For our sample task, we first add a `prefix` property. This property is used when we print the Gradle version instead of the text `'Current Gradle version:'`. We give it a default value, so when we use the task and don't set the property value, we still get a meaningful prefix. We can mark our property as optional, because of the default value, with the annotation `@Optional`. This way, we have documented that our property doesn't need to be configured when we use the task:

```
task info(type: InfoTask)

defaultTasks 'info'

class InfoTask extends DefaultTask {
    @Optional
    String prefix = 'Current Gradle version'

    @TaskAction
    def info() {
        println "$prefix: $project.gradle.gradleVersion"
    }
}
```

If we want another prefix in our output, we can configure the `info` task in our build file. We assign the `'Running Gradle'` value to the prefix property of our `InfoTask`:

```
task info(type: InfoTask) {
    prefix = 'Running Gradle'
}

defaultTasks 'info'

class InfoTask extends DefaultTask {

    String prefix = 'Current Gradle version'

    @TaskAction
    def info() {
        println "$prefix: $project.gradle.gradleVersion"
    }
}
```

Now, if we run our build file, we can see our new prefix value in the output:

```
$ gradle
:info
Running Gradle: 1.1


BUILD SUCCESSFUL


Total time: 2.139 secs
```

# Using incremental build support

We know Gradle supports incremental builds. This means that Gradle can check if a task has any dependencies for input or output on files, directories, and properties. If none of these have changed since the last build, the task is not executed. We will learn how we can use annotations with our task properties to make sure our task supports Gradle's incremental build feature.

We have seen how we can use the `inputs` and `outputs` properties of tasks we have created so far. To indicate which properties of our new enhanced tasks are `input` and `output` properties, the ones used by Gradle's incremental support, we must add certain annotations to our class definition. We can assign the annotation to the field property or the getter method for the property.

In a previous chapter, we have created a task that reads a XML source file and converts the contents to a text file. Let's create a new enhanced task for this functionality. We use the `@InputFile` annotation for the property that holds the value for the source XML file. The `@OutputFile` annotation is assigned to the property that holds the output file:

```
task convert(type: ConvertTask) {
    source = file('source.xml')
    output = file("$buildDir/convert-output.txt")
}


/**
 * Convert XML source file to text file.
 */
class ConvertTask extends DefaultTask {

    @InputFile
    File source

    @OutputFile
    File output

    @TaskAction
    void convert() {
        def xml = new XmlSlurper().parse(source)
        output.withPrintWriter { writer ->
            xml.person.each { person ->
                writer.println "${person.name},${person.email}"
            }
        }
        println "Converted ${source.name} to ${output.name}"
    }
}
```

Let's create an XML file with the name `source.xml` in the current directory, with the following code:

```
<?xml version="1.0"?>
<people>
    <person>
        <name>mrhaki</name>
        <email>hubert@mrhaki.com</email>
    </person>
</people>
```

Now, we can invoke the `convert` task in our build file. We can see in the output that the file is converted:

```
$ gradle convert
:convert
Converted source.xml to convert-output.txt


BUILD SUCCESSFUL


Total time: 3.8 secs
```

If we look at the contents of the `convert-output.txt` file, we see the following values from the source file:

```
$ cat build/convert-output.txt
mrhaki,hubert@mrhaki.com
```

When we invoke the `convert` task for the second time, we can see Gradle's incremental build support has noticed that the input and output file haven't changed, so our task is up-to-date:

```
$ gradle convert
:convert UP-TO-DATE

BUILD SUCCESSFUL

Total time: 1.664 secs
```

The following table shows the annotations we can use to indicate the input and output properties of our enhanced task:

| Annotation Name | Description |
| --- | --- |
| @Input | Indicates property specifies an input value. When the value of this property changes, the task is not longer up-to-date. |
| @InputFile | Indicates property is an input file. Use this for properties that reference a single file of type `File`. |
| @InputFiles | Mark property as input files for a property that holds a collection of `File` objects. |
| @InputDirectory | Indicates property is an input directory. Use this for a `File` type property that references a directory structure. |
| @OutputFile | Indicates property as output file. Use this for properties that reference a single file of type `File`. |

| Annotation Name | Description |
| --- | --- |
| @OutputFiles | Mark property as output files for a property that holds a collection of File objects. |
| @OuputDirectory | Indicates property is an output directory. Use this for a File type property that references a directory structure. If the output directory doesn't exist, it will be created. |
| @OutputDirectories | Mark property is an output directory Use this for a property that references a collection of File objects, which are references to directory structures. |
| @Optional | If applied to any of the above annotations, we mark it as optional. The value doesn't have to be applied for this property. |
| @Nested | We can apply this annotation to a Java Bean property. The bean object is checked for any of the above annotations. This way, we can use arbitrary objects as input or output properties. |

# Creating a task in the project source directory

In the previous section we have defined and used our own enhanced task in the same build file. Next, we are going to extract the class definition from the build file and put it in a separate file. We are going to place the file in the buildSrc project source directory.

Let's move our InfoTask to the buildSrc directory of our project. We first create the buildSrc/src/main/groovy/sample directory. We create a file named InfoTask.groovy in this directory, with the following code:

```groovy
package sample

import org.gradle.api.*
import org.gradle.api.tasks.*

class InfoTask extends DefaultTask {

    String prefix = 'Current Gradle version'

    @TaskAction
    def info() {
        println "$prefix: $project.gradle.gradleVersion"
    }
}
```

Notice that we must add import statements for the classes of the Gradle API. These imports are implicitly added to a build script by Gradle, but if we define the task outside the build script, we must add the import statements ourselves.

In our project build file, we only have to create a new info task of type `InfoTask`. Notice that we must use the package name to identify our `InfoTask` class or add an `import sample.InfoTask` statement:

```
task info(type: sample.InfoTask) {
    prefix = 'Running Gradle'
}

defaultTasks 'info'
```

If we run the build, we can see that Gradle first compiles the `InfoTask.groovy` source file:

```
$ gradle
:buildSrc:compileJava UP-TO-DATE
:buildSrc:compileGroovy
:buildSrc:processResources UP-TO-DATE
:buildSrc:classes
:buildSrc:jar
:buildSrc:assemble
:buildSrc:compileTestJava UP-TO-DATE
:buildSrc:compileTestGroovy UP-TO-DATE
:buildSrc:processTestResources UP-TO-DATE
:buildSrc:testClasses UP-TO-DATE
:buildSrc:test
:buildSrc:check
:buildSrc:build
:info
Running Gradle: 1.1

BUILD SUCCESSFUL

Total time: 4.2 secs
```

As a matter of fact, the build task of the buildSrc directory is executed. We can customize the build of the buildSrc directory by adding a build.gradle file. In this file, we can configure the tasks, add new tasks, and do practically anything we can in a normal project build file. The buildSrc directory can even be a multi-project build.

Let's add a new build.gradle file in the buildSrc directory. We add a simple action to the build task, which prints the value 'Done building buildSrc':

```
// File: buildSrc/build.gradle
build.doLast {
    println 'Done building buildSrc'
}
```

If we run our project build, we can see the following output:

```
$ gradle
:buildSrc:compileJava UP-TO-DATE
:buildSrc:compileGroovy UP-TO-DATE
:buildSrc:processResources UP-TO-DATE
:buildSrc:classes UP-TO-DATE
:buildSrc:jar UP-TO-DATE
:buildSrc:assemble UP-TO-DATE
:buildSrc:compileTestJava UP-TO-DATE
:buildSrc:compileTestGroovy UP-TO-DATE
:buildSrc:processTestResources UP-TO-DATE
:buildSrc:testClasses UP-TO-DATE
:buildSrc:test UP-TO-DATE
:buildSrc:check UP-TO-DATE
:buildSrc:build
Done building buildSrc
:info
Running Gradle: 1.1

BUILD SUCCESSFUL

Total time: 3.198 secs
```

# Writing tests

As the `buildSrc` directory is similar to any other Java/Groovy project, we can also create tests for our task. We have the same directory structure as that of a Java/Groovy project, and we can also define extra dependencies in the `build.gradle` file.

If we want to access a `Project` object in our test class, we can use the `org.gradle.testfixtures.ProjectBuilder` class. With this class, we can configure a `Project` object and use it in our test case. We can optionally configure the name, parent, and project directory before using the `build()` method to create a new `Project` object. We can use the `Project` object, for example, to add a new task with the type of our new enhanced task and see if there are any errors. `ProjectBuilder` is meant for low-level testing. The actual tasks are not executed.

In the following JUnit test, we test if the property value can be set. We have a second test to check if the task of type `InfoTask` is added to the task container of a project:

```
package sample

import org.junit.*
import org.gradle.api.*
import org.gradle.testfixtures.ProjectBuilder

class InfoTaskTest {

    @Test
    void createTaskInProject() {
        final Task newTask = createInfoTask()
        assert newTask instanceof InfoTask
    }

    @Test
    void propertyValueIsSet() {
        final Task newTask = createInfoTask()
        newTask.configure {
            prefix = 'Test'
        }
        assert newTask.prefix == 'Test'
    }

    private Task createInfoTask() {
        // We cannot use new InfoTask() to create a new instance,
        // but we must use the Project.task() method.
        final Project project = ProjectBuilder.builder().build()
        project.task('info', type: InfoTask)
    }

}
```

In our `build.gradle` file in the `buildSrc` directory, we must add a Maven repository and the dependency on the JUnit libraries by using the following lines of code:

```
repositories.mavenCentral()

dependencies {
    testCompile 'junit:junit:4.10'
}
```

Our test is automatically executed because the `test` task is part of the build process for the `buildSrc` directory.

# Creating a task in a standalone project

To make a task reusable for other projects, we must have a way to distribute the task. Also, other projects that want to use the task must be able to find our task. We will see how we can publish our task in a repository and how other projects can use the task in their projects.

We have seen how we can place the task implementation from the build file into the `buildSrc` directory. The `buildSrc` directory is similar to a normal Gradle build project, so it is easy to create a standalone project for our task. We only have to copy the contents of the `buildSrc` directory to our newly created project directory.

Let's create a new project directory and copy the contents of the `buildSrc` directory. We must edit the `build.gradle` file of our standalone project. Gradle implicitly added the Groovy plugin and dependencies on the Gradle API and Groovy for us when the `build.gradle` file is in the `buildSrc` directory. Now we have a standalone project, and we must add those dependencies ourselves.

The following `build.gradle` file has all the definitions necessary to build and deploy our artifact to a local distribution directory. We could also define a corporate intranet repository so that other projects can re-use our `InfoTask` in their projects.

```
apply plugin: 'groovy'
apply plugin: 'maven'

version = '1.0'
group = 'sample.infotask'
archivesBaseName = 'infotask'

repositories.mavenCentral()
```

```
dependencies {
    compile gradleApi()
    groovy localGroovy()
    testCompile 'junit:junit:4.10'
}

uploadArchives {
    repositories.mavenDeployer {
        repository(url: 'file:../lib')
    }
}
```

When we invoke the `uploadArchives` task to publish our packaged `InfoTask` in the `../lib` directory, we see the following output:

```
$ gradle uploadArchives
...
:uploadArchives
Uploading: sample/infotask/infotask/1.0/infotask-1.0.jar to repository
remote at file:../lib
Transferring 5K from remote
Uploaded 5K

BUILD SUCCESSFUL

Total time: 3.431 secs
```

We have published our task, and other projects can use it in their builds. Remember that anything in the `buildSrc` directory of a project is added automatically to the classpath of the build. But if we have a published artifact with the task, this will not happen automatically. We must configure our build and add the artifact as a dependency of the build script.

We use the `buildscript{}` script block in our build to configure the classpath of our Gradle project. To include our published `InfoTask` in a new project, we must add the artifact as a `classpath` configuration dependency for our build.

We create a new directory and add the following `build.gradle` file to the directory:

```
buildscript {
    repositories {
        maven {
```

```
                url 'file:../lib'
        }
    }
    dependencies {
        classpath group: 'sample.infotask', name: 'infotask', version:
'1.0'
    }
}

task info(type: sample.InfoTask)

defaultTasks 'info'
```

Next, we can run the build and see in the output that the `InfoTask` is executed:

```
$ gradle
:info
Current Gradle version: 1.1

BUILD SUCCESSFUL

Total time: 3.452 secs
```

# Creating a custom plugin

One of the great features of Gradle is the support for plugins. A plugin can contain tasks, configurations, properties, methods, concepts, and more to add extra functionality to our projects. For example, if we apply the Java plugin to our project, we can immediately invoke the compile, test, and build tasks. Also, we have new dependency configurations we can use and extra properties we can configure. The Java plugin itself applies the java-base plugin. The java-base plugin doesn't introduce tasks, but the concept of source sets. This is a good pattern for creating our own plugins, where a base plugin introduces new concepts and another plugin derives from the base plugin and adds explicit build logic-like tasks.

So a plugin is a good way to distribute build logic that we want to share between projects. We can write our own plugin, give it an explicit version, and publish it to, for example, a repository. Other projects can then re-use the functionality by simply applying the plugin to a project. We can create our own plugins and use them in our projects. We start by defining the plugin in the build file.

# Creating a plugin in the build file

We can create a custom plugin right in the project build file. Similar to a custom task, we can add a new class definition with the logic of the plugin. We must implement the `org.gradle.api.Plugin<T>` interface. The interface has one method named `apply()`. When we write our own plugin, we must override this method. The method accepts an object as a parameter. The type of the object is the same as the generic type `T`. When we create a plugin for projects, the type `Project` is used. We can also write plugins for other Gradle types, like tasks. Then we must use the `Task` type.

We are going to create a simple plugin that will print out the Gradle version. The plugin adds a new `info` task to the project. The following sample build file defines a new plugin with the name `InfoPlugin`. We override the `apply()` method and add a new task to the project, with the name `info`. This task prints out the Gradle version. At the top of the build file, we use the `apply()` method and reference the plugin by the name `InfoPlugin`, which is the class name of the plugin:

```
apply plugin: InfoPlugin

class InfoPlugin implements Plugin<Project> {

    void apply(Project project) {
        project.task('info') << {
            println "Running Gradle: $project.gradle.gradleVersion"
        }
    }
}
```

From the command line, we can invoke the `info` task when we run Gradle. We can see the Gradle version in the following output:

```
$ gradle info
:info
Running Gradle: 1.1


BUILD SUCCESSFUL


Total time: 2.503 secs
```

The info task always prints the same text before the Gradle version. We can rewrite the task and make the text configurable. A Gradle Project has an associated ExtensionContainer object. This object can hold all settings and properties we want to pass to a plugin. We can add a Java Bean to ExtensionContainer so that we can configure the bean's properties from the build file. The Java Bean is a so-called extension object.

In our sample build file, we first add a new class InfoPluginExtension with a property prefix of type String. This is the Java Bean-compliant class we add to ExtensionContainer. In the apply() method, we use the create() method of ExtensionContainer to add InfoPluginExtension with the name info to the project. In the build file, we configure the prefix property using the info configuration closure. Or we can simply reference the prefix property through the info extension object:

```
apply plugin: InfoPlugin

// Configure the InfoPlugin through the
// InfoPluginExtension.
info {
    prefix = 'Gradle version'
}
// Or info.prefix = 'Gradle version'

class InfoPlugin implements Plugin<Project> {
    void apply(Project project) {
        // Add the Java Bean InfoPluginExtension with the
        // name info to the project ExtensionContainer.
        project.extensions.create('info', InfoPluginExtension)

        project.task('info') << {
            // Use project.info.prefix from the extension.
            println "$project.info.prefix: $project.gradle.
gradleVersion"
        }
    }
}

class InfoPluginExtension {
    String prefix = 'Running Gradle'
}
```

If we run the `info` task, we see our configured prefix in the output:

```
$ gradle info
:info
Gradle version: 1.1

BUILD SUCCESSFUL

Total time: 7.345 secs
```

# Creating a plugin in the project source directory

We have defined the plugin and used the plugin in the same build file. We will see how we can extract the plugin code from the build file and put it in a separate source file in the project source directory. Also, we will learn how we can test the plugin.

When we define the plugin in our build file, we cannot re-use it in other projects. And we now have the definition and usage of the plugin in the same file. To separate the definition and usage, we can create the plugin class in the `buildSrc` directory of a Gradle project. In a Gradle multi-project, we must use the `buildSrc` directory of the root project. This means, for a multi-project build, we can re-use the plugin in the other projects of the multi-project build.

We already learned when we wrote a custom task that any sources in the `buildSrc` directory are automatically compiled and added to the classpath of the project. First, we create the directory `buildSrc/src/main/groovy/sample`. In this directory, we create a file called `InfoPlugin.groovy` with the following code:

```
package sample

import org.gradle.api.*

class InfoPlugin implements Plugin<Project> {

    void apply(Project project) {
        project.extensions.create('info', InfoPluginExtension)

        project.task('info') << {
            println "$project.info.prefix: $project.gradle.
gradleVersion"
        }
    }
}
```

Next, we create the file `InfoPluginExtension.groovy` in the directory:

```
package sample

class InfoPluginExtension {
    String prefix
}
```

In our build file in the root of the project, we reference our plugin with the package and class name:

```
apply plugin: sample.InfoPlugin

info {
    prefix = 'Gradle version'
}
```

When we run the `info` task, we see in the output that first the plugin code is compiled, and then the `info` task is executed:

```
$ gradle
:buildSrc:compileJava UP-TO-DATE
:buildSrc:compileGroovy
:buildSrc:processResources UP-TO-DATE
:buildSrc:classes
:buildSrc:jar
:buildSrc:assemble
:buildSrc:compileTestJava UP-TO-DATE
:buildSrc:compileTestGroovy UP-TO-DATE
:buildSrc:processTestResources UP-TO-DATE
:buildSrc:testClasses UP-TO-DATE
:buildSrc:test
:buildSrc:check
:buildSrc:build
:info
Gradle version: 1.1

BUILD SUCCESSFUL

Total time: 2.743 secs
```

# Testing a plugin

One of the tasks that are executed for the project in the `buildSrc` directory is the `test` task. We can write test cases for testing the plugin code, just like in any other project. We add a `build.gradle` file in `buildSrc` and define the dependencies for the JUnit test framework. In the following sample build file, we add a dependency for JUnit:

```
repositories.mavenCentral()

dependencies {
    testCompile 'junit:junit:4.10'
}
```

Next, we can add a test case named `InfoPluginTest.groovy` in the `buildSrc/src/test/groovy/sample` directory:

```
package sample

import org.gradle.api.*
import org.gradle.testfixtures.ProjectBuilder
import org.junit.*

class InfoPluginTest {

    @Test
    void infoTaskIsAddedToProject() {
        final Project project = ProjectBuilder.builder().build()
        project.apply plugin: sample.InfoPlugin
        assert project.tasks.findByName('info')
    }

    @Test
    void configurePrefix() {
        final Project project = ProjectBuilder.builder().build()
        project.apply plugin: sample.InfoPlugin
        project.info.prefix = 'Sample'
         assert project.info.prefix == 'Sample'
    }
}
```

We use the `ProjectBuilder` class to create a fixture for the `Project` object. We can apply the plugin to the project and then test to see if the `info` task is available. The `Project` object cannot execute tasks in the project; it is only for simple checks like this one.

When we invoke the `info` task from the command line, our test class is compiled and executed. If a test fails, the project will abort, but if all tests pass, the project continues.

# Creating a plugin in a standalone project

We have defined our plugin in the project source directory, but we cannot re-use it in another project. We will learn how we can distribute our plugin logic, using a standalone project. Also, we will see how we can use the plugin in other projects.

By placing the plugin code in the `buildSrc` directory, we have separated the definition of the plugin and the usage. The plugin still cannot be used by other projects. To make the plugin reusable, we create a standalone project and create an artifact with the plugin code and publish the artifact to a repository. Other projects can then get the plugin from the repository and use the build logic from the plugin in the project.

We already have the code for the plugin and the test code in the `buildSrc` directory (from the previous section). We can copy this code to a new directory with the project for the plugin. In this new directory, we must also create a `build.gradle` file. The implicit dependencies and plugin added to a project in the `buildSrc` directory must be made explicit in a standalone project.

Let's create a new Gradle project in the directory `plugin`, and create the file `build.gradle` with the following content:

```
apply plugin: 'groovy'
apply plugin: 'maven'
version = 1.0
group = 'sample.infoplugin'
archivesBaseName = 'infoplugin'
repositories.mavenCentral()
dependencies {
    compile gradleApi()
    groovy localGroovy()
    testCompile group: 'junit', name: 'junit', version: '4.10'
}

uploadArchives {
    repositories.mavenDeployer {
        repository(url: 'file:../lib')
    }
}
```

Next, we create the `plugin/src/main/groovy/sample` and `plugin/src/test/groovy/sample` directories. We copy the `InfoPlugin.groovy` and `InfoPluginExtension.groovy` files to the `src/main/groovy/sample` directory, and the `InfoPluginTest.groovy` file to the `plugin/src/test/groovy/sample` directory.

So far we have all the ingredients to create an artifact JAR file with the plugin code. The artifact is deployed to the local `../lib` directory. We can, of course, define any Maven or Ivy repository to deploy the plugin artifact into.

To make sure Gradle can find the plugin, we must provide a properties file in the `plugin/src/main/resources/META-INF/gradle-plugins` directory with the name of our plugin. The properties file has a property key `implementation-class` with the full class name of the `Plugin` class.

We want to name our plugin as `info`, so in the `plugin/src/main/resources/META-INF/gradle-plugins` directory we create the `info.properties` file with the following code:

```
implementation-class = sample.InfoPlugin
```

We are ready to create the artifact with the plugin and upload it to our repository. We invoke the `uploadArchives` task, and we get the following output:

```
$ gradle uploadArchives
:compileJava UP-TO-DATE
:compileGroovy UP-TO-DATE
:processResources
:classes
:jar
:uploadArchives
Uploading: sample/infoplugin/infoplugin/1.0/infoplugin-1.0.jar to
repository remote at file:../lib
Transferring 8K from remote
Uploaded 8K


BUILD SUCCESSFUL


Total time: 3.076 secs
```

The plugin is now in the repository. To use the plugin, we must create a new Gradle project. We must extend the classpath of this new project, and include the plugin as a dependency. We use the `buildscript{}` script block, where we can configure the repository location and a classpath dependency. For our sample we reference the local `../lib` directory. In the dependencies section we set the `classpath` configuration to the `InfoPlugin` artifact.

The following sample build file contains the definitions:

```
buildscript {
    repositories {
        maven {
            url 'file:../lib'
        }
    }
    dependencies {
        classpath group: 'sample.infoplugin', name: 'infoplugin',
version: '1.0'
    }
}

apply plugin: 'info'

info.prefix = 'Gradle version'
```

Our project now has the `info` task from the plugin. We can configure the plugin extension through the `info` object or the configuration closure.

If we run the `info` task, we get the following output:

```
$ gradle info
:info
Gradle version: 1.1

BUILD SUCCESSFUL

Total time: 3.073 secs
```

# Summary

In this chapter we have learned how to create our own enhanced task. We have seen how to add the class definition in our build file and use it directly in the build.

If we put the task definition in the `buildSrc` directory of a Gradle project or multi-project build, we can re-use the task in the context of the Gradle build. Also, we now have a good separation of the definition and configuration of the task.

Finally, we have learned how to publish the task as an artifact to a repository. Other projects can include the task in their classpath by using the `buildscript{}` script block. Then, we can configure and use the task in the project.

In this chapter we also learned how to write our own Gradle plugin. We have seen how to add a plugin class to our Gradle build file. Then we learned to use the `buildSrc` directory and place the source code of the plugin in there.

Finally, to make the plugin really reusable by other projects, we put the plugin code in a separate project. The plugin code is then packaged into a JAR file and published to a repository. Other projects can then define a dependency on the plugin and use the build logic from the plugin.

In the next chapter we see how we can use Gradle in continuous integration tools.

# 11
# Using Gradle with Continuous Integration

It is good practice to have a continuous integration tool in a software project. With a continuous integration tool, we can automatically build our software in a controlled environment. In this chapter, we are going to take a look at the support for Gradle in several continuous integration tools.

First, we are going to create a sample Java project and use Git as a version control repository. Then, we are going to see how the continuous integration servers Jenkins, JetBrains TeamCity, and Atlassian Bamboo support Gradle.

## Creating a sample project

Before we can see the support for Gradle in the several continuous integration servers, we must have a sample project. We are going to create a very simple Java project with a test class and add it to a Git repository, in this section.

We already created a Java project earlier. We are going to re-use the code in this chapter for our sample project. We want to have a test in our project, so that we can see how the continuous integration tools can handle test results. Finally, we want to have more than one artifact for our project; we want to have a JAR file with the compiled classes, source code, and Javadoc generated documentation.

We first create a `build.gradle` file in a directory, with the following contents:

```
// We create a Java project so we need the Java plugin
apply plugin: 'java'

// Set base name for archives.
archivesBaseName = 'gradle-sample'

// Version of the project.
version = '1.0'

// Definine Maven central repository for downloading
// dependencies.
repositories {
    mavenCentral()
}

// We have a single dependency on JUnit
// for the testCompile configuration
dependencies {
    testCompile 'junit:junit:[4.8,)'
}

// Extra task to create a JAR file with the sources.
task sourcesJar(type: Jar) {
    classifier = 'sources'
    from sourceSets.main.allSource
}

// Extra task to create a JAR file with Javadoc
// generated documentation.
task docJar(type: Jar, dependsOn: javadoc) {
    classifier = 'docs'
    from javadoc.destinationDir
}

// Add extra JAR file to the list of artifacts
// for this project.
artifacts {
    archives sourcesJar
    archives docJar
}
```

Next, we create three Java source files in the `src/main/java/gradle/sample` directory. First, we have an interface with a single method to return a welcome message:

```
// File: src/main/java/gradle/sample/ReadWelcomeMessage.java
package gradle.sample;

/**
 * Read welcome message from source and return value.
 */
public interface ReadWelcomeMessage {

    /**
     * @return Welcome message
     */
    String getWelcomeMessage();
}
```

Next, we create an implementation of this interface and return a `String` value:

```
// File: src/main/java/gradle/sample/ReadWelcomeMessageImpl.java
package gradle.sample;

import java.util.ResourceBundle;

/**
 * Simple implementation to return welcome message.
 */
public class ReadWelcomeMessageImpl implements ReadWelcomeMessage {

    public ReadWelcomeMessageImpl() {
    }

    /**
     * Return "Welcome to Gradle." String value.
     *
     * @return Welcome to Gradle.
     */
    public String getWelcomeMessage() {
        return "Welcome to Gradle.";
    }
}
```

Finally, we have a Java application class that uses the interface and implementation class we already added:

```java
// File: src/main/java/gradle/sample/SampleApp.java
package gradle.sample;

import java.util.ResourceBundle;

public class SampleApp {

    public SampleApp() {
    }

    public static void main(final String[] arguments) {
        final SampleApp app = new SampleApp();
        app.welcomeMessage();
    }

    public void welcomeMessage() {
        final String welcomeMessage = readMessage();
        showMessage(welcomeMessage);
    }

    private String readMessage() {
        final ReadWelcomeMessage reader = new
ReadWelcomeMessageImpl();
        final String message = reader.getWelcomeMessage();
        return message;
    }

    private void showMessage(final String message) {
        System.out.println(message);
    }
}
```

Let's create a test to verify that our `ReadWelcomeMessageImpl` class returns the expected `String` value. We add the file `ReadWelcomeMessageTest.java` in the directory `src/test/java/gradle/sample`:

```java
// File: src/test/gradle/sample/ReadWelcomeMessageTest.java
package gradle.sample;

import org.junit.Assert;
```

```
import org.junit.Test;

public class ReadWelcomeMessageTest {

    @Test
    public void readWelcomeMessage() {
        final ReadWelcomeMessage reader = new
ReadWelcomeMessageImpl();
        final String realMessage = reader.getWelcomeMessage();

        final String expectedMessage = "Welcome to Gradle.";

        Assert.assertEquals("Get text from implementation",
expectedMessage, realMessage);
    }
}
```

To check if everything is okay, we run Gradle with the `build` task. We should see the following output:

```
$ gradle build
:compileJava
:processResources UP-TO-DATE
:classes
:javadoc
:docJar
:jar
:sourcesJar
:assemble
:compileTestJava
:processTestResources UP-TO-DATE
:testClasses
:test
:check
:build

BUILD SUCCESSFUL

Total time: 9.031 secs
```

We have all the source code, so let's put it in a version control repository. We can use any version control system we want, as long as the continuous integration server supports the version control system. We create a Git repository for our example, because it is easy to set up a local repository and then to use it in the continuous integration tools. In order to use Git, we must have it installed on our computers. We create a new Git repository in the current project directory, with the `init` command in Git:

```
$ git init
Initialized empty Git repository in /Users/mrhaki/Projects/java-project
```

Next, we add the file to the Git staging area, with the `add` command:

```
$ git add .
```

We commit the code to the repository, with the `commit` command in Git:

```
$ git commit -m "First commit."
[master (root-commit) e80a23f] First commit.
 6 files changed, 121 insertions(+), 0 deletions(-)
 create mode 100644 build.gradle
 create mode 100644 src/main/java/gradle/sample/ReadWelcomeMessage.java
 create mode 100644 src/main/java/gradle/sample/ReadWelcomeMessageImpl.
java
 create mode 100644 src/main/java/gradle/sample/SampleApp.java
 create mode 100644 src/test/java/gradle/sample/ReadWelcomeMessageTest.
java
```

Our project is ready to be used in the continuous integration tools.

# Using Jenkins

One of the most popular open source continuous integration tools is Jenkins. The good news is that Jenkins has support for Gradle via the Gradle plugin. Let's see how we can use the plugin to add our little Java project to Jenkins.

To install Jenkins on our computer, we must first download the installation files from the Jenkins website. A native installer is available for Mac OS X, Windows, and Linux. We simply run the installer software to install Jenkins on our computer. We can also download a WAR file and deploy it to a Java web container to install Jenkins. The WAR file is also a Java executable archive. This means that we can simply run the WAR file with the `java -jar` command to execute Jenkins.

# Adding the Gradle plugin

First, we must install the Gradle plugin in Jenkins. We launch a web browser and access the URL `http://localhost:8080`. From the Jenkins main page, we select the link **Manage Jenkins**, which takes us to the appropriate page:

Here, we select **Manage plugins**. On the **Plugin Manager** page, we can use the **Filter** box at the top-right corner to search for Gradle Plugin:

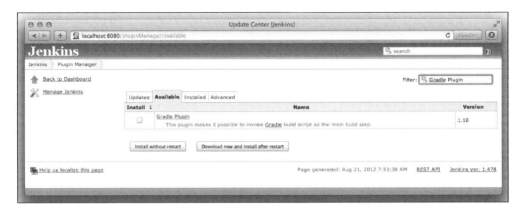

We select the plugin and click on the button **Install without restart**. If the installation of the plugin is successful, we see the following screen:

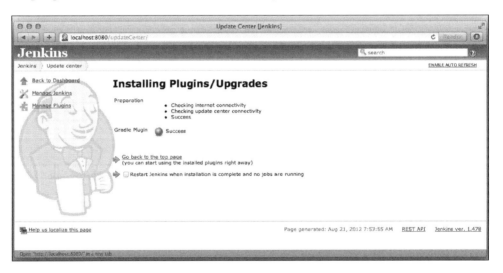

We need to restart Jenkins to make the plugin active and usable for our Jenkins projects.

# Configuring Jenkins job

Jenkins is now set up with the Gradle plugin, and it is time to create a job. From the main page, we select the **New job** link. We get a screen where we can fill in a name for the job and select the **Build a free-style software project** radio button:

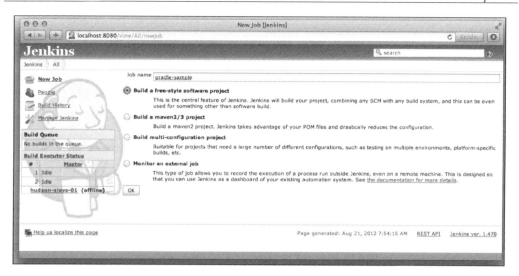

If we have filled in the name and selected the radio button, we can click on the **OK** button. We go to the **configuration** page of our job. The name of the job is already filled with the value from the previous screen:

We must at least define our Git repository in the **Source Code Management** section. Also, we must add a build step in the **Build** section. We select the **Git** radio button to define the location of our Git repository in the **URL of repository** field. If we select the button **Add build step**, in the **Build** section, we can see the option **Invoke Gradle script**. Thanks to the Gradle plugin, we now have this option highlighted in the following screenshot:

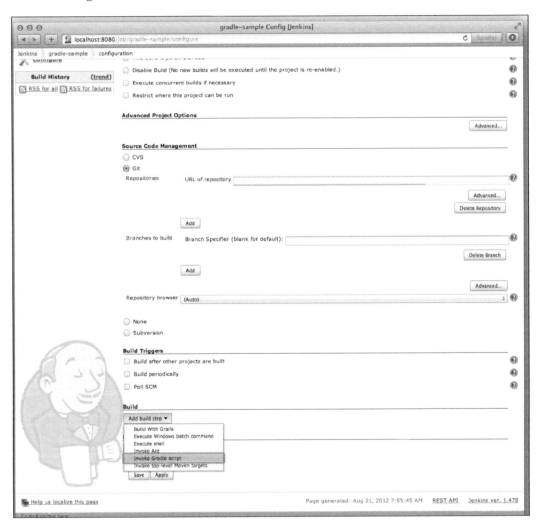

We select the option **Invoke Gradle script**, and Jenkins adds new fields to configure our Gradle build:

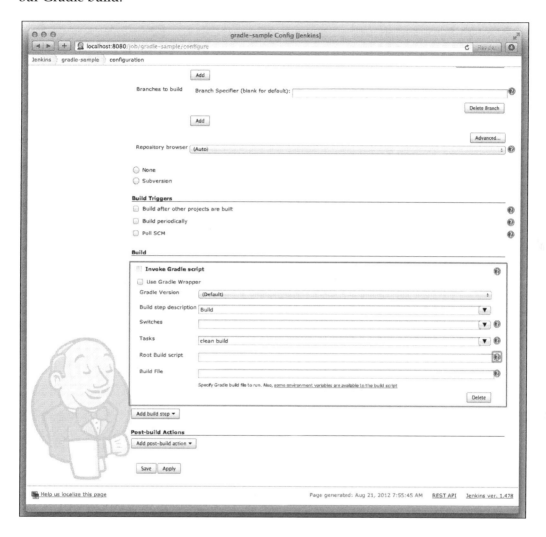

First, we can choose if we want to use the Gradle wrapper for this project. We don't need it for our project, so we leave this unchecked.

Next, we can choose a Gradle version. We can install multiple Gradle versions for Jenkins, and we can choose which version we want to use. The default version is the one that is available on the system path. We will learn later how we can add more Gradle versions to Jenkins.

We can give our build step a short description in the **Build step description** field. The **Switches** field can contain the Gradle command-line options we want to use. For example, to exclude a task, we can set the value `-x taskName`. The **Tasks** field must contain the tasks we want to execute. If our project has default tasks set and we want to run those, we can leave the **Tasks** field empty. For our project, we want to invoke the `clean` and `build` tasks, so we set the value to **clean build**.

The **Root Build script** field is for a multi-project build where the root script is not in a default location. We can define the custom location here.

If a Gradle project has a build file name other than the default `build.gradle`, we can set the value in the **Build File** field.

# Running the job

We have the basic setup for running our Gradle project. We click on the **Save** button and close the configuration. We return to the job page. At the left, we see a menu with the link **Build now**. We click on the link, and Jenkins starts the job:

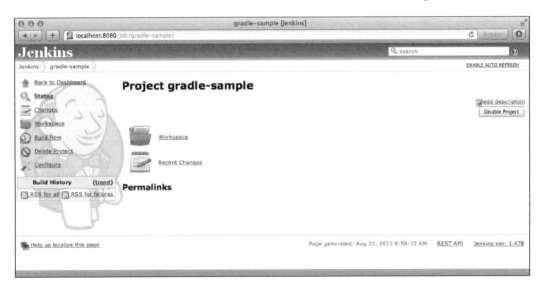

Our code will be checked out from the Git repository, and the Gradle tasks `clean` and `build` are run. If the job is done, we can see the build result. From the build result page, we can see the console output when we click on the **Console Output** link:

At the left, we even see all Gradle tasks that have been executed. We can click on
the links and jump directly to any output of the task.

# Configuring artifacts and test results

To see the generated artifacts and test results, we must add two post-build actions to the job configuration. First, we select the **Configure job** link. At the **Post-build Actions** section, we click on the **Add post-build action** button. Here, we first select **Archive the artifacts**:

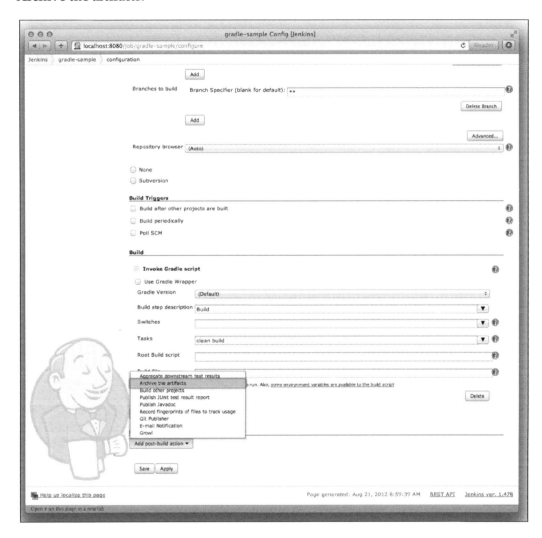

Next, we select **Publish JUnit test result report**:

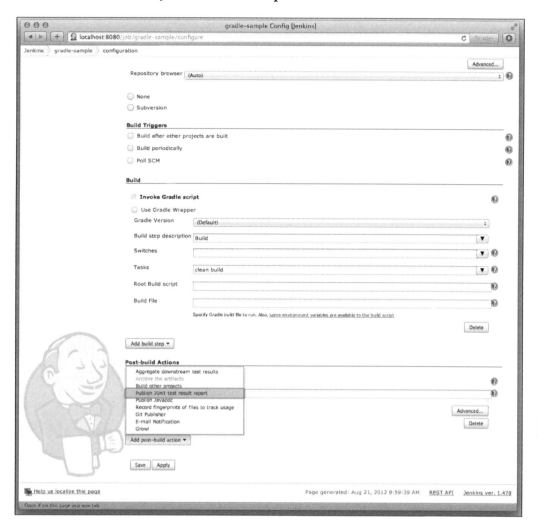

The artifacts are saved in the `build/libs` directory of our project. So, in the **Files to archive** field, we enter `build/libs/*.jar`. And, we set the value for the field **Test report XMLs** to **build/test-results/*.xml**:

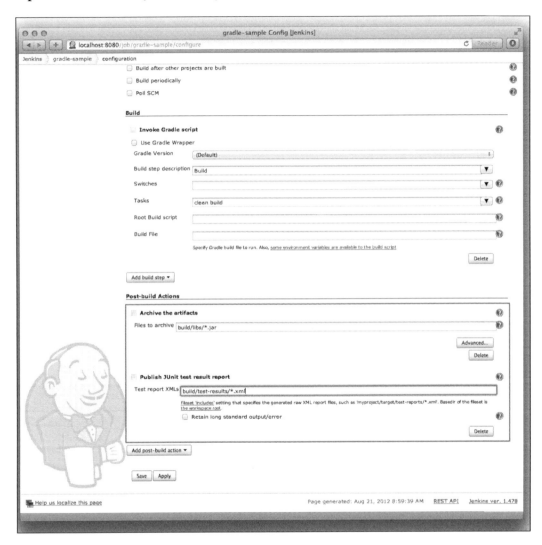

The configuration is done, so we click on the **Save** button. We can run the job again, and this time, we see the artifacts of our projects as downloadable links on the job page. The test results are also shown, and we can even see more details if we click on the **Test Result** link:

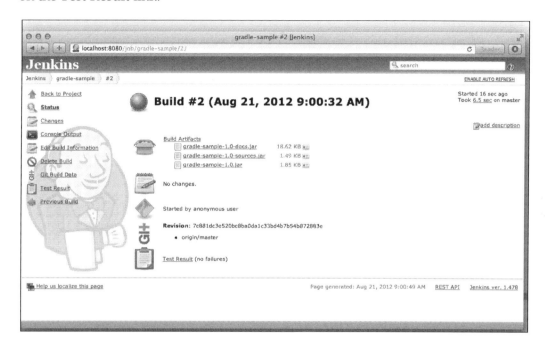

# Adding Gradle versions

We can add extra Gradle versions to Jenkins. If, for example, some projects rely on Gradle 1.0 and others on Gradle 1.1, we must be able to add the Gradle versions.

From the **Manage Jenkins** page, we select **Configure System**. The page has a **Gradle** section, where we can add new Gradle installations:

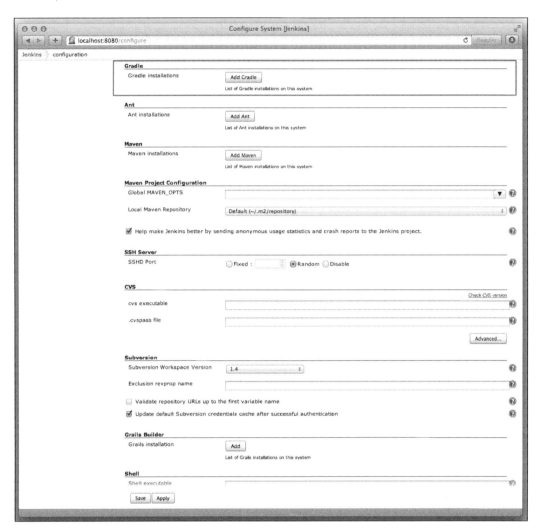

If we click on the **Add Gradle** button, we can define a name for our Gradle installation in the **Gradle name** field. We also see a checkbox, **Install automatically**. If this is checked, Jenkins will download a Gradle version for us from the Internet. We select the version from the **Version** drop-down box:

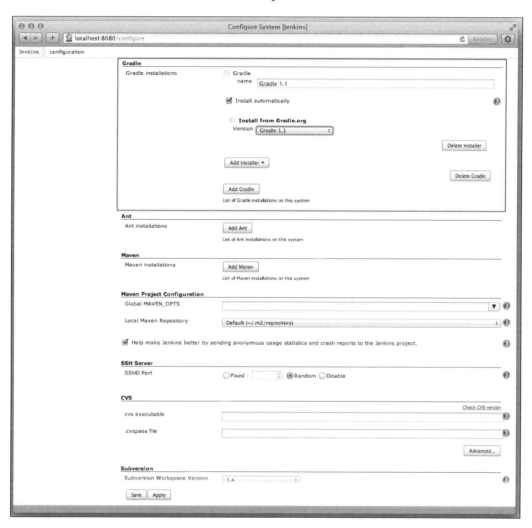

If we want to use a locally installed instance of Gradle, we must uncheck the **Install automatically** checkbox. Now, we can set the Gradle location in the **GRADLE_HOME** field:

We must click on the **Save** button to save the changes. Now, we can choose the correct Gradle version in the jobs.

# Using JetBrains TeamCity

JetBrains TeamCity is a commercial continuous integration server. TeamCity has a Professional Server license. This means that we can create 20 build configurations and one build agent. If we need more configurations or build agents, we can purchase other licenses. In this section, we will see how we can create a build plan with Gradle.

We can download installer software for Mac OS X, Windows, and Linux, from the JetBrains TeamCity website. We run the installer software to install TeamCity on our computer. TeamCity is also available as an archive for all platforms. To install the archive, we only have to unpack the contents to a directory on our computer. TeamCity is also available as a WAR file, which can be deployed to a Java web container.

# Creating a project

After we install TeamCity, we open a web browser and go to the URL http://localhost:8011/. We can create a new project from the **Administration** page. We can define the name of our project and provide a short description:

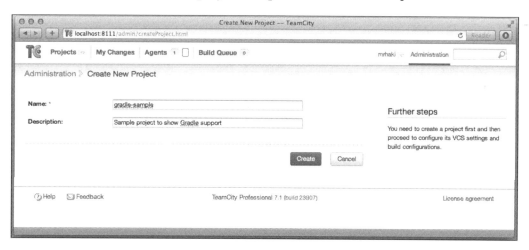

We click on the **Create** button to create the project and go to an overview page of our project:

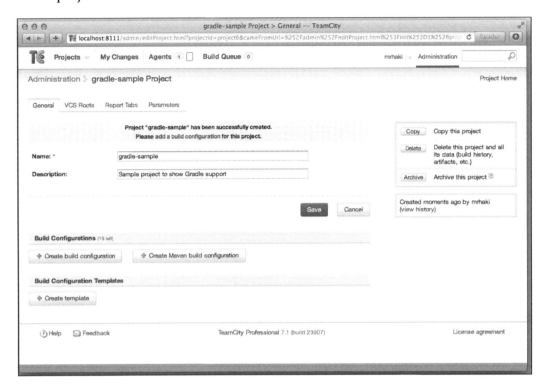

It is time to add a new build configuration. We click on the **Create build configuration** button in the **Build Configurations** section to add a build configuration. On the following screen, we can define the path of the artifacts in our project in the **Artifact paths** field. Here, we fill in build/libs/*.jar:

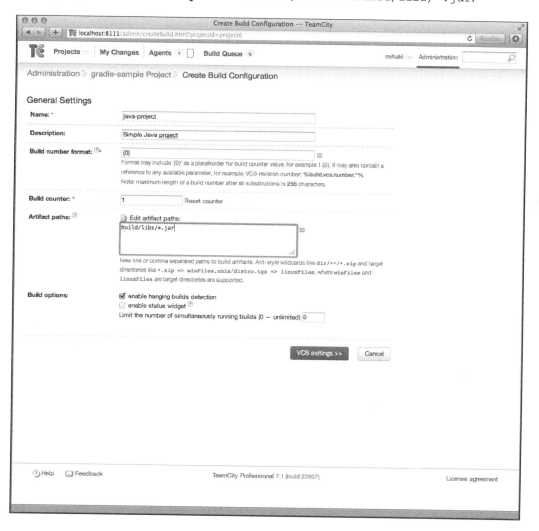

We must click on the **VCS settings** button to go to the next page and define our Git repository as version controller repository. Here, we must set the **Fetch URL** field with the location of the Git repository:

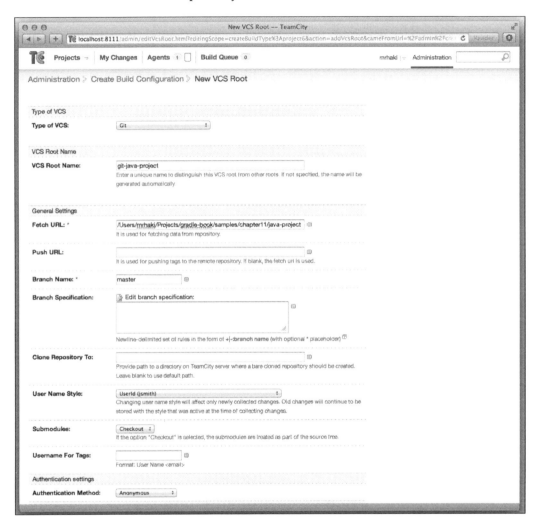

We save the configuration and return to an overview page with the VCS:

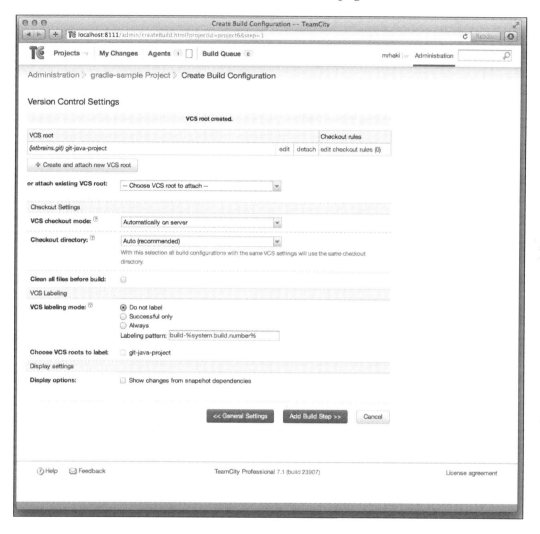

On this screen, we click on the **Add Build Step** button. We are taken to a new screen, where we can select the **Runner type** of the build. Here, we select the **Gradle** runner and click on the **Save** button:

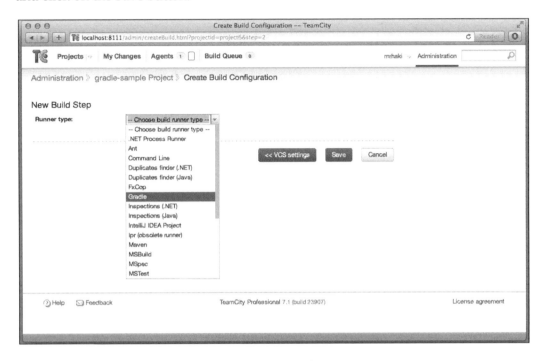

We are on the configuration page for the build step:

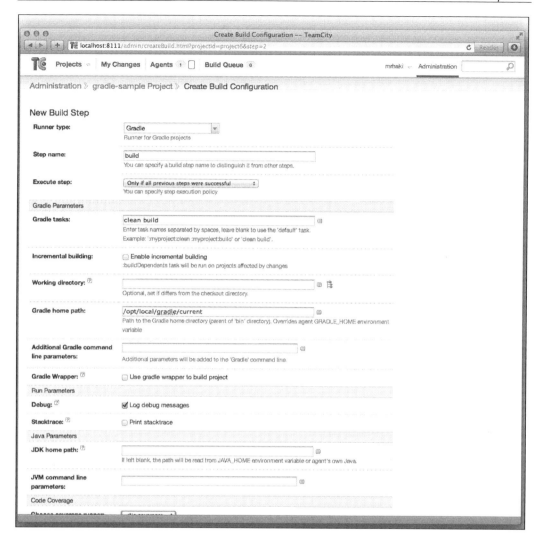

We can fill in a descriptive name for this build step in the **Step name** field. In the
**Gradle Parameters** section, we can set the tasks in the **Gradle tasks** field. For our
project, we want to invoke the `clean` and `build` tasks, so we fill in `clean build`.
Note that we can enable **Incremental building** for multi-project builds. TeamCity
will use the `buildDependents` task.

To set the Gradle version, we fill in the **Gradle home path** field. Extra command-line parameters can be filled in the **Additional Gradle command line parameters** field.

If our project has a Gradle wrapper, we can check the checkbox **Gradle Wrapper**. TeamCity will then use the `gradlew` or `gradlew.bat` scripts, instead of the **Gradle home path** location, to run Gradle.

# Running the project

We can save the build configuration, and we are ready to run it. At the top right, we can see the **Run** button with an ellipsis. When we click on the ellipsis, we get a dialog window with options that we can set before we run the build:

We leave all options unchanged and click on the **Run Build** button.

TeamCity instructs the build agent to run our build configuration. The code is checked out from the repository, and the Gradle tasks `clean` and `build` are invoked. On the **Projects** page, we see a summary of the build:

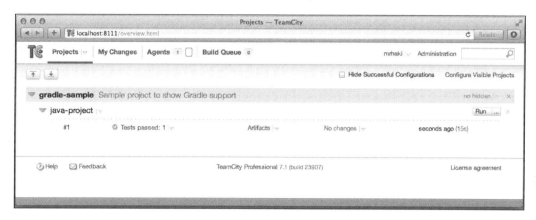

We can click on the project and see more details. The overview page of the project shows the date of the project build, the build agent used, and a summary of test results:

If we click on the **Tests** tab, we see the tests that have run and the time it took to execute them:

The **Build Log** tab page shows the output of the build process. Because we selected the debug level on the build configuration page, we see very detailed information here:

Finally, on the **Artifacts** page, we see the generated JAR files. We can click on the filename and see the contents of the files:

# Using Atlassian Bamboo

The last continuous integration tool we are going to configure is Atlassian Bamboo. Bamboo is a commercial continuous integration server. There is a 30-day evaluation license available from the Atlassian website. We will see how we can configure Bamboo to use Gradle as a build tool for our Java project.

We can install Bamboo on our local computer. We first need to download the installation package from the Bamboo website. We can choose native installers for Mac OS X, Windows, and Linux. Alternatively, we can simply download a packaged version and unzip it to a directory on our computer. Finally, we can download a WAR file and deploy it to a web container.

# Defining a build plan

Bamboo has no Gradle runner or plugin, but we can define a build plan and add a so-called `script` task. A `script` task can run any script as part of the build plan. To make sure Bamboo can build our Java project, we must add the Gradle wrapper scripts to the project.

We change our `build.gradle` file and add the task `createWrapper`:

```
// We create a Java project so we need the Java plugin
apply plugin: 'java'

// Set base name for archives.
archivesBaseName = 'gradle-sample'

// Version of the project.
version = '1.0'

// Definine Maven central repository for downloading
// dependencies.
repositories {
    mavenCentral()
}

// We have a single dependency on JUnit
// for the testCompile configuration
dependencies {
    testCompile 'junit:junit:[4.8,)'
}

// Extra task to create a JAR file with the sources.
task sourcesJar(type: Jar) {
    classifier = 'sources'
    from sourceSets.main.allSource
}

// Extra task to create a JAR file with Javadoc
// generated documentation.
```

```
task docJar(type: Jar, dependsOn: javadoc) {
    classifier = 'docs'
    from javadoc.destinationDir
}

// Add extra JAR file to the list of artifacts
// for this project.
artifacts {
    archives sourcesJar
    archives docJar
}

// Create Gradle wrapper
task createWrapper(type: Wrapper)
```

We run the `createWrapper` task from the command line. We now have the script files `gradlew` and `gradlew.bat`. Also, the directory `gradle` is created with the configuration for the Gradle wrapper. We add the directory and files to our Git repository:

```
$ git add .
```

```
$ git commit -m "Add Gradle wrapper output."
```

We are ready to create a new build plan in Bamboo. We start a web browser and open the URL `http://localhost:8085/`. After we have logged in to Bamboo, we select the **Create Plan** link. A new page is opened, where we can choose to create a new plan or Maven project:

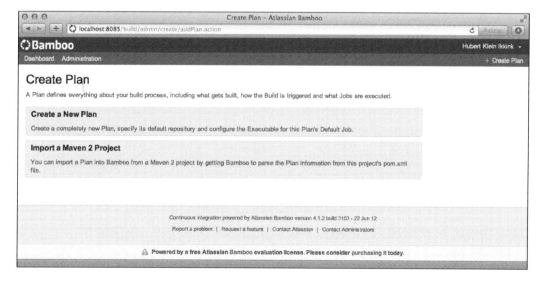

We select the option **Create a New Plan**. We go to a new page, where we can set the properties of the build plan:

We must define a project name in the **Project Name** field. Bamboo also expects a short identifier in uppercase characters, as the project key, in the **Project Key** field. The plan that is part of the project also has a name and key; we fill these the **Plan Name** and **Plan Key** fields. We can set a short description in the **Plan Description** field.

In the **Source Repositories** section, we can define the Git repository location for our project.

Finally, in the **Build Strategy** section, we set the value of the **Build Strategy** drop-down box to **Manual**. This means we manually start the build via the run action in the Bamboo user interface.

We click on the **Configure Tasks** button to add tasks to our plan. A task contains some logic we want to execute as part of the plan.

The first task is automatically added and is responsible for checking out the source code of the Git repository. We click on the **Add Task** button to create a new task.

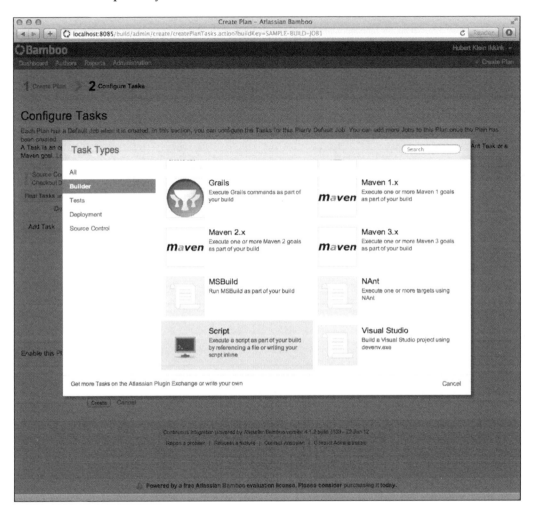

A dialog window is shown, and we select the **Script** task from the **Builder** section. With this task, we can configure the Gradle wrapper scripts to be executed.

We return to the tasks window, and we can fill in the fields under **Script Configuration**:

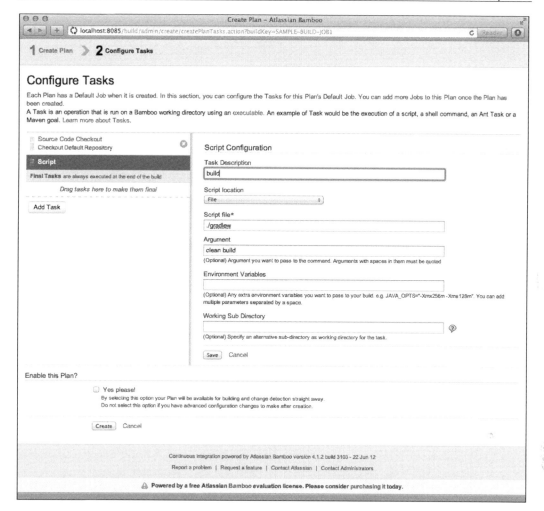

We fill in a description in the **Task Description** field. **Script location** must be set to **File** instead of **Inline**. The **Script file** field has the location of the gradlew or gradlew.bat script we want invoked.

In the **Argument** field, we pass the arguments to the gradlew script. We want to invoke the clean and build tasks, so we set the value to **clean build**.

We are ready to click on the **Save** button to save our `script` task configuration. The task is added to the list of tasks:

We enable the plan in the **Enable this Plan?** section by checking the checkbox **Yes please!**. Next, we click on the **Create** button to finish the configuration and save the plan in Bamboo.

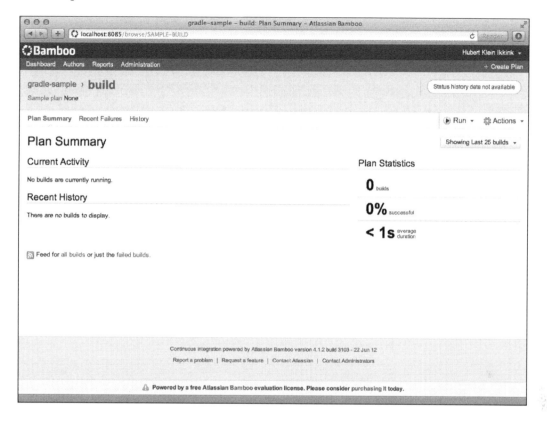

# Running the build plan

We are ready to run the build and click on the **Run** button at the top right of the page. While the build is running, we can see some of the log output. At the end of the log output, we can see that the `gradle-1.1-bin.zip` file is downloaded because of the Gradle wrapper script:

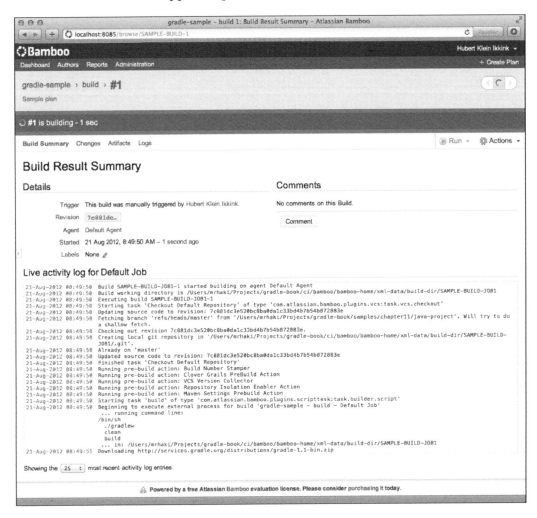

After the build is finished, we can see the results. We also want to add the project artifacts to our plan, and the test results as well. Therefore, we select the option **Configure plan** from the **Actions** menu:

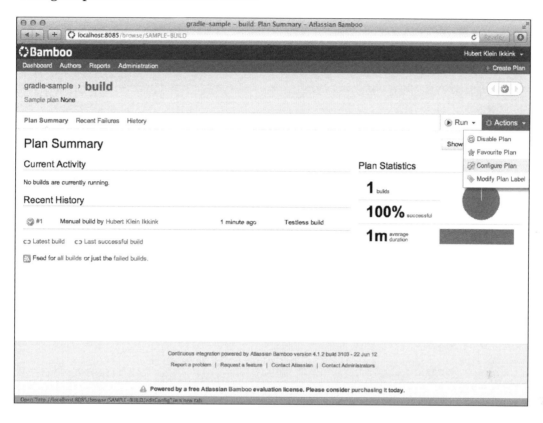

We go to the **Artifacts** tab page and click on the **Create Definition** button to add a new artifact definition:

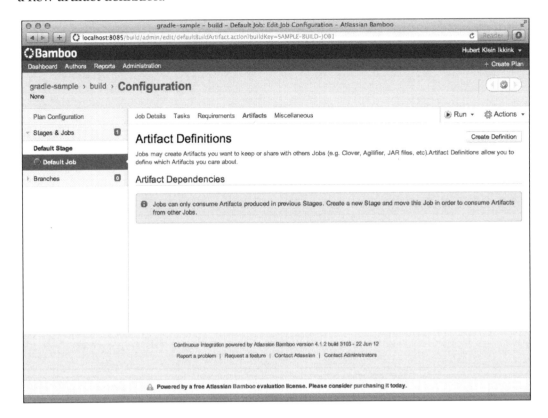

We see a dialog window, and we can define the name, location, and pattern of the artifacts:

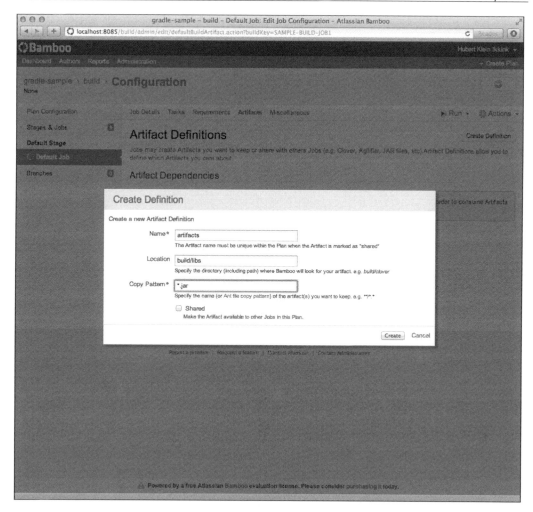

We fill in `artifacts` in the **Name** field and `build/libs` in the **Location** field. The **Copy Pattern** field is filled with the value `*.jar`, to include all JAR files. We click on the **Create** button to finish the configuration of the artifacts.

Next, we select the **Tasks** tab page and click on the **Add Task** button to create a new task:

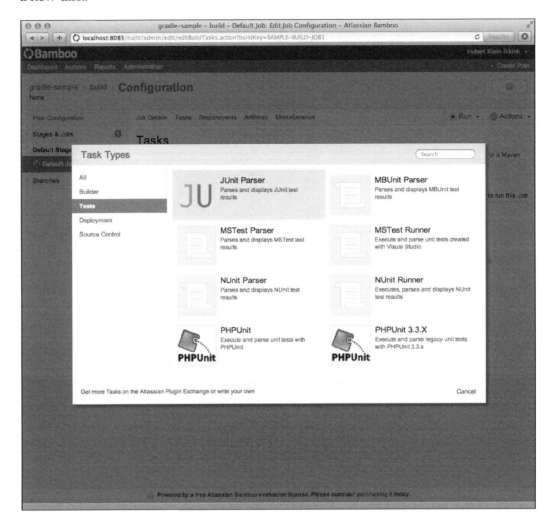

In the dialog window with task types, we select **JUnit Parser** from the **Tests** section. Bamboo shows the configuration fields for this task:

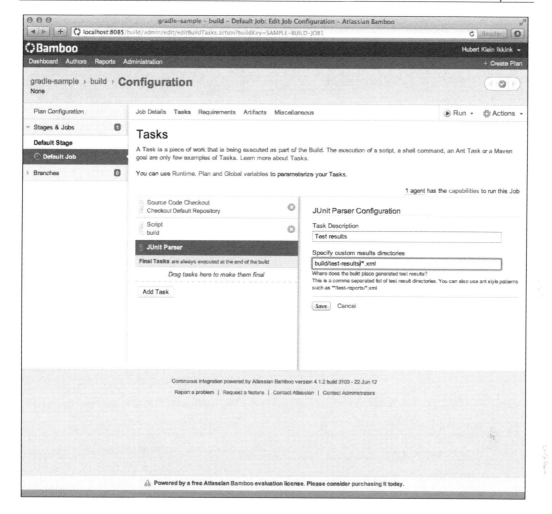

We set the **Task Description** with the value `Test results`. In the field **Specify custom results directories**, we set the pattern `build/test-results/*.xml`.

We are ready to run our plan again, but this time we have test results:

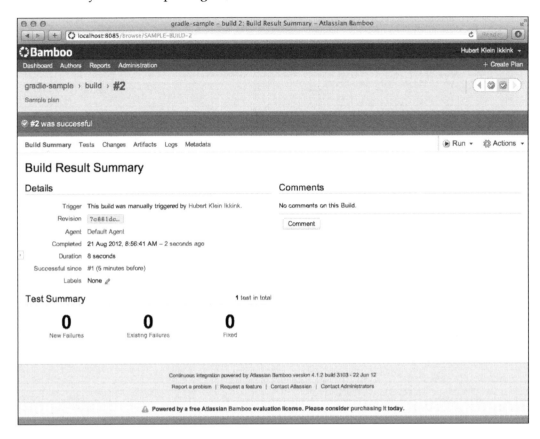

We click on the **Artifacts** tab and see that the plan has produced artifacts:

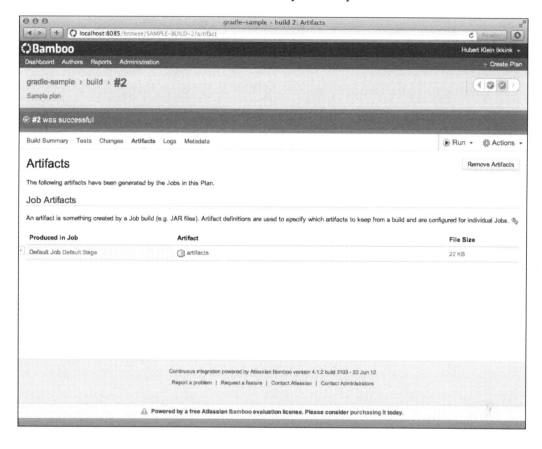

If we click on the **artifacts** link, we are taken to a page where we can download each artifact JAR file:

# Summary

In this chapter, we have learned how we must configure continuous integration tools Jenkins, JetBrains TeamCity, and Atlassian Bamboo to build our Java project with Gradle.

Jenkins and TeamCity have good support for Gradle builds. We can choose to use either a locally installed Gradle version or the Gradle task wrapper scripts. Defining which tasks to run is easy.

Bamboo has no real support for Gradle builds. We can use the script build option and the Gradle task wrapper support to work around this. This way, we can still run Gradle builds with Bamboo.

In the next chapter, we will learn how we can integrate Gradle with **Integrated Development Environments (IDEs)** Eclipse and JetBrains IntelliJ.

# 12
# IDE Support

When we develop applications, we usually use an **Integrated Development Environment** (IDE). An IDE provides support for writing code for our applications. We can write our code in Java, Groovy, or Scala. We have seen how we can use Gradle to define, for example, library dependencies to compile the code. We want to use the same information that we have defined in a Gradle build file in a project in our favorite IDE.

In this chapter, we will learn how we can use Gradle plugins to generate the project files with classpath dependencies for **Eclipse** and **JetBrains IntelliJ IDEA**. We will also learn how we can customize the file generation to add extra configuration data.

Next, we will see the Eclipse and IntelliJ IDEA support for running Gradle tasks from within the IDE.

## Using the Eclipse plugin

The Eclipse plugin can generate the project files necessary to import the project in Eclipse. In this section, we will see which tasks are added by the plugin and how we can customize the generated output.

If we have a Java project and want to import the project into Eclipse, we must use the Eclipse plugin to generate the Eclipse project files. Each Eclipse project has as minimum a `.project` file and a `.classpath` file. The `.project` file contains metadata about the project, such as the project name. The `.classpath` file contains classpath entries for the project. Eclipse needs this to be able to compile the source files in the project. The Eclipse plugin will try to download the artifact with source files belonging to a dependency as well. So, if we import the project into Eclipse and the source files are available, we can directly see the source of dependent class files.

For a Java project, an additional **Java Development Tools** (JDT) configuration file is created in the .settings folder. The name of the file is org.eclipse.jdt. core.prefs.

Let's create a simple Gradle build file for a Java project. The code for the build file is shown in the following code snippet:

```
apply plugin: 'java'
apply plugin: 'eclipse'

version = 1.0

sourceCompatibility = 1.6
targetCompatibility = 1.6

description = 'Sample project'

ext {
    slf4jVersion = '1.6.6'
    slf4jGroup = 'org.slf4j'
}

configurations {
    extraLib
}

repositories {
    mavenCentral()
}

dependencies {
    testCompile 'junit:junit:4.8'

    extraLib "$slf4jGroup:slf4j-api:$slf4jVersion",
"$slf4jGroup:slf4j-simple:$slf4jVersion"
}
```

We apply the Java and Eclipse plugins for our project. We set some project properties, such as version, description, source, and target compatibility. We define a dependency on **JUnit** for the testCompile configuration. Also, we add an extra custom configuration with a dependency on the slf4j logging library.

First, let's see which tasks are added to our project by the Eclipse plugin. We invoke the `tasks` task and look at all the tasks in our plugin, shown in the following code snippet:

```
$ gradle tasks --all
...
IDE tasks
---------
cleanEclipse - Cleans all Eclipse files.
    cleanEclipseClasspath
    cleanEclipseJdt
    cleanEclipseProject
eclipse - Generates all Eclipse files.
    eclipseClasspath - Generates the Eclipse classpath file.
    eclipseJdt - Generates the Eclipse JDT settings file.
    eclipseProject - Generates the Eclipse project file....
...
```

The `eclipse` task is dependent on the following three tasks: `eclipseClasspath`, `eclipseJdt`, and `eclipseProject`. Each task generates a single file. The `eclipseClasspath` task generates the `.classpath` file, `eclipseProject` generates the `.project` file, and `eclipseJdt` generates `org.eclipse.jdt.core.prefs`.

When we execute the `eclipse` task from the command line, we get the following output:

```
$ gradle eclipse
:eclipseClasspath
Download http://repo1.maven.org/maven2/junit/junit/4.8/junit-4.8.pom
Download http://repo1.maven.org/maven2/junit/junit/4.8/junit-4.8-sources.
jar
Download http://repo1.maven.org/maven2/junit/junit/4.8/junit-4.8.jar
:eclipseJdt
:eclipseProject
:eclipse

BUILD SUCCESSFUL

Total time: 8.672 secs
```

Note that the sources of the JUnit library are downloaded. We now have the `.classpath` and `.project` files in our project folder. In the `.settings` folder we have the `org.eclipse.jdt.core.prefs` file.

The `.project` file has the following contents:

```xml
<?xml version="1.0" encoding="UTF-8"?>
<projectDescription>
        <name>chapter12</name>
        <comment>Sample project</comment>
        <projects/>
        <natures>
                <nature>org.eclipse.jdt.core.javanature</nature>
        </natures>
        <buildSpec>
                <buildCommand>
                        <name>org.eclipse.jdt.core.javabuilder</name>
                        <arguments/>
                </buildCommand>
        </buildSpec>
        <linkedResources/>
</projectDescription>
```

The `name` element is filled with the project's folder name. We will learn how to change this later in the chapter. The `comment` element contains our project description. We have applied the Java plugin in our project, and hence the Java nature and build command are added to the project configuration.

If we look at the `.classpath` file, we can see a `classpathentry` element with the JUnit dependency, as shown in the following code snippet:

```xml
<?xml version="1.0" encoding="UTF-8"?>
<classpath>
        <classpathentry kind="output" path="bin"/>
        <classpathentry kind="con" path="org.eclipse.jdt.launching.
JRE_CONTAINER" exported="true"/>
        <classpathentry sourcepath="/Users/mrhaki/.gradle/
caches/artifacts-14/filestore/junit/junit/4.8/source/
abe171e0fc1242d1fe10e8dc43bce031e3f65560/junit-4.8-sources.jar"
kind="lib" path="/Users/mrhaki/.gradle/caches/artifacts-14/filestore/
junit/junit/4.8/jar/4150c00c5706306ef0f8f1410e70c8ff12757922/junit-
4.8.jar" exported="true"/>
</classpath>
```

The `classpathentry` element has a reference to the location in the Gradle cache of the downloaded JUnit library. Note that the `sourcepath` attribute references the source files.

The last generated `org.eclipse.jdt.core.prefs` file has the following contents:

```
#
#Thu Aug 21 09:36:25 CEST 2012
org.eclipse.jdt.core.compiler.debug.localVariable=generate
org.eclipse.jdt.core.compiler.compliance=1.6
org.eclipse.jdt.core.compiler.codegen.unusedLocal=preserve
org.eclipse.jdt.core.compiler.debug.sourceFile=generate
org.eclipse.jdt.core.compiler.codegen.targetPlatform=1.6
org.eclipse.jdt.core.compiler.problem.enumIdentifier=error
org.eclipse.jdt.core.compiler.debug.lineNumber=generate
eclipse.preferences.version=1
org.eclipse.jdt.core.compiler.codegen.inlineJsrBytecode=enabled
org.eclipse.jdt.core.compiler.source=1.6
org.eclipse.jdt.core.compiler.problem.assertIdentifier=error
```

We can see that the source and target compatibility we defined in the Gradle build file are used for the properties `org.eclipse.jdt.core.compiler.source`, `org.eclipse.jdt.core.compiler.codegen.targetPlatform`, and `org.eclipse.jdt.core.compiler.compliance`.

We have added the Java plugin to our project and the Eclipse plugin knows this, so the Java nature and builder are added to the generated `.project` file. If we use the Groovy and Scala plugins, the Eclipse plugin will add the correct nature and build configurations to the `.project` file.

# Customizing generated files

We have several options to customize the configuration in the generated files. The Eclipse plugin adds a **DSL** to configure model objects that represent Eclipse configuration objects. If we use the DSL to configure the objects, these newly configured objects are merged with existing configuration before the file is generated. We can also hook into the generation process and work directly on the model objects before and after the configuration is merged and the file is generated. Finally, we can even use a hook to work directly on the XML structure before the configuration file is generated.

The following steps describe the complete configuration file generation lifecycle:

1. First, the file is read from disk or a default file is used if the file is not available.

2. Next, the `beforeMerge` hook is invoked. The hook accepts the model object for the configuration file as an argument.

3. The implicit configuration information from the Gradle build file and the configuration defined using the DSL are merged.

4. Then, the `whenMerged` hook is executed. The hook accepts the model object for the configuration file as an argument.

5. The `withXml` hook is invoked. XML manipulation can happen here before the file is written to disk.

6. Finally, the configuration file is written to disk.

# Customizing using DSL

When the Eclipse plugin generates the files, it will look in the Gradle build file for the necessary information. For example, if we set the `description` property of the `Project` object, the comment section in the `.project` file is filled with the value of that property:

The Eclipse plugin also adds a configuration script block with the name `eclipse`. The configuration can be described using a simple DSL. At the top level we can add path variables that will be used for replacing absolute paths in classpath entries. The `org.gradle.plugins.ide.eclipse.model.EclipseModel` object is used and the `pathVariables()` method of this class must be used to define a path variable.

Next, we can define the configuration information for the `.project` file in the `project` section. The model object `org.gradle.plugins.ide.eclipse.model. EclipseProject` is used to model the Eclipse project configuration. We can, for example, use the `name` property to change the name of the project in the generated `.project` file. It is good to know that Gradle can generate unique project names for a multi-project build. A unique name is necessary to import the projects into Eclipse. During the `.project` file generation, all projects that are part of the multi-project must be known. So, it is best to run the `eclipse` or `eclipseProject` task from the root of the project. Also, methods for adding project natures and new build commands are available.

To customize the `.classpath` file generation, we can use the classpath section of the eclipse configuration closure. Here, the `org.gradle.plugins.ide.eclipse. model.EclipseClasspath` object is used to model the classpath entries of the Eclipse project. We can use the properties `plusConfigurations` and `minusConfigurations` to add or remove dependency configurations from the generated `.classpath` file. By default, the associated source files for a dependency are downloaded, but we can also set the `downloadJavadoc` property to `true` to download the Javadoc associated with the dependency.

The `jdt` section of the eclipse configuration closure can be used to change the source and target compatibility versions. By default, the Gradle Java plugin settings are used, but we can overrride it here. The `org.gradle.plugins.ide.eclipse.model.EclipseJdt` object is used to model the Eclipse configuration.

In the following build file, we see an example of all the possible methods and properties we can use with the DSL to customize the generated `.project` file:

```
apply plugin: 'java'
apply plugin: 'eclipse'

eclipse {
    pathVariables 'APPSERVER_HOME': file('/apps/appserver/1.0')

    project {
        name = 'sample-eclipse'

        comment = 'Eclipse project file build by Gradle'

        // Add new natures like Spring nature.
        natures 'org.springframework.ide.eclipse.core.springnature'

        // Add build command for Spring.
        buildCommand 'org.springframework.ide.eclipse.core.
springbuilder'

        // If using location attribute then type 1 is file, 2 is
folder
        linkedResource name: 'config', type: '2', location: file('/
opt/local/config')

        // If using locationUri attribute then type 1 for file/folder,
2 is virtual folder
        linkedResource name: 'config2', type: '1', locationUri:
'file:../config'

        // Define reference to other project. This is not
        // a build path reference.
        referencedProjects 'other-project'
    }
}
```

In the following example build file, we see the options to change the `.classpath` file:

```
apply plugin: 'java'
apply plugin: 'eclipse'

eclipse {
    classpath {
        // Add extra dependency configurations.
        plusConfigurations += configurations.extraLib

        // Remove dependency configurations.
        minusConfigurations += configurations.testCompile

        // Included configurations are not exported.
        noExportConfigurations += configurations.testCompile

        // Download associated source files.
        downloadSources = true

        // Download Javadoc for dependencies.
        downloadJavadoc = true

        // Add extra containers.
        containers 'ApacheCommons'

        // Change default output dir (${projectDir}/bin)
        defaultOutputDir file("$buildDir/eclipse-classes")
    }
}
```

The following example build file shows the configuration options to generate the `org.eclipse.jdt.core.prefs` file:

```
apply plugin: 'java'
apply plugin: 'eclipse'

eclipse {
    jdt {
        sourceCompatibility = 1.6
        targetCompatibility = 1.6
    }
}
```

# Customizing with merge hooks

Using the DSL to customize file generation is very elegant. Remember from the configuration file generation steps that this information is used right after the beforeMerged and before the whenMerged hooks. These hooks take a model object as an argument that we can use to customize. We can use the merge hooks if we want to do something that is not possible using the project configuration or DSL.

The merge hooks can be defined in the eclipse configuration closure. For each file, we can define a configuration closure for the beforeMerged and whenMerged hooks. These methods are part of the org.gradle.plugins.ide.api. XmlFileContentMerger class. Gradle will delegate the configuration closures to the methods of this class. The beforeMerged hook is useful to overwrite or change existing sections in the configuraton file. The cleanEclipse task cleans all the sections in a configuration file, and by using the beforeMerged hook we can ourselves define which parts need to be cleaned or overwritten.

The whenMerged hook is the preferred way of changing the model object. When this hook is invoked, the model object is already configured with all settings from the project configuration and DSL.

Each file is represented by the file property of the eclipse configuration closures. For example, to add a merge hook to the .project file generation, we define it 353using the eclipse.project.file property.

The following table shows the class that is passed as an argument for the merge hooks closures:

| Model | Merge hook argument | Description |
|-------|---------------------|-------------|
| Project | org.gradle.plugins.ide. eclipse.model.Project | Model object with properties for .project file generation. |
| Classpath | org.gradle.plugins.ide. eclipse.model.Classpath | Model object with properties for .classpath file generation. |
| Jdt | org.gradle.plugins.ide. eclipse.model.Jdt | Model object with properties for org.eclipse.jdt.core.prefs file generation. |

For the Jdt model, we have an additional method named withProperties(), to change the contents of the file. This method has a closure with an argument of type java.util.Properties.

In the following example build file, we use the merged hooks to change the configuration in the .project file:

```
apply {
    plugin 'java'
    plugin 'eclipse'
}

eclipse {
    project {
        file {
            beforeMerged { project ->
                // We can access the internal object structure
                // using merge hooks.
                project.natures.clear()
            }

            afterMerged { project ->
                project.name = 'sample-eclipse'

                project.comment = 'Eclipse project file build by
Gradle'

                project.natures.add 'org.springframework.ide.eclipse.
core.springnature'

                buildCommand.add 'org.springframework.ide.eclipse.
core.springbuilder'

                linkedResources.add name: 'config', type: '2',
location: 'file:/opt/local'

                referencedProjects.add 'other-project'
            }
        }
    }
}
```

In the following example build, we use the merged hooks to change the `.classpath` and `org.eclipse.jdt.core.prefs` files:

```
apply {
    plugin 'java'
    plugin 'eclipse'
}

eclipse {
    classpath {
        file {
            beforeMerged { classpath ->
                // Remove lib classpath entries.
                classpath.entries.removeAll {
                    it.kind == 'lib'
                }
            }

            whenMerged { classpath ->
                classpath.entries.add kind: 'output', path:
"$buildDir/eclipse-classes"
            }
        }
    }

    jdt {
        file {
            beforeMerged { jdt ->
            }

            whenMerged { jdt ->
                jdt.sourceCompatibility = 1.6
                jdt.targetCompatibility = 1.6
            }

            whenProperties { properties ->
                properties.extraProperty = 'value'
            }
        }
    }
}
```

# Customizing with XML manipulation

We have seen how to customize the configuration file generation with project configuration, DSL, and the merge hooks. At the lowest level, there is a hook to change the XML structure before it is written to disk. Therefore, we must implement the `withXml` hook. We define a closure, and the first argument of the closure is of type `org.gradle.api.XmlProvider`. The class has the `asNode()` method, which returns the root of the XML as a Groovy node. This is the easiest object with which to alter the XML contents. The `asString()` method returns a `StringBuilder` instance with the XML contents. Finally, the `asElement()` method returns an `org.w3c.dom.Element` object.

The `asNode()` method returns the Groovy `groovy.util.Node` class. With this node class, we can easily add, replace, or remove nodes and attributes.

In the following example build file, we can see different ways to manipulate the XML structure:

```
apply {
    plugin 'java'
    plugin 'eclipse'
}

eclipse {
    project {
        file {
            withXml { xml ->
                def projectXml = xml.asNode()
                projectXml.name = 'sample-eclipse'

                def natures = projectXml.natures
                natures.plus {
                    nature {
                        'org.springframework.ide.eclipse.core.
springnature'
                    }
                }
            }
        }
    }

    classpath {
        file {
            withXml { xml ->
```

```
            def classpathXml = xml.asNode()
            classpathXml.classpathentry.findAll { it.@kind ==
'con' }*.@exported = 'true'
                }
            }
        }
    }
```

We have seen all the different options to change the configuration files. Configuration changes, which we would normally make in Eclipse, can now be done programmatically in a Gradle build file.

# Merging configuration

If a file already exists, Gradle will try to merge extra information with the existing information. Depending on the section, the information will be amended to existing configuration data or will replace existing configuration data. This means that if we make changes to our project settings in Eclipse, they will not be overwritten even if we invoke one of the eclipse tasks.

To completely rebuild the project files, we must use the cleanEclipse tasks. For each project file, there is a corresponding cleanEclipse task. For example, to rebuild the .project file, we invoke the cleanEclipseProject task before eclipseProject. Any changes we have made manually are removed, and a new .project file is generated by Gradle, with the settings from our Gradle build file.

# Configuring WTP

We can add **Web Tools Platform (WTP)** to Eclipse, to add support for Java enterprise applications. We get support for web applications (WAR) and enterprise applications (EAR). To generate the correct configuration files, we must add another plugin to our Gradle build file. We add the Eclipse WTP plugin to the project and also the War or Ear plugin.

Let's create a build file and add the War and Eclipse WTP plugins, as follows:

```
apply plugin: 'java'
apply plugin: 'war'
apply plugin: 'eclipse-wtp'

version = 1.0

description = 'Sample project'
```

```
repositories {
    mavenCentral()
}

dependencies {
    testCompile 'junit:junit:4.8'
}
```

The Eclipse WTP plugin adds several new tasks to our Gradle build. In the following snippet, we invoke the tasks task to see which tasks are added:

```
$ gradle tasks --all

...

IDE tasks
---------

cleanEclipse - Cleans all Eclipse files. [cleanEclipseWtp]
    cleanEclipseClasspath
    cleanEclipseJdt
    cleanEclipseProject
cleanEclipseWtp - Cleans Eclipse wtp configuration files.
    cleanEclipseWtpComponent
    cleanEclipseWtpFacet
eclipse - Generates all Eclipse files. [eclipseWtp]
    eclipseClasspath - Generates the Eclipse classpath file.
    eclipseJdt - Generates the Eclipse JDT settings file.
    eclipseProject - Generates the Eclipse project file.
eclipseWtp - Generates Eclipse wtp configuration files.
    eclipseWtpComponent - Generates the Eclipse WTP component settings
file.
    eclipseWtpFacet - Generates the Eclipse WTP facet settings file.

...
```

The Eclipse WTP plugin includes the Eclipse plugin as well. We get all the tasks that we have seen earlier, but new tasks are also added for WTP configuration files. The task eclipseWtp depends on eclipseWtpComponent and eclipseWtpFacet, to generate the corresponding configuration files. Note that the eclipse task itself also now depends on eclipseWtp.

For each of these tasks, there is a corresponding clean task. These clean tasks will delete the configuration files.

If we execute the `eclipse` task, we get the following configuration files: `.project`, `.classpath`, and `org.eclipse.jdt.core.prefs`. We also get additional configuration files in the `.settings` folder, with the names `org.eclipse.wst.common.component` and `org.eclipse.wst.common.project.facet.core.xml`.

```
$ gradle eclipse
:eclipseClasspath
:eclipseJdt
:eclipseProject
:eclipseWtpComponent
:eclipseWtpFacet
:eclipseWtp
:eclipse


BUILD SUCCESSFUL


Total time: 4.264 secs
```

The contents of the `.project` file show that the Eclipse WTP plugin added additional natures and build commands, which is shown as follows:

```xml
<?xml version="1.0" encoding="UTF-8"?>
<projectDescription>
        <name>chapter12</name>
        <comment>Sample project</comment>
        <projects/>
        <natures>
                <nature>org.eclipse.jdt.core.javanature</nature>
                <nature>org.eclipse.wst.common.project.facet.core.
nature</nature>
                <nature>org.eclipse.wst.common.modulecore.
ModuleCoreNature</nature>
                <nature>org.eclipse.jem.workbench.JavaEMFNature</
nature>
        </natures>
        <buildSpec>
                <buildCommand>
                        <name>org.eclipse.jdt.core.javabuilder</name>
                        <arguments/>
                </buildCommand>
                <buildCommand>
                        <name>org.eclipse.wst.common.project.facet.
core.builder</name>
```

```
                    <arguments/>
                </buildCommand>
                <buildCommand>
                        <name>org.eclipse.wst.validation.
validationbuilder</name>
                        <arguments/>
                </buildCommand>
        </buildSpec>
        <linkedResources/>
</projectDescription>
```

In the .classpath configuration file, an additional container named org.eclipse.
jst.j2ee.internal.web.container is added, as shown in the following
code snippet:

```
<?xml version="1.0" encoding="UTF-8"?>
<classpath>
        <classpathentry kind="output" path="bin"/>
        <classpathentry kind="con" path="org.eclipse.jdt.launching.
JRE_CONTAINER" exported="true"/>
        <classpathentry kind="con" path="org.eclipse.jst.j2ee.
internal.web.container" exported="true"/>
        <classpathentry sourcepath="/Users/mrhaki/.gradle/
caches/artifacts-14/filestore/junit/junit/4.8/source/
abe171e0fc1242d1fe10e8dc43bce031e3f65560/junit-4.8-sources.jar"
kind="lib" path="/Users/mrhaki/.gradle/caches/artifacts-14/filestore/
junit/junit/4.8/jar/4150c00c5706306ef0f8f1410e70c8ff12757922/junit-
4.8.jar" exported="true">
                <attributes>
                        <attribute name="org.eclipse.jst.component.
nondependency" value=""/>
                </attributes>
        </classpathentry>
</classpath>
```

The contents of the org.eclipse.jdt.core.prefs file in the .settings folder are
not different from the standard Eclipse plugin. The org.eclipse.wst.common.
component file has the following contents:

```
<?xml version="1.0" encoding="UTF-8"?>
<project-modules id="moduleCoreId" project-version="2.0">
        <wb-module deploy-name="chapter12">
                <property name="context-root" value="chapter12"/>
                <wb-resource deploy-path="/" source-path="src/main/
webapp"/>
        </wb-module>
</project-modules>
```

Here, we find information for the web part of our project.

The last generated file in the `.settings` folder is `org.eclipse.wst.common. project.facet.core.xml` file, here we see the servlet and Java versions. The file has the following contents:

```
<?xml version="1.0" encoding="UTF-8"?>
<faceted-project>
        <fixed facet="jst.java"/>
        <fixed facet="jst.web"/>
        <installed facet="jst.web" version="2.4"/>
        <installed facet="jst.java" version="6.0"/>
</faceted-project>
```

# Customizing file generation

The Eclipse WTP plugin uses the same configuration options as the standard Eclipse plugin. The plugin uses project information to set the value in the configuration files. We can use a DSL to configure the values we want in the generated files. We can also use the merge hooks and work with model objects to change information. The XML structure can be changed using the `withXml` hook with a configuration closure.

To use the DSL, we can add an additional `wtp` script block to the `eclipse` script block. In the `wtp` script block, we can change the component configuration in a component configuration closure and the facet settings in the facet configuration closure.

In the following example build file, we see some of the options we can set by using the DSL:

```
apply plugin: 'java'
apply plugin: 'war'
apply plugin: 'eclipse-wtp'


eclipse {
    wtp {
        component {
            // Change context path of the Web application.
            // Default value is project.war.baseName.
            contextPath = '/sample-web'

            // Customize wb-resource elements of type WbResource.
            // Default for war plugin is
            // [deployPath: '/', sourcePath: project.webAppDirName]
```

and
```
            // for ear plugin is []
            resources += [deployPath: '/css', sourcePath: 'src/main/
css']
            // We can also use the resource() method    resource
deployPath: '/css', sourcePath: 'src/main/css'

            // Remove configurations from
            // the deployed configurations.
            minusConfigurations += project.configurations.testCompile

            // Add dependency configurations to
            // the deployLibPath location.
            libConfigurations += project.configurations.testCompile

            // Extra source directory.
            sourceDirs += file('src/main/css')
        }

        facet {
            // Add extra facet via property.
            facets += [name: 'extra', version: '1.0']

            // Or via facet() method.
            facet name: 'gradle', version: '1.1'
        }
    }
}
```

Another method to customize file generation is by using the merge hooks.
The beforeMerged and whenMerged hooks accept a configuration closure to
set properties on a model object. In the following table, we see the types of
the model object that is passed as argument to the closure:

| Model | Merge hook argument | Description |
| --- | --- | --- |
| Component | org.gradle.plugins.ide. eclipse.model.WtpComponent | Model object with properties for org.eclipse.wst. common.component file generation. |
| Facet | org.gradle.plugins.ide. eclipse.model.WtpFacet | Model object with properties for org.eclipse.wst. common.project.facet. core.xml file generation. |

In the following example build file, we use the merge hooks to customize
the configuration:

```
apply plugin: 'java'
apply plugin: 'war'
apply plugin: 'eclipse-wtp'

version = 1.0

description = 'Sample project'

repositories {
    mavenCentral()
}

dependencies {
    testCompile 'junit:junit:4.8'
}

eclipse {
    wtp {
        component {
            file {
                beforeMerged { wtpComponent ->
                    wtpComponent.wbEntries.clear()
                }

                whenMerged { wtpComponent ->
                    wtpComponent.contextPath = '/sample-web'
                    wtpComponent.deployName = 'sample'
                }
            }
        }

        facet {
            file {
                beforeMerged { wtpFacet ->
                }

                whenMerged { wtpFacet ->
                    def java = wtpFacet.facets.find { it.facet ==
'jst.java' }

                    java.version = '5.0'
                }
            }
        }
    }
}
```

Finally, we can manipulate the XML with the `withXml` hook. The argument is of type `XmlProvider`, just like the standard plugin. In the closure, we can change nodes and attributes.

The following example build file shows how we can manipulate the XML:

```
apply plugin: 'java'
apply plugin: 'war'
apply plugin: 'eclipse-wtp'

version = 1.0

description = 'Sample project'

repositories {
    mavenCentral()
}

dependencies {
    testCompile 'junit:junit:4.8'
}

eclipse {
    wtp {
        component {
            file {
                withXml { componentXml ->
                    def root = componentXml.asNode()
                    root.'wb-module'.@'deploy-name' = 'sample'
                }
            }
        }

        facet {
            file {
                withXml { facetXml ->
                    def root = facetXml.asNode()
                    root.installed.find { it.@facet == 'jst.web' }.@
version = '2.5'
                }
            }
        }
    }
}
```

# Using the IntelliJ IDEA plugin

**IntelliJ IDEA** from **JetBrains** is another IDE we can use to develop applications. Gradle has the IDEA plugin to generate the project files for IntelliJ IDEA. This means we can simply open the project in IntelliJ IDEA. The dependencies are set correctly so as to compile the project in the IDE. In this section, we will see how we can generate those files and customize file generation.

IntelliJ IDEA supports a folder-based and file-based format for the project files. The IDEA plugin generates files for the file-based format. The file format for the project files is XML. The workspace project file has the extension `.iws` and contains personal settings. The project information is stored in a file with extension `.ipr`. The project file can be saved in a version control system, because it doesn't have reference to local paths. The workspace project file has a lot of personal settings and shouldn't be put in a version control system.

For a Java project, we have a third project file with the exension `.iml`. This file contains dependency references with local path locations. We shouldn't put this file in a version control system. The IDEA plugin can just, like the Eclipse plugin, download associated source files for a dependency. We can also configure and download the associated Javadoc files. The IDEA plugin works together with the Java plugin. If we have a Gradle build file and apply both the Java and IDEA plugins, a specific Java configuration is added to the project files.

Let's create an example build file and apply the IDEA plugin, as shown in the following code snippet:

```
apply plugin: 'java'
apply plugin: 'idea'

version = 1.0

sourceCompatibility = 1.6
targetCompatibility = 1.6

description = 'Sample project'

ext {
    slf4jVersion = '1.6.6'
    slf4jGroup = 'org.slf4j'
}

configurations {
    extraLib
}
```

```
repositories {
    mavenCentral()
}

dependencies {
    testCompile 'junit:junit:4.8'
    extraLib "$slf4jGroup:slf4j-api:$slf4jVersion",
"$slf4jGroup:slf4j-simple:$slf4jVersion"
}
```

First, we execute the `tasks` task and see which tasks are added by the plugin, as follows:

```
$ gradle tasks --all

...

IDE tasks
---------

cleanIdea - Cleans IDEA project files (IML, IPR)
    cleanIdeaModule
    cleanIdeaProject
idea - Generates IDEA project files (IML, IPR, IWS)
    ideaModule - Generates IDEA module files (IML)
    ideaProject - Generates IDEA project file (IPR)
    ideaWorkspace - Generates an IDEA workspace file (IWS)

...
```

We have an `idea` task that is dependent on the following three other tasks: `ideaWorkspace`, `ideaModule`, and `ideaProject`. Each of these tasks can generate a project file. To remove the module and project files, we can execute the `cleanIdeaModule` and `cleanIdeaProject` tasks or simply the `cleanIdea` task. There is no `cleanIdeaWorkspace` task, because the workspace file contains personal settings. These settings are probably set via the user interface of IntelliJ IDEA and shouldn't be removed by a Gradle task.

When we run the `idea` task from the command line and look at the output which is as follows, we see that all the tasks are executed and we now have three project files:

```
$ gradle idea
:ideaModule
```

```
:ideaProject
:ideaWorkspace
:idea


BUILD SUCCESSFUL


Total time: 4.477 secs
```

# Customizing file generation

The IDEA plugin has several ways to customize the configuration in the generated files. The plugin will look in the project settings and use the information in the generated files. For example, we can set the source and target compatibility versions in our Gradle project and the plugin will use them to set a correct value in the generated project file.

We can use a DSL to change the configuration information before the file is generated. Gradle also offers hooks where we can manipulate model objects before and after the project information and DSL configuration is applied. To change the generated XML structure, we can implement the `withXml` hook. We can alter the XML just before it is written to disk. To change the contents of the workspace file, we should use the `withXml` hook. The workspace file has an empty model object and has no DSL, because the contents are very specific and they contain a lot of personal settings.

# Customizing using DSL

The IDEA plugin adds a new idea configuration script block that is used to change the project files' contents. For the module and project files, we can use a DSL to set the configuration settings. Each file has its own configuration script block.

For module file generation, we can change the name of the file. But, it is best to leave it unchanged. Gradle will make sure the file names are unique within a multi-project build. IntelliJ IDEA requires that the module names be unique for a multi-module project.

IntelliJ IDEA has several scopes for dependencies. We can customize which dependency configuration apply to which scope. The following table shows the default mapping of IntelliJ IDEA scopes with Gradle dependency configurations:

| IntelliJ IDEA scope | Gradle configuration |
|---|---|
| Compile | `project.configurations.compile` |
| Runtime | `project.configurations.runtime-project.configurations.compile` |
| Test | `project.configurations.testRuntime-project.configuations.runtime` |
| Provided | Not set |

Each scope has a `plus` and `minus` key. We can add additional configurations using the `plus` key and remove configurations with the `minus` key.

In the following example build file, we see the different options and methods of the DSL used to change the project file contents:

```
apply plugin: 'java'
apply plugin: 'idea'

idea {
    project {
        // Set JDK name. Default is from Java version
        // used to run Gradle.
        jdkName = '1.6'

        // Set Java language level for the project.
        // Default value is project.sourceCompatibility.
        languageLevel = '1.6'  // Or JDK_1_6

        // For multi-project builds we can define other modules.
        // Default value is project.allprojects*.idea.module.
        modules = project(':other').idea.module

        // Set resource wildcard pattern.
        // Default value is ['!?*.java', '!?*.groovy']
        wildcards += '!?*.xsd'
    }
}
```

The following example build file shows some of the options we can use to change the module file:

```
apply plugin: 'java'
apply plugin: 'idea'

configurations { extraLib }
sourceSets { api }

idea {
    module {
        // Download associated Javadoc files for dependencies.
        // Default value is false.
        downloadJavadoc = true

        // Download associated source files for dependencies.
        // Default value is true.
        downloadSources = true

        // Set which directories to exclude.
        excludeDirs += file('.settings')

        // Set specific JDK for this module, or use the value
'inherited'
        // to use project JDK. Default value is 'inherited'.
        jdkName = 'inherited'

        // Directory with the source files.
        // Default value is project.sourceSets.main.allSource
        sourceDirs += project.sourceSets.api.allSource

        // Directory with the test source files.
        // Default value is project.sourceSets.test.allSource
        testSourceDirs += project.sourceSets.api.allSource

        // Set configurations for the IntelliJ IDEA scopes.
        scopes.COMPILE.plus += configurations.extraLib
        scopes.TEST.minus += configurations.extraLib
    }
}
```

# Customizing with merged hooks

With the merge hooks, we can access the model objects and manipulate them to customize file generation. In the following table, we can see the type of argument that is passed to the beforeMerged and whenMerged hooks:

| Model | Merge hook argument | Description |
| --- | --- | --- |
| Project | org.gradle.plugins.ide.idea.model.Project | Model object with properties for project file generation. |
| Module | org.gradle.plugins.ide.idea.model.Module | Model object with properties for module file generation. |

The project script block has an ipr script block that we must use to define the beforeMerged and whenMerged hooks. The module script block has the iml configuration script block to define those hooks.

In the following example build file, we see some of the things we can do by using the merge hooks:

```
apply plugin: 'java'
apply plugin: 'idea'

version = 1.0

description = 'Sample project'

repositories {
    mavenCentral()
}

dependencies {
    testCompile 'junit:junit:4.8'
}


idea {
    project {
        ipr {
            beforeMerged { iprProject ->
                iprProject.wildCards.removeAll()
            }
```

```
                whenMerged { iprProject ->
                    iprProject.wildCards.add '!?*.xsd'
                }
            }
        }

    module {
        iml {
            beforeMerged { imlModule ->
                imlModule.outputDir = null
            }

            whenMerged { imlModule ->
                imlModule.jdkName = '1.6'
                module.dependencies*.exported = true
                imlModule.excludeFolders.add file('.svn')
            }
        }
    }
}
```

# Customizing with XML manipulation

At the lowest level, we can manipulate the XML before it is written to disk. For workspace file configuration changes, this is the best way. We can also use it for the project and module files. We must implement a closure with the `withXml` hook to customize the XML structure. The closure has a single argument of type `org.gradle.api.XmlProvider`. We can use the `asNode()` method to get a Groovy `groovy.util.Node` object. This is the easiest way to manipulate the XML. The `asString()` method returns a `StringBuilder` object and the `asElement()` returns an `org.w3c.dom.Element` object.

In the following example build file, we make some changes to the XML for the project, module, and workspace files:

```
apply plugin: 'java'
apply plugin: 'idea'

idea {
    project {
        ipr {
            withXml { xml ->
                def projectRoot = xml.asNode()
```

```
                    projectRoot.component.find {
                        it.@name == 'ProjectRootManager'
                    }.@'assert-keyword' = true

                    def javadoc = projectRoot.component.find {
                        it.@name == 'JavadocGenerationManager'
                    }
                    javadoc.option.find {
                        it.@name == 'OPEN_IN_BROWSER'
                    }.@value = false
                }
            }
        }

    module {
        iml {
            withXml { xml ->
                def moduleRoot = xml.asNode()
                def facetManager = moduleRoot.component.find {
                    it.@name == 'FacetManager'
                }
                facetManager.plus {
                    facet(type: 'Spring', name: 'Spring') {
                        configuration {
                            fileset(id: 'fileset1', name: 'XML
Application Context') {
                                file 'file://$MODULE_DIR$/src/main/
resources/applicationContext.xml'
                            }
                        }
                    }
                }
            }
        }
    }

    workspace {
        iws {
            withXml { xml ->
```

```
def workspaceRoot = xml.asNode()
def coverageViewManager = workspaceRoot.component.find
{
    it.@name == 'CoverageViewManager'
}
coverageViewManager.option.find {
    it.@name == 'myFlattenPackages'
}.@value = 'false'
        }
    }
  }
}
```

# Running Gradle in Eclipse

We can generate the Eclipse project files using the Eclipse plugin. We can also import a Gradle build file in Eclipse and then execute the Gradle tasks from within Eclipse. In this section, we see how to install the Gradle plugin in Eclipse and also how we can use it to import a Gradle build file and execute tasks.

The Gradle plugin is part of **SpringSource Tool Suite (STS)**. SpringSource Tool Suite is based on Eclipse and adds support for building Spring-based applications through already-installed plugins. We can install SprintSource Tool Suite as a standalone IDE. If we want to re-use our existing Eclipse IDE, we can install STS as a plugin. The plugin has an import wizard to import existing Gradle builds. Multi-project builds are also supported by it.

The plugin keeps track of dependencies defined in the Gradle build file as project dependencies. This means that if we change a dependency in the build file, the Eclipse classpath will be updated with the change, so that the compiler can use it.

To execute tasks, the plugin adds an additional view to Eclipse. From the view we can execute tasks. The Eclipse launching framework is used to execute tasks.

If we have installed the Groovy Eclipse plugin, we get Gradle DSL support. This means we get code completion and Javadoc tooltips in the editor when we edit Gradle build files.

# Installing Gradle plugin

To install the Gradle plugin, we use the update site, `http://dist.springsource.com/release/TOOLS/gradle`. From the **Help** menu, we select **Install New Software....**, we then see a new dialog window. Click on the **Add...** button to add a new update site. In the dialog window that appears, we fill in the correct values shown in the following screenshot:

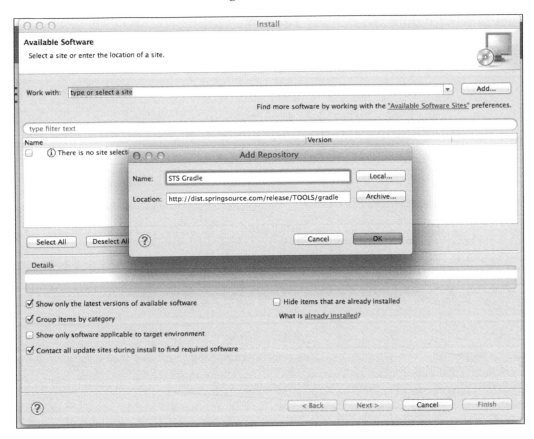

Eclipse will fetch the information from the update site. In the **Install** dialog window, all components are shown. We click on the **Select All** button and continue, as shown in the following screenshot:

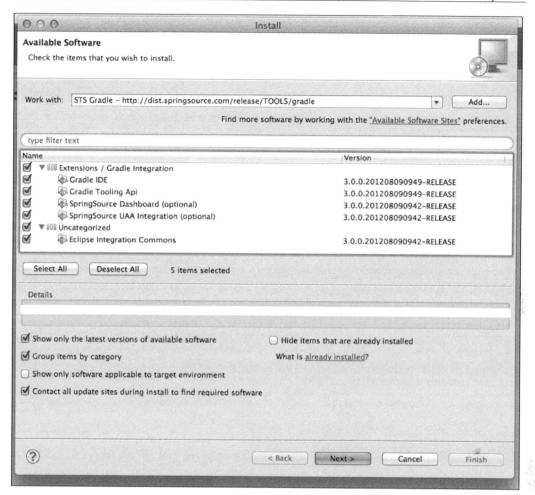

We have to accept the licenses, and Eclipse downloads the plugin components. Restart Eclipse after all the plugin components have been downloaded.

If we want DSL support for the Gradle build files, we must also install the Groovy Eclipse plugin. We go to **SpringSource Dashboard** and select the **Extension** tab. In the **Find:** field, we type in **groovy-eclipse** and select the **Groovy-Eclipse** option from the search results, as shown in the following screenshot:

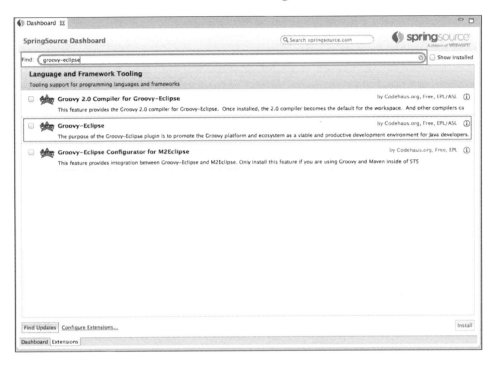

We click on the **Install** button to install the plugin into Eclipse.

# Importing Gradle project

After we have installed the plugin, we can use the import wizard to import a Gradle project. We use a very simple Java project with the following build file:

```
apply plugin: 'java'

version = '1.0'
group = 'sample.gradle'

description = 'Sample Java project'

repositories {
    mavenCentral()
}
```

```
dependencies {
    testCompile 'junit:junit:4.8'
}
```

In Eclipse, we select the **Import...** option from the **File** menu. In the **Import** dialog window, we type **gradle** in the search field. We select the **Gradle Project** option before we click on the **Next** button, as shown in the following screenshot:

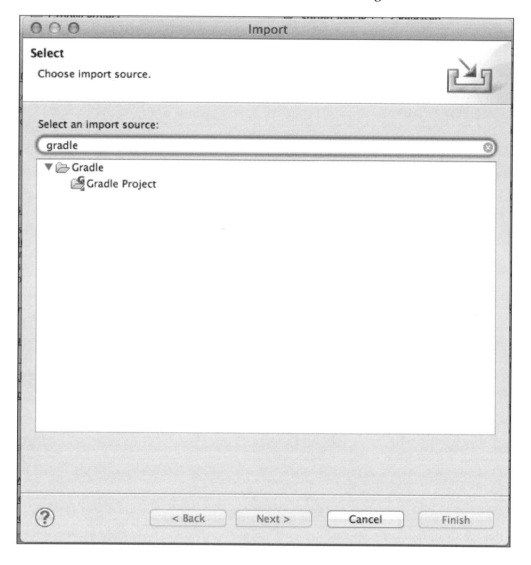

In the next step of the import wizard, we must specify the root folder for our Gradle project. For a multi-project build, we should select the root folder. If we only have a single project, we can then select the project folder. After we have selected the folder, we must click on the **Build Model** button. The folder is then scanned for information, and after the model is built, we can see our project displayed as shown in the following screenshot:

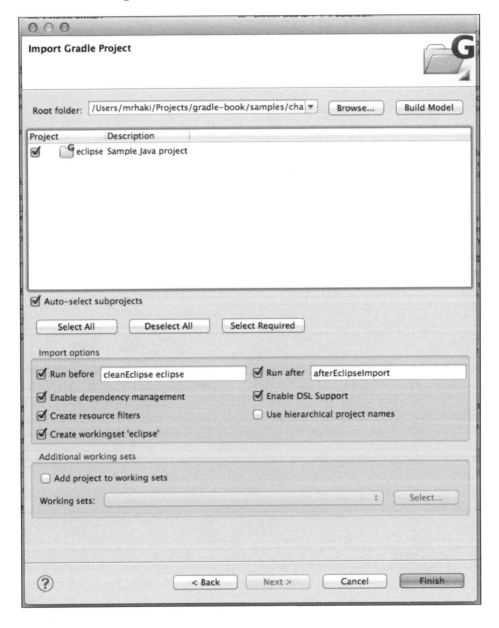

We can select the project and click on the **Finish** button to import the project into our Eclipse workspace.

But before we do that, first take a closer look at the **Import options**. The option **Run before** allows us to define Gradle tasks to be executed before the import. The default value **cleanEclipse eclipse** will regenerate the Eclipse project files from the Eclipse plugin in our Gradle build file. We don't need it for Java projects, because the Gradle plugin in Eclipse will make sure everything works. For web or enterprise applications with WTP support, we can still invoke the `eclipse` tasks.

The **Run after** option has the default **afterEclipseImport** task. This task name is a hook for the import process. We must implement the task ourselves in the build file, if we want to do some customization after the import wizard is finished.

With the **Enable dependency management** option, we instruct Eclipse to build the dependencies based on the Gradle build file contents. The **Enable DSL Support** is useful if we have also installed the Groovy-Eclipse plugin.

The **Create resource filters** option can be used for multi-project builds. The Gradle plugin will create linked projects to be able to import multiple projects, but this means a project can occur multiple times in the project view. If we enable this option, a resource filter is created, so that we see the project displayed only once in the project view.

Also, with multi-project build, the option **Use hierarchical project names** can be used. If we enable this option, the name of the root project is also used in the project name. Finally, if we enable the option **Create workingset 'eclipse'**, a new working set is created with all the projects that we import.

We don't want to execute any Gradle tasks before and after the import, so we must uncheck those options. After unchecking the **Run before** and **Run after** options, we are now ready to click on the **Finish** button, as shown in the following screenshot:

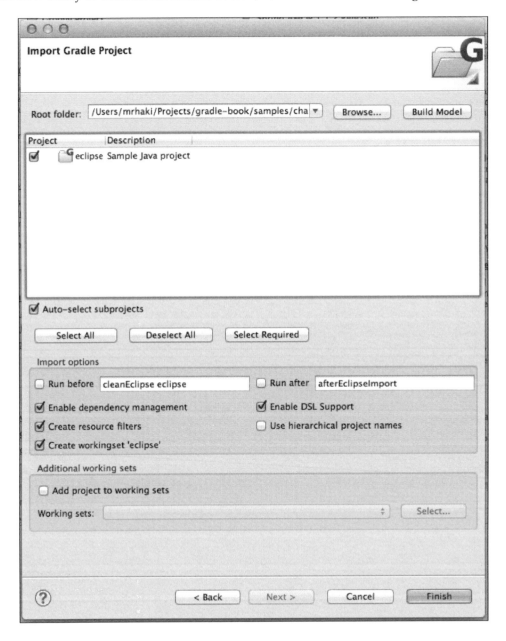

After the import wizard is done, we can see our project in the **Package Explorer**, as shown in the next screenshot:

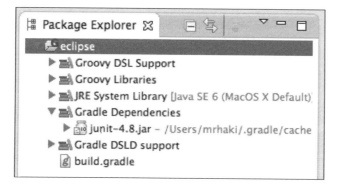

The **Gradle Dependencies** node has the dependency that we have defined in our Gradle build file. If we add new dependencies, we can update the project by right-clicking on the project name. From the submenu, we select **Gradle** and **Refresh Dependencies**.

# Running tasks

To execute tasks, we first open the **Gradle Tasks** view. From the **Window** menu, we select **Show View** and then **Other...**. We type **gradle** in the search field, to search for the **Gradle Tasks** view, as shown in following screenshot:

We select the view and click on the **OK** button.

In our workspace, we now have the **Gradle Tasks** view. We select a project from the **Project** selection list. The tasks for that project are then displayed as shown in the following screenshot:

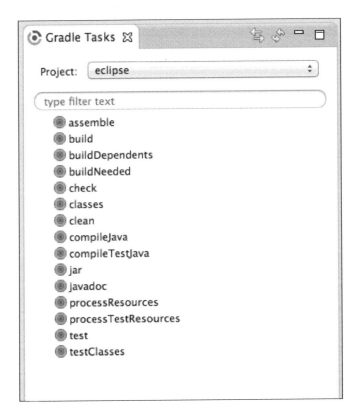

To execute a task, we simply have to double-click on the task name, and in the **Console view**, we can see the output of the executed task.

We can also use the launch framework of Eclipse to run tasks. We must right-click on the project and select the **Gradle Build** or **Gradle Build...** option from the **Run As** option. The launch configuration is opened, and here we can configure the tasks to be executed, as shown in following screenshot:

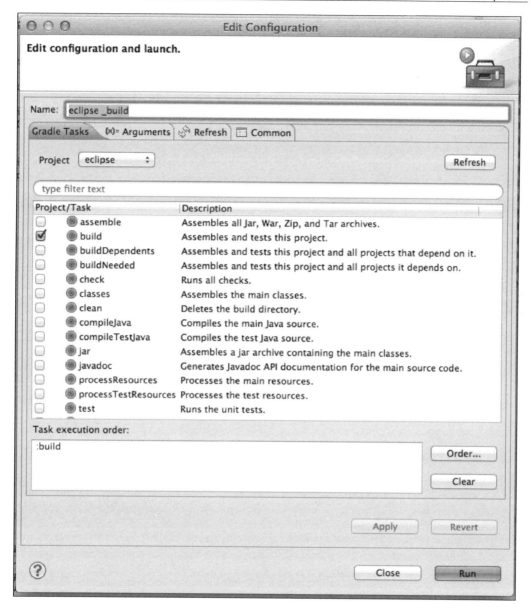

If we have multiple tasks to execute, we can set the order in the **Task execution order** section.

# Editing build files

We have installed the Groovy-Eclipse plugin, and if we open the `build.gradle` file, we get code completion support for the Gradle DSL. For example, if we type **ar** and enter the key combination for code completion, we can see the option **artifacts**, as shown in the following screenshot:

```
 Dashboard       *build.gradle
 apply plugin: 'java'

    version = '1.0'
    group = 'sample.gradle'

    description = 'Sample Java project'

    repositories {
        mavenCentral()
    }

    dependencies {
        testCompile 'junit:junit:4.8'
    }

    ar
         artifacts : ArtifactHandler – Project (Groovy)
         artifacts(Closure configureClosure) : void – Project (Groovy)
                          Press '^Space' to show Template Proposals
```

# Running Gradle in IntelliJ IDEA

We can generate IDEA project files with the IDEA plugin in our build file. IntelliJ IDEA has a Gradle plugin to import a Gradle project without first creating the project files. In this section, we learn how to use the Gradle plugin with IntelliJ IDEA 11.1.

We use the same project that was used with the Eclipse Gradle plugin to import the project into IntelliJ IDEA.

# Installing the plugin

The Gradle plugin can be installed through the IntelliJ IDEA plugin manager. We need to go to IDE Settings in the **Settings** window, as shown in the following screenshot:

We select the **Gradle** plugin to install it in the IDE. Once we have installed the plugin, we can then import a project.

# Importing a project

To import an existing Gradle project, we start the **New project** wizard. We select the **New Project...** option from the **File** menu. IntelliJ IDEA shows a dialog window in which we can choose the source of the new project. We select the **Import project from external model** option, as shown in the following screenshot:

We click on the **Next** button and select **Gradle** as external model, as shown in the following screenshot:

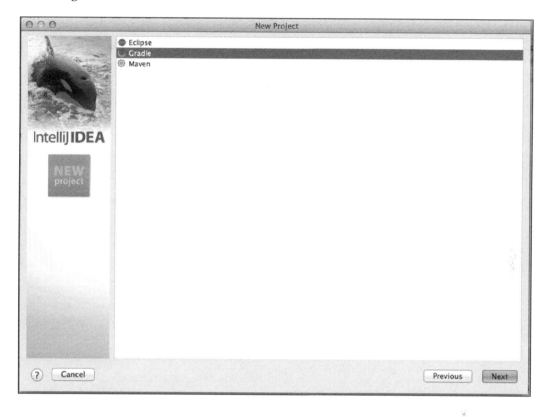

Now we can click on the **Next** button, and in the following window, we must fill in the location of the `build.gradle` file and the location of our Gradle installation as shown in the following screenshot:

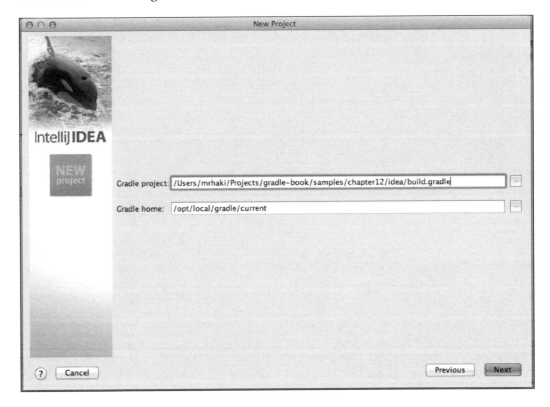

After we have filled in the values, we click on the **Next** button. IntelliJ IDEA will parse the build file and then show the determined **Project structure** in the following window. We can change the properties for the **project**, **module**, and **content-root** properties. In the following screenshot, we can see the properties that are set for the project property:

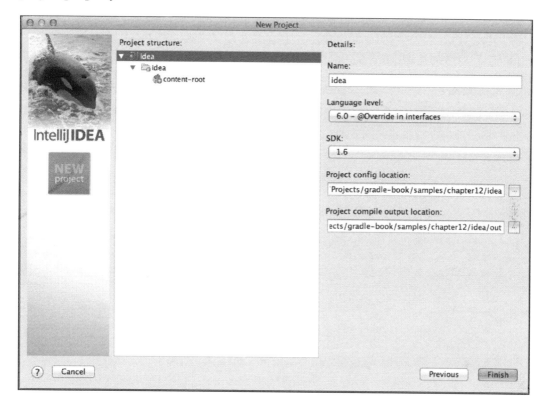

Next, we can see the properties that are set for the module property, as shown in the following screenshot:

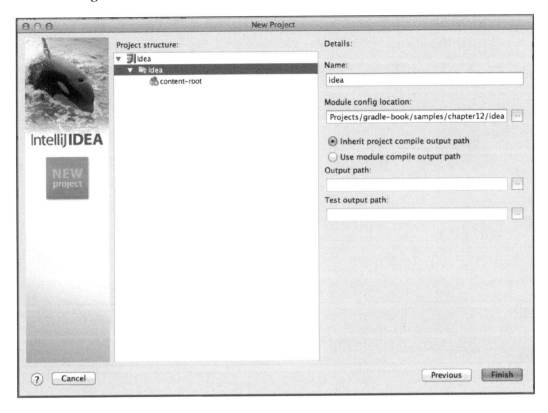

In the following screenshot, we can see the properties that are set for the content-root property:

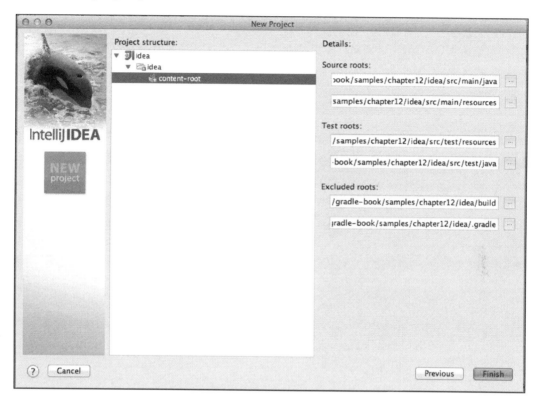

We click on the **Finish** button, and IntelliJ IDEA opens the new project. We can see the project and its dependencies, as shown in the following screenshot:

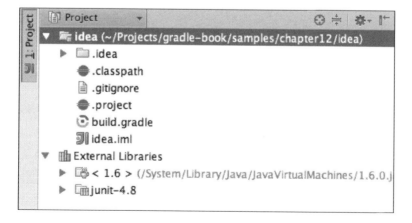

To see the Gradle project dependency structure, we can also open the **JetGradle** window. Here, we can see the differences between the IDEA module dependencies and the Gradle dependencies. We must click on the **Refresh** button to use the latest changes in the `build.gradle` file. For example, if we add a new compile dependency `org.slf4j:slf4j-api:1.6.4`, we must click on the **Refresh** button to see the changes, as shown in the following screenshot:

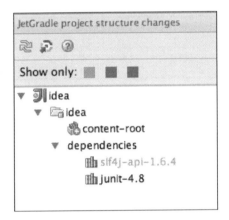

Notice that dependency name is in green. This means that the dependency is defined in the Gradle build file, but not in the IntelliJ IDEA module. We right-click on the dependency and then select **Import** to add the dependency to the IDEA module, as shown in the following screenshot:

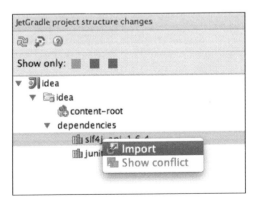

If dependencies were added to the IDEA module, but not defined in the Gradle build file, the color of the dependency will be blue. Conflicting dependencies are shown in red.

# Running tasks

To execute Gradle tasks, we use IntelliJ IDEA's run/debug configurations. From the **Run** menu, select **build**. A pop-up menu is shown, and from here select the **Edit...** option, as shown in the following screenshot:

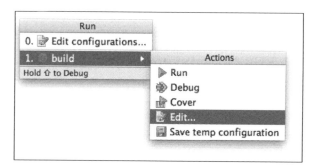

The **Edit Configuration settings** dialog window is then shown. This is the Groovy configuration dialog. In the **Script parameters** field, we can type the task names that we want to execute, as shown in the following screenshot:

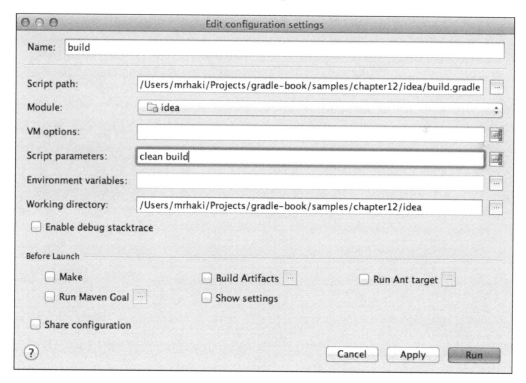

We click on the **Run** button to execute the tasks. After the tasks are executed, we can see the output of the tasks in the **Run** window. The new configuration is added to the list of configurations. We can choose the configuration again to re-run the tasks.

# Summary

When we develop applications, we usually develop the code with an IDE. In this chapter, we have seen how we can use the Gradle plugins in Eclipse, Eclipse WTP, and IDEA, to generate project files for Eclipse and IntelliJ IDEA.

The plugins have a DSL to change the configuration before the files are generated. We can also use hooks to change the model objects before and after the DSL is applied. At the lowest level, we can use the withXml hook to alter the XML content before the file is written to disk.

Both Eclipse and IntelliJ IDEA have plugins to import an existing Gradle project. We can then work with the project from within the IDE. Extra dependencies or changes are reflected in the classpath project files, so that the code can be compiled with the IDE's compiler. We can also run Gradle tasks from within the IDE, so we don't have to leave our favorite IDE if we want to use Gradle.

In this book, we have seen the power of Gradle as a build tool. The Gradle syntax is very consistent and compact. If we know the basics, we can accomplish many things. We learned how to add functionality to a build file, with tasks. We have seen how we can use Gradle in Java, Groovy, and Scala projects. We saw Gradle's features for working with multi-projects. We have learned how to create custom tasks and plugins to enable the re-use of build logic across projects. After reading this book, we will be able to use Gradle in our software development. By using Gradle, we can have great flexibility in our projects and still rely on sold convention-over-configuration defaults. We can start simple and gradually expand the build script with more functionality. With this book, we should get started quickly and have successful Gradle implementation in our projects.

# Index

## Symbols

## A

## B

# S

# T

## Thank you for buying
# Gradle Effective Implementation Guide

## About Packt Publishing

Packt, pronounced 'packed', published its first book "*Mastering phpMyAdmin for Effective MySQL Management*" in April 2004 and subsequently continued to specialize in publishing highly focused books on specific technologies and solutions.

Our books and publications share the experiences of your fellow IT professionals in adapting and customizing today's systems, applications, and frameworks. Our solution based books give you the knowledge and power to customize the software and technologies you're using to get the job done. Packt books are more specific and less general than the IT books you have seen in the past. Our unique business model allows us to bring you more focused information, giving you more of what you need to know, and less of what you don't.

Packt is a modern, yet unique publishing company, which focuses on producing quality, cutting-edge books for communities of developers, administrators, and newbies alike. For more information, please visit our website: www.packtpub.com.

## About Packt Open Source

In 2010, Packt launched two new brands, Packt Open Source and Packt Enterprise, in order to continue its focus on specialization. This book is part of the Packt Open Source brand, home to books published on software built around Open Source licences, and offering information to anybody from advanced developers to budding web designers. The Open Source brand also runs Packt's Open Source Royalty Scheme, by which Packt gives a royalty to each Open Source project about whose software a book is sold.

## Writing for Packt

We welcome all inquiries from people who are interested in authoring. Book proposals should be sent to author@packtpub.com. If your book idea is still at an early stage and you would like to discuss it first before writing a formal book proposal, contact us; one of our commissioning editors will get in touch with you.

We're not just looking for published authors; if you have strong technical skills but no writing experience, our experienced editors can help you develop a writing career, or simply get some additional reward for your expertise.

## Apache Maven 3 Cookbook

ISBN: 978-1-84951-244-2        Paperback: 244 pages

Over 50 recipes towards optimal Java software
engineering with Maven 3

1. Grasp the fundamentals and extend Apache
   Maven 3 to meet your needs

2. Implement engineering practices in your
   application development process with Apache
   Maven

3. Collaboration techniques for Agile teams with
   Apache Maven

4. Use Apache Maven with Java, Enterprise
   Frameworks, and various other cutting-edge
   technologies

## Java 7 New Features Cookbook

ISBN: 978-1-84968-562-7        Paperback: 384 pages

Over 100 comprehensive recipes to get you
up-to-speed with all the exciting new features of Java 7

1. Comprehensive coverage of the new features of
   Java 7 organized around easy-to-follow recipes

2. Covers exciting features such as the
   try-with-resources block, the monitoring
   of directory events, asynchronous IO and
   new GUI enhancements, and more

3. A learn-by-example based approach that
   focuses on key concepts to provide the
   foundation to solve real world problems

Please check **www.PacktPub.com** for information on our titles

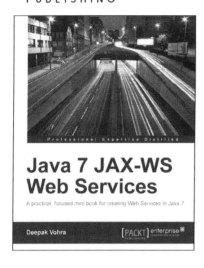
## Java 7 JAX-WS Web Services

ISBN: 978-1-84968-720-1        Paperback: 64 pages

A practical, focused mini book for creating Web Services in Java 7

1. Develop Java 7 JAX-WS web services using the NetBeans IDE and Oracle GlassFish server

2. End-to-end application which makes use of the new clientjar option in JAX-WS wsimport tool

3. Packed with ample screenshots and practical instructions

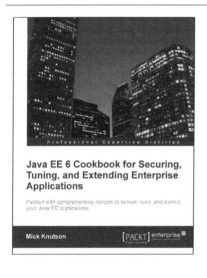

## Java EE 6 Cookbook for Securing, Tuning, and Extending Enterprise Applications

ISBN: 978-1-84968-316-6        Paperback: 356 pages

Packed with comprehensive recipes to secure, tune, and extend your Java EE applications

1. Secure your Java applications using Java EE built-in features as well as the well-known Spring Security framework

2. Utilize related recipes for testing various Java EE technologies including JPA, EJB, JSF, and Web services

3. Explore various ways to extend a Java EE environment with the use of additional dynamic languages as well as frameworks

Made in the USA
Lexington, KY
12 September 2013